SHELBY
AMERICAN

SHELBY AMERICAN

The Renegades Who Built the Cars,
Won the Races, and Lived the Legend

PRESTON LERNER

octanepress.com

Octane Press is based in Austin, Texas

Printed in the United States

To my parents, Isabel and Joseph Lerner,
who instilled in me a love of the written word.

CONTENTS

INTRODUCTION

Ted Sutton had just created a monster.

Sutton was a resourceful young mechanic at Shelby American, the company Carroll Shelby had assembled in Southern California to build the Cobra. Engineered by motorsports savants and equipped with a 289-cubic-inch Ford V-8, the Cobra was the most fearsome sports car in the world, circa 1964. But Shelby wasn't content with what he had wrought; he wanted something even more menacing. Sutton was assigned to play mad scientist. Performing surgery in a broad, red-brick building nestled incongruously in a blue-collar enclave in Venice, he retrofitted a standard Cobra with a big-block 427. When the conversion was complete, he did what any self-respecting twenty-five-year-old gearhead would have done: He climbed into the cockpit, cranked the ignition, and careened through the neighborhood, breaking the tires loose at every opportunity and sending gloriously obnoxious blasts of big-block bedlam out the straight pipes. When he got back to the shop, he heard his name being called. Mr. Shelby wanted to see him.

Gulp.

Recovering from knee surgery, Shelby hobbled down the stairs from his office. Sutton waited glumly, sure he was about to be fired. Instead, Shelby asked him, "Was that you that drove that car?"[1] Sutton warily acknowledged that it was. "Well, how did it go?"

"It was just fine, sir," Sutton said.

"Let's see. You wanna ride along?"

Sutton explained that he'd pulled out the passenger seat so he could run the down tube for the U-shaped roll bar through the cockpit.

"Well, you can sit on the floor, can't you?"

As soon as Sutton wedged himself into place, Shelby started sling-ing the Cobra through a nearby field in four-wheel drifts and wind-ing out the 427 to redline as he blew past stop signs. Sutton hadn't adjusted the brakes or swapped out the narrow tires and wimpy wire wheels that had been mounted on the car while he was building it, and it was only by the grace of God that there were no schoolkids or other pedestrians happening past as they skirted around a trailer park. As he desperately hung on, with one hand wrapped around the roll bar and the other clutching Shelby's crutch, Sutton kept thinking that he was trapped inside a flimsy deathtrap with a certifiable lunatic. "I was absolutely purple by the time we got back to the shop," he said. "To say he scared the shit out of me would be a gross understatement—I was truly afraid for my life. I just knew we were going to hit something or someone."[2]

Shelby killed the ignition while Sutton lingered in the car, drained and ashen-faced. "That's real nice," Shelby drawled nonchalantly before limping back up to his office.

Six decades ago, the shop in Venice where he parked the Cobra was the beating heart of Shelby American, and even today, though the building now houses high-tech sound recording studios, 1042 Princeton Drive remains hallowed ground for fans of Shelby's iconic creations. Shelby had founded the company in 1962 with a relatively modest goal—to build a car fast enough to outrun the Chevrolet Corvette. Yet by the end of 1964, Shelby American was the biggest, baddest, most successful motorsports-cum-high-performance automotive operation in the country and second in the world only to Ferrari. If you'd walked through the shop during the week before Christmas you would have seen the Ford GTs that would eventually sweep Le Mans; Daytona Coupes being prepped to win the GT World Championship; the King Cobras that had just starred in the precursor to the Can-Am series; 289-cubic-inch competition Cobras destined for privateers; the big-block prototype race car formerly known not so fondly as The Turd; and the first of what would be thousands of Mustangs being transformed into GT350s. Across the street, a production crew was knocking out leaf-spring Cobras as fast as possible.

Dozens of books have been written about Shelby American, from rich memoirs by Shelby, John Morton, Dave Friedman, Peter Brock, Chuck Cantwell, and Phil Henny to the invaluable and stunningly detailed registries published by the Shelby American Automobile Club—and that doesn't include all the biographies and other histories that touch upon elements of the Shelby American story. Most of the books reflect the particular interests (obsessions?) of the writers and readers. Some geek out on coil-spring Cobras. Others can't get enough of Shelby Mustangs. For one group of fans, the Shelby American saga ends when the company left the fabled shop in Venice. Another cares only about the team's racing exploits.

This book covers it all, from the origin of the Cobra in 1961 to the end of the 1969 Trans-Am season and the introduction of the 1970 GT350 and GT500. It includes not only the well-documented triumphs but also the often-overlooked failures—the star-crossed Indianapolis 500 turbine car, the close-but-no-cigar Toyota 2000GT program, the day-late-and-dollar-short Can-Am efforts, even the sadly forgotten Lone Star. But this isn't a car book per se. Because cars don't design themselves. They don't build themselves. They don't race themselves. This is the saga of the men and women who brought Shelby American to life, and insofar as is possible, it's told in their own words.

Sixty years have passed since the first Cobra thundered through the oil fields of Santa Fe Springs. And while most of the people who worked at Shelby American have died since then, their legacy lives on. Not merely in the priceless artifacts they created but also in the practices they pioneered. Shelby American was the first genuinely professional road-racing team in the United States, and it helped liberate sports car racing from the snobby amateur straitjacket that had prevented it from finding a wider audience. On the street car front, the Cobras and, to a lesser degree, the Shelby Mustangs managed to maintain artisanal quality on an industrial scale—what we now call small-batch production.

It's a complicated story, and there's no simple way to tell it, especially because so much has been said and written about it already. It's comforting to think of a historian as a scholar revealing universal principles, like a mathematician discovering the Pythagorean theorem. But, really, he's more like an archaeologist trying to make sense of the disconnected remnants of a lost civilization. If history tells us anything, it's that there's no such thing as absolute truth in human affairs. Different participants bring different perspectives to the same events. Memory is notoriously fallible, so recollections don't always track with contemporary accounts. Sources have axes to grind and scores to settle. Shelby himself was the quintessential example of what literary theorists refer to as an unreliable narrator. His versions of stories varied so wildly that they sometimes said more about his state of mind than the events in question.

Shelby American is the subject of a vast mythology that wraps the milestones of the 1960s in a nostalgic haze that mercilessly romanticizes the past. But the chronicle of Carroll Shelby and his merry band of Southern California mavericks doesn't require any Hollywood sweetening because, in this case, fact really *is* stranger than fiction. If you want to know the true story of Shelby American, then you have to go beyond the legend.

CHAPTER ONE

BUILDING A BETTER BEAST

1962

People rarely realize that they're in the process of making history. They're too busy making it. So the small cohort of men working in a cramped bay of a garage on the fringe of Los Angeles in February 1962 had no idea that the car they were assembling would sell at auction for $13.75 million five decades later or that the lanky, laid-back Texan overseeing the project would become one of the most enduring legends in automotive history. But there's another reason—a much better reason—that they couldn't imagine the glory to come. The way they looked at it, they weren't working on anything unusual, much less monumental. They were simply doing what Southern California car guys had been doing for as long as any of them could remember:

They were building a hot rod.

Granted, this wasn't a '32 Model A with a flathead Ford. It was a two-seat roadster aimed at the sporty-car set instead of blue-collar gearheads. The chassis had been welded up by a small British company called AC Cars, based in the strange-sounding village of Thames Ditton. The aluminum bodywork had been hand formed into a barchetta shape popularized by the Ferrari 166 MM back in 1948. Nobody was going to confuse it with a Deuce Coupe or a lead sled or a road-racing special like the intimidating Scarab, which had been built a few miles away.

Still, the car was being put together in the well-known Santa Fe Springs hot-rod speed shop owned by Dean Moon, of Mooneyes fame. And while the engine wasn't a flathead, it was a Ford V-8—a spanking-new 260-cubic-inch model designed to compete with the small-block Chevy. This particular motor had been thoroughly massaged by Mel Chastain, who would later be enshrined in the Dry Lakes Racing Hall of Fame. The headers had been fabricated by Fred Larsen, who eventually earned a slot in the Bonneville Salt Flats 300 MPH Club. Roy Gammell, Moon's chief mechanic, was in charge of assembling the car. Among the people helping him was Dean Jeffries, soon to become a luminary on the SoCal custom-car scene.

Ironically, the man who'd commissioned the project was the one who understood the least about the nuts and bolts of the operation. Carroll Shelby was many things—son of a rural mail carrier in East Texas, World War II aviator, bankrupt chicken farmer, one-time concrete contractor, former exotic sports car dealer, and, most famously, Le Mans-winning race car driver—but he damn sure wasn't a mechanic, much less a designer or an engineer. A few years earlier, while racing in a 1,000-kilometer race in Argentina, the engine of his Allard-Cadillac had caught fire. After peering under the hood and realizing he didn't have the mechanical know-how to fix the flaming Caddy, he solved the problem by pissing on it.

Has the motorsports world ever produced a more colorful or complicated character than Carroll Shelby? Movie-star handsome and dangerously charismatic, he amassed a vast coterie of powerful friends and beautiful women, not counting his seven "official" wives. "Tall, skinny, wearing striped overalls, always with a pretty girl and always enjoying himself hugely, he was the very essence of what a race driver ought to be," James T. Crow wrote in *Road & Track*.[1] But race driver was only one of the many roles he played during his long and eventful life. More often, he was a serial entrepreneur with a cavalier attitude toward money—other people's money, that is. Not for nothing did friends call

Although he later became famous for other exploits, Carroll Shelby was first and foremost a race car driver. Here, he balances an Aston Martin DBR1 in a textbook four-wheel drift through Madgwick Corner during the Tourist Trophy race at Goodwood in 1958. The following year, in a sister car, he and Roy Salvadori would win the 24 Hours of Le Mans—the capstone of his career as a driver.
Revs Institute / George Phillips Photograph Collection

him "Billie Sol," alluding to the Texas con man who infamously faked mortgages on nonexistent agricultural ammonia tanks. As Don Frey once said about Shelby, "Whenever I walked out of his office after a meeting, I felt in my pockets to make sure everything was still there."[2]

Frey was joking, of course. Well, half joking. As the assistant general manager of Ford Division, Frey was the executive who'd signed off on the decision to give Shelby the engine he was now installing in the chassis from AC Cars even though he'd just met Shelby and didn't really know anything about him. But this was par for the course. Closing deals with a raspy drawl and twinkling eyes, Shelby was a salesman for the ages and a bottomless repository of Texas tall tales that only occasionally intersected with the truth. "He could sell white blackbirds," his first wife once said of him.[3] But what he was really selling, most of the time, was himself.

Shelby was born in 1923 in the small country town of Leesburg, roughly equidistant from Dallas, Texarkana, and Shreveport. He was a child of the Great Depression who saw military service as the route to a more prosperous and secure future. He enlisted in the army seven months before the attack on Pearl Harbor, hoping to fly airplanes, then spent World War II as an instructor pilot who never left the United States. Come to find out, Shelby felt constrained by the restrictions and limitations of military life. After the war, he tried a couple of businesses on for size, but none of them fit his personality or ambition. Cars had fascinated him since he was a child, and he was a gifted natural athlete who effortlessly picked up new sports. (Later in life, he became a scratch golfer.) Car racing seemed like it might be a pleasant diversion. In 1952, he drove a friend's MG-TC in a pissant sports car race in Norman, Oklahoma. After waxing the field in the small-bore race, Shelby moved up in class and embarrassed drivers in much more powerful Jaguar XK120s. "It wasn't much," he said. "I stayed sideways all the time."[4]

Sports car racing was just getting off the ground in the 1950s. The Sports Car Club of America (SCCA) was the only game in town, and it was strictly an amateur proposition. Shelby didn't have the money or social credentials to crash the no-crowds-and-no-crowding scene. But he had the skill and courage to drive big, hairy sports cars the way they were supposed to be driven, and he had the charm and moxie to persuade the sportsmen who could afford these imported extravagances to hire him. He was paid under the table while he drove Allards and Jags for Roy Cherryhomes, then a whole succession of exotic Ferraris and Maseratis for Allen Guiberson, Tony Parravano, Dick Hall, Jim Kimberly, Temple Buell, John Edgar, Lucky Casner, and Frank Harrison. "I drove cars professionally in an amateur sport," Shelby liked to say.[5] Among his American road-racing contemporaries, his only equal was Phil Hill, who would become the country's first Formula 1 World Champion. But the more mercenary Shelby had Hill beat hands down in the cash-on-the-barrelhead department.

Before long, Shelby made his way to Europe because that's where the money was. But even overseas, the pay was paltry. In 1956, Enzo Ferrari offered him a factory ride for $70 a month—mere chicken feed. Shelby turned him down. "Instead," he said later, "I went to drive for John Wyer, and he let me make a living."[6] At the time, Wyer managed the Aston Martin sports car operation. Over the years, he would employ superstars ranging from Stirling Moss to Jacky Ickx, yet he called Shelby "one of the really great sports car drivers."[7] Teamed by Wyer with Roy Salvadori, Shelby won Le Mans in an Aston Martin DBR1 in 1959. It was the capstone of his driving career.

But winning Le Mans didn't transform Shelby into a celebrity. Back then, Americans didn't consider racing, especially road racing, a major-league sport, and Indianapolis 500 winners were the only drivers who registered on the radar of the general public. But from the start, Shelby appreciated the power of publicity, and he understood how to generate it. Early on, without thinking, he wore a pair of Carhartt striped bib overalls in a race on a sweltering afternoon at the Eagle Mountain National Guard Base near Fort Worth. When he saw how much attention they drew, he kept on wearing them. He made sure he was in bib overalls when he was photographed for the cover of *Sports Illustrated* after being named the 1957 Driver of the Year, and he changed into a pair shortly before starting his final stint before taking the checkered flag at Le Mans in 1959. As Shelby himself put it: "They wrote about a cowboy from Texas. It was a lot of show business."[8] The ease with which he could manipulate the narrative amused him.

Shelby suffered for several years from angina pectoris, a condition that causes severe chest pain due to insufficient blood supply to the heart. Though not fatal, the disease was serious—and dangerous—enough to compel him to retire at the end of the 1960 season. He finished the year racing with his front pocket full of nitroglycerin pills that he'd pop whenever he had an attack of angina. Despite agonizing chest pains, he scored his last big win in a Birdcage Maserati in the *Los Angeles Herald-Express* Grand Prix at Riverside. He needed four pills to make it through the second-to-last race of the year and seven for the season ender. But by finishing second to Moss in his final race, Shelby clinched the United States Auto Club (USAC) Road Racing Championship.

Despite his successes on the track, Shelby entered his post-driving career in a precarious financial situation. With a wife (whom he soon divorced) and three teenage children, he hadn't saved much money. He moved to Southern California, which was then the center of the American race car industry. A proposal to build a racetrack fizzled. He formulated plans to run a high-performance driving school at Riverside International Raceway, but an ad in a local racing magazine didn't generate enough enthusiasm to justify scheduling any classes. Fortunately, his friend Tony Webner gave him the distribution rights to sell Goodyear racing tires in eleven western states, and he had a couple of side hustles representing Koni shock absorbers and Champion spark plugs. This brought in enough income for Shelby to rent a tiny office from Dean Moon and hire his live-in girlfriend, Joan Sherman, as his assistant. But it was a hand-to-mouth existence. His friend Bill Neale, a genial Dallas advertising executive, made it a point to buy Shelby dinner during business trips to LA. "He didn't say he didn't have any money," Neale remembered, "but it was obvious—boy, he was broke."[9]

But Shelby had something more valuable than cash: he had an idea—to build an American sports car and put it into production. (Actually, for some strange reason, he always referred to them as "sport" cars.) It's impossible to say exactly when Shelby came up with the concept. The stories he told changed repeatedly over the years, and there's no foolproof way to decide where the truth ended and the revisions began. But Shelby insisted that he first began working on a tube-frame chassis with a flathead Ford in 1951 with Ed Wilkins, who owned the MG he drove in his first race. "We decided to put a Hemi in it," Shelby said. "We were building it in a garage I had there in Dallas. But we were making so damn much noise that my wife ran us out of the garage."[10] He also said the dream of building his own car was one of the major reasons he'd jumped at the chance to race in Europe. "That's the reason that I hung around Ferrari, Aston Martin, Maserati—trying to learn how those little companies operated."[11]

Shelby had already taken a few swings at the ball without making solid contact. He'd commissioned the design and drawing of a tube-frame chassis, but no metal was ever cut, and there had been some talks with Donald Healey of Austin-Healey fame, but they'd led nowhere. Then Shelby had gotten the blessing of General Motors executive Ed Cole, father of the small-block Chevy, to rebody three Corvettes in Modena, Italy, at Carrozzeria Scaglietti, best known as Ferrari's preferred coachbuilder. Against all odds, the project panned out. But when Zora Arkus-Duntov, Chevrolet's in-house Corvette whisperer, heard about the cars, he raised holy hell, and a chastened Cole told Shelby,

The saga begins! In February 1962, a small cadre of hot-rodders began assembling the first Cobra in Dean Moon's speed shop. Peering at the engine is Moon's chief mechanic, Roy Gammell, who spearheaded the project. Next to him is his son, Doyle, and Doyle's high school bud, Ralph Maldonado. Behind them is the inventory for the Goodyear distributorship that kept Shelby afloat while he was struggling to put the Cobra into production. *Ford Motor Company*

"I never gave you those three sons of bitches, and don't you ever tell anybody that I did."[12] (Evidently, Ferrari wasn't too happy with Scaglietti either.) Shelby had even floated a proposal to scratch-build a sports car with Max Balchowsky, the creator of Ol' Yaller, the shockingly quick junkyard dog that Shelby had raced shortly before retiring, but that would-be project was another nonstarter.

By this time, Shelby was palling around with the Petersen Publishing editors behind *Hot Rod*, *Motor Trend*, and *Sports Car Graphic* magazines. In fact, he was even listed on the masthead of *Sports Car Graphic* as a contributing editor for a few issues in 1961. A spiffy ad in the magazine for the Carroll Shelby School of Race Car Driving ("Do you want to become a racing driver BUT don't know how to begin?") drew an unexpectedly robust response. This galvanized Shelby into actually putting together what he hoped would be the first school of its kind in the country. Shelby had planned to go into business with Paul O'Shea, a prominent East Coast hot shoe who'd won several SCCA national championships in Mercedes-Benz 300 SLs. The two of them met at Riverside to hash out the details. Instead, there was an explosion. "You've got to understand that both of these guys were top egos,"[13] Peter Brock said. "Shelby thought that O'Shea would be his assistant and run the school for him, and O'Shea thought just the opposite. When reality set in, O'Shea said, 'Fuck you,' and walked off."[14]

Brock had recently left a job as a designer at GM and moved to Southern California to pursue his goal of racing cars for a living. While working as a parts chaser for Balchowsky, he'd befriended Shelby and accompanied him to Riverside for the abortive meeting with O'Shea. After O'Shea stormed off, an exasperated Shelby turned to Brock and said, "I don't have time to do this. Do you want to do it?" At the time, Brock had a grand total of a dozen or so races in his logbook. But he knew that fortune favors the brave. "You bet!" he said.[15] He therefore would become America's first official race car driving instructor.

With Brock taking care of business in Riverside, Shelby stayed abreast of car industry goings-on by attending weekly three-martini lunches with the Petersen mafia in West Hollywood. During the summer, he heard that the Bristol Aeroplane Company was ending production of the motor that powered the British AC Ace sports car. Wheels started turning in Shelby's head. In the best of all possible worlds, he wanted to build a car from the ground up. But the Ace seemed like a plausible alternative. It was a handsome two-seat roadster based on a simple ladder-style frame that John Tojeiro had laid down in 1952. The rudimentary suspension—transverse leaf springs and lower wishbones, front and rear—had been inspired by the prewar Fiat Topolino. Better still, it had been proven in the wildly successful rear-engine single-seaters built by John Cooper. Fitted with a Bristol powerplant, the Ace offered reasonably peppy performance and had dominated the SCCA's 2.0-liter class for the previous five years.

Just looking at the long hood, Shelby was sure the car was large enough to accommodate a bigger engine. He immediately wrote to AC owner Charles Hurlock to find out if he'd be interested in modifying a chassis to accept an American V-8. Initially, Shelby was thinking about the slick, new all-aluminum 215-cubic-inch V-8 from Buick-Oldsmobile-Pontiac (which would ultimately find its way into countless Rovers, Land Rovers, Triumphs, MGBs, and Morgans). But by the time Hurlock wrote back to say he was on board, Shelby had come up with a better idea.

Through his magazine contacts, Shelby had caught wind of the impending introduction of a new V-8 developed by Ford. Thanks to an innovative thin-wall casting process, the 221-cubic-inch engine was nearly the same weight—but almost twice as powerful—as the Bristol it would be replacing. The previous month, while attending the Pikes Peak Hill Climb as the Goodyear rep, Shelby had met Ford motorsports executive Dave Evans. Shelby wrote him a letter outlining his plans to stick an American engine in the AC Ace. To Shelby's delight, he received a phone call from Evans a few days later.

"That AC chassis may be just the thing for our new engine," Evans said. "Tell you what we're going to do. We're sending you a couple of these new engines. Play around with them; put them in your chassis and see what you come up with. Let me know."[16]

Shelby could hardly believe what he was hearing. But sure enough, a pair of V-8s were delivered to Santa Fe Springs, where Shelby hired Chastain to give the engines the old hot-rod hocus-pocus. Ford had already decided to bore out the 221 to displace 260 cubic inches, and while the standard motor was earmarked for humdrum Fairlane family sedans, Shelby was being given a high-performance version with solid lifters, more compression and bigger ports and valves. A third engine materialized unexpectedly in Thames Ditton in a wood crate with a mysterious legend stenciled on it. AC mechanics warily regarded the unidentified foreign object. "FoMoCo—what does that mean?" one of them asked.[17] What it meant was that Shelby had performed a remarkable sleight of hand. He'd secured Ford Motor Company engines on the strength of AC chassis he didn't have, and he'd drummed up AC chassis on the strength of Ford engines he didn't own. Shelby wasn't so much a magician as he was an alchemist, creating something out of nothing.

Before flying to England to check on the progress at AC Cars, Shelby made a detour to Dearborn to dazzle the men who would, he hoped, underwrite his project. Exactly whom he met with and precisely what was said is impossible to verify. Different people told different stories—not only different from each other, mind you, but different from the stories they themselves told on different occasions. Without question, Shelby saw Evans and Frey, and maybe Lee Iacocca as well. Hal Sperlich, best known as the architect of the minivan, later claimed that *he* was the first Ford executive to meet Shelby. What they saw in Shelby is also a matter of debate. In some versions, they were laboring under the misimpression that he was a deep-pocketed Texas oilman, and they were stunned to find out later that he was poorer than an out-of-work roughneck. Other accounts

A Cobra at Le Mans in 1957? Nope. This is an AC Ace, the car whose ladder-style frame and barchetta bodywork formed the foundation of Shelby's Southern California roadster. Ken Rudd and Peter Bolton finished second in class (and tenth overall) with an Ace powered by a 2.0-liter Bristol engine. Five years later, Shelby would sub in a small-block Ford V-8, and the Cobra would motor into automotive history. *Revs Institute / Karl Ludvigsen Photograph Collection*

say they took him for a rube lost in the big city and couldn't believe it when he turned out to have enough business savvy to pull off the deal.

As usual, Shelby's recollection is the most entertaining, though not necessarily the most accurate. "Dave Evans and Don Frey took me into Iacocca's office," he said, relishing the story. "I told him I needed twenty-five thousand dollars, and I'd build a car that would outrun the Corvettes. I'm told—Iacocca says he don't remember—but I'm told he told Don Frey, 'Give that son of a bitch twenty-five thousand dollars before he bites somebody.'"[18]

Shelby got an even warmer reception in Thames Ditton. To say that Charles Hurlock and his nephew Derek saw Shelby as a source of salvation who would deliver them from financial ruin is overly dramatic. But AC Cars was looking for work, and it looked like Shelby was in a position to provide it. Still, it wasn't clear then—or now, for that matter—which one of the parties was the lead dog during the early days of their partnership. As with the Ford GT40, the product of another strained Anglo-American collaboration, British historians promote the hypothesis that the Brits were the prime movers while the Americans provided little more than engines and money. According to this theory, the Cobra was merely a gussied-up Ace that Shelby more or less snaked away from the Hurlocks. Americans, on the other hand, maintain that Shelby made so many improvements that, at a certain point, there was nothing left of the original car. To them, the Ace is best thought of as the blank canvas upon which a masterpiece was painted.

In the beginning, at least, the changes Shelby requested were minimal. The Ace recently had been reconfigured to accept the 2.6-liter inline-6 found in the Ford Zephyr. For Shelby's purposes, the bodywork was largely unchanged other than discreetly reshaping the fender arches to accommodate a slightly wider track. Under the skin, the modifications were equally modest. Thicker tubes were used in the frame and cross bracing added to withstand the additional grunt of the bigger, torque-ier engine. A big Salisbury rear end like the one in the E-type Jaguar was installed, and the rear brakes were moved inboard to avoid brake pad contamination. Heavier-duty half shafts and hubs were also retrofitted. Nothing approaching rocket science, in other words, and the conversion didn't take long.

On a cold, damp day at the end of January 1962, Shelby drove the prototype for the first time on the broad, featureless expanses of Silverstone. Shelby rarely talked about the experience, which was odd, considering that this represented the realization of a goal he'd been chasing on and off for the past decade. The most likely explanation for this atypical reticence was that he wasn't very impressed. The engine was a stock 221, which hardly qualified as a world-beater, and judging from all the development work done after the car arrived in the States, the handling must have been underwhelming. Remember, too, that Shelby was accustomed to driving the fastest and most sophisticated race cars in the world. Less than two years earlier, he'd planted an Aston Martin DBR4 Formula 1 car sixth on the grid during the British Grand Prix, outqualifying Moss, Bruce McLaren, and Graham Hill.

Now that he'd actually driven the car, Shelby first understood—really understood—just how far he still had to go to transform his dream into reality. It's important to recognize that, from the start, he was aiming higher than building a one-off race car. Known generically as specials, these sports racers ranged from impeccably built cars such as the Scarab and the Troutman & Barnes Chaparral to shade-tree contraptions that mated unsuitable chassis with impractical engines. Shelby's stated objective was to build one hundred cars—the minimum number to be eligible to compete against the Corvette in the SCCA's A Production class. Because if his new baby could beat the Corvette on the track, then it would be anointed as the best sports car in America.

Three weeks later, the prototype—less engine and transmission—arrived at Los Angeles International Airport. Shelby picked it up with a borrowed trailer. But before heading back to Santa Fe Springs, he granted an interview at the airport to Gus Vignolle, the editor-in-chief of *MotoRacing*, a small but feisty biweekly published on newsprint. Vignolle's presence at LAX—by invitation—was emblematic of Shelby's symbiotic relationship with the press.

There was undoubtedly a mercenary aspect to Shelby's embrace of the media. He recognized the power of the pen, and he wasn't above unleashing a charm offensive to make sure he got the coverage he wanted. But Shelby genuinely enjoyed the company of the gentlemen of the press. He was comfortable with the profane banter and disdain for pomposity that characterized the Fourth Estate. Shelby, in turn, was catnip for the reporters who covered him. He made himself available rather than hiding behind a phalanx of public relations operatives, he was always good for a lively quote, and he told stories that had the patina of truth even if they weren't 100 percent true.

"Back when I was still racing," he remembered, "they used to ask me what I'd do when I finished. Sometimes, I would say I was a bat guano distributor just for the fun of it. Nobody knew what a bat guano distributor was, so they'd go ahead and print it. Later, they'd come back to me and say, 'You son of a bitch, you snuck that one in on me.'"[19]

In magazine stories, credited to writers who'd followed him for years, Shelby was often referred to as Ol' Shel. The phrase was used as a written version of a wink, as if to say, *We know that this is all a bunch of bat guano, but we're in on the joke.* They were and, then again, they weren't. Or maybe it's more correct to say that the joke was *on* them. Because wittingly or not, they were the ones who happily repeated the tall tales that burnished his reputation. Like the newspaper editor in the classic John Ford Western, *The Man Who Shot Liberty Valance*, they subscribed to the dictum: "When the legend becomes fact, print the legend."[20]

Vignolle's article in *MotoRacing*, the first ever written about Shelby's new car, was an exemplar of gullible reporting: "'It is an honest one hundred seventy-five mile per hour touring car,' [Shelby] said as he loaded the car at the airport. 'They are building the car in volume, and it won't be long before one hundred of them will be available. I think we'll be able to flatten the Corvettes and E-Jags any time.'"[21] The plan, Shelby told Vignolle with a straight face, was to race the car at Santa Barbara in May. For those keeping score at home, the car—a different one, actually—didn't race until October, and the hundredth Cobra wouldn't be available for more than a year. Oh, and the only way it could have reached 175 miles per hour was if it'd had been dropped out of an airliner flying at thirty-five thousand feet.

The most interesting part of Vignolle's story was the headline: "Shelby AC Cobra Unveiled." Yes, Shelby had chosen a name for his car even before it technically existed. He always insisted that "Cobra" had come to him in a dream, and when he woke up in the middle of the night, he'd written it down on a notepad next to his bed so that he wouldn't forget. It wasn't clear whether he'd had this dream years earlier and squirreled the name away for future use or if the epiphany arrived after he started working with AC Cars. Either way, it was one of the most evocative names in automotive history, and it was a fitting testament to Shelby's promotional genius.

According to the Cobra creation myth, the prototype was towed back to Santa Fe Springs, where a small crew quickly assembled the drivetrain, and Shelby and Moon went joyriding in the car that night, a mere eight hours after the engine installation process began. Alas, this is more bat guano, which becomes obvious when you do the math. Picking up and loading the car—actually a rolling chassis—would have taken a few hours. Ditto for the drive from the airport across town on surface streets to Santa Fe Springs, then maneuvering the chassis into Moon's garage. Although the installation wasn't complicated, the crew working on the car had never seen an AC Ace before. The job required all sorts of fussy custom work, from fabricating brackets to fitting the trim to hanging the exhaust. Welding seams had to be filed, and countless hours and boxes of steel-wool pads were consumed getting the aluminum bodywork to shine. It wasn't the work of a day. More like a week, according to Doyle Gammell, the son of the man ramrodding the project.

At the time, Gammell was a senior at nearby Santa Fe Springs High School. The previous October, he'd welded up square tubing into a tire rack for Shelby's fledgling Goodyear distributorship, which was operated out of the Mooneyes shop. Now, he and his high-school buddy Larry Maldonado were part of a makeshift crew of about a half dozen guys who came and went while working twelve to fifteen hours a day. Before long, word made the rounds on the street. "I mean everybody and anybody in the Southern California hot-rod scene had heard about what Shelby was trying to do," he recalls. "You wouldn't believe all the people—and celebrities—who came through Moon's to see this thing in process. It only lasted for four or five days, but it was like Grand Central Station for movers and shakers."[22]

Legend has it that immediately after the Cobra was pronounced street worthy—after a mere eight hours of labor—Shelby and Moon took it out in search of Corvettes to humiliate. Not true, the younger Gammell said. "When he got the Cobra done, Dean and I took that sucker out into the oil fields [behind the shop]," he recalls.[23] The dirt roads cut between oil derricks and pump jacks were a perfect test track even if the car left something to be desired. "There were no seats in it," Gammell recalled. "Dean sat on a milk carton, and I sat on the belly pan, but we got it running real good. Right off the bat, it outperformed the Corvette. We made a couple of turns and brought it back to the shop before Shelby got there because he would've shit a brick. He did *not* want anybody to have the first ride other than him. To think that I got to ride in a car that sold for $13.75 million, and I ain't got a picture to prove it."

As part of the assembly process, Shelby removed the AC badges and had "Shelby" hand-painted in script on the nose by German hot-rod artist Dick Bolik. When the car was buttoned up, Shelby asked Gammell, "Okay, Doyle, you're the rebel in the neighborhood. Where do we go to find a Corvette?" Gammell told Shelby to check out Harvey's Broiler, the Googie-style drive-in restaurant on Firestone Boulevard in nearby Downey, or the Wich Stand in Inglewood, where epic street races on a closed-off stretch of the 405 freeway were negotiated. Shelby didn't find any victims that night. But he felt confident enough to telephone *Sports Car Graphic* editor-in-chief John Christy the next morning. "C'mon out, 'rat now—got sumpthin' to show you," Shelby said without preamble.[24]

Christy and Shelby shared plenty of history. It was Christy who'd given Shelby a sinecure as a contributing editor when he needed a job, and it was Christy who'd encouraged him to run the ad that had gotten the driving school off the ground. Now, Shelby was returning the favors. As soon as Christy climbed into the Cobra, Shelby punched the throttle and laid down two black streaks of rubber down Norwalk Boulevard in front of Dean Moon's shop. "Over the years," Christy wrote later, "I'd ridden in and driven some reasonably ferocious machinery from hot rods and track roadsters to such exotica as a Porsche RS-60 and a few examples of Ferrari, but that car, for that time, was pure Billy Bad-Ass. Later Cobras were quicker and a number were some bit faster, but none ever left the impression between the shoulder blades I felt—and still feel—during those first few minutes in CSX0001."[25] (The car was later redesignated CSX2000.)

When the thrill ride was over, Christy got an even bigger surprise: Shelby tossed him the keys and drawled, "Come back in three days."[26]

This was Shelby at his best—generous, fearless, and awesomely cool. To be sure, he was expecting a quid pro quo in the form of a flattering magazine article. But he could have given the first ride to one of the bigger, more influential magazines. And remember, this was the only Cobra in existence. It had barely been shaken down, much less tested. There was a very real possibility that a major component would fail or the experimental motor would go kablooey. Not to worry. The Cobra didn't miss a beat, and Christy bagged the marque's first Corvette scalp during an impromptu "speed contest" on the Ventura Freeway after roaring away from Moon's shop. His story, in the May 1962 issue of *Sports Car Graphic*, listed a top speed of 145 mph—and a projected 170 mph for the upcoming race model, which was being prepared for SCCA

Sports Car Graphic editor John Christy puts CSX2000 through its paces for a magazine story days after the car was assembled at Dean Moon's shop. At this point, the body is still in bare aluminum, with "Shelby" hand-painted in script on the hood where the AC Cars badge had been. "For those wishing to cause consternation in the hairy big-bore Production ranks," Christy wrote in the May 1962 issue, "the line forms on the right." *Dave Friedman*

A Production class. The list price was $5,995, or roughly comparable with a Bristol-powered Ace or a fully optioned Corvette. "For those wishing to cause consternation in the hairy big-bore Production ranks," Christy wrote, "the line forms on the right."[27]

Ford didn't know what to make of the Cobra. The car looked familiar, and other than the engine, the design was positively archaic, from the worm-and-sector steering to the buggy-spring suspension. As for Shelby himself, nobody was sure whether he was a player or a poseur. Ford decided to send somebody from the comptroller's office to LA to assess the situation. The assignment went to Ray Geddes, in part because he happened to be working late on the Friday night when the call for a body came down. He turned out to be a propitious choice. Although he'd joined Ford less than a year earlier, he'd been to law school, earned a business degree, and briefly run his own company. Bright, enterprising, and diplomatic, he became one of Shelby's staunchest allies. "His job was to look after Ford's interests out here," said Bruce Junor, who later worked for Shelby on several projects. "But he had real rapport with Shelby, and he knew how to work with Ford management."[28]

Geddes met Shelby in Dean Moon's shop, where the first and only Cobra was still in bare aluminum, and he returned to Dearborn with a favorable report. Ford agreed to supply engines to Shelby in return for "Powered by Ford" plaques on the front fenders—a finely calibrated solution designed to soak up reflected glory if the Cobra program took off while offering plausible deniability if the project went south. This emboldened Shelby and Sherman to craft a grandiloquent press release trumpeting the imminent introduction of "a new 150 mph sports roadster—the Shelby AC Cobra—designed for fast touring and world-wide road racing competition." The debut was scheduled for the New York International Automobile Show in April.

First, the Cobra had to be painted. But what color? Moon was partial to a proprietary shade of yellow that he had specially blended in a paint shop in Whittier. "Nothing leaves Moon's unless it's yellow," he told Shelby.[29]

"I don't want to paint it yellow," Shelby said.

"It's going to be yellow, dammit!"

"We're not painting that car yellow!"

Eventually, they compromised on a unique pearlescent yellow to be painted by Jeffries. This was the color it was wearing in the New York Coliseum. The car was still yellow when it appeared in an ad in the October issue of *Playboy*. "Fair warning from the Cobra!" the ad copy read. "From this day on, drivers of the world's proudest sports cars are advised to stick to the right-hand side of the road. For at any moment an AC/Cobra can come storming past, belly low to the road with twin pipes ripping out a curt 'good-by!'" Gotta love the tagline, too: "Cobra: Buy it . . . or watch it go by."[30]

At the end of May, Vignolle breathlessly reported in *MotoRacing* that twenty-five Cobras had been built and 250 more were in the pipeline. Presumably, Shelby himself was the source of these whoppers. In fact, he'd built only one car, the prototype, which officially bore serial number CSX2000. ("C" was AC's internal designation for the Ace chassis, "S" stood for Shelby and "X" for Export.) But he managed to fool magazine editors and make the rounds of the show circuit with his single Cobra, thanks to a liberal application of snake oil. "He painted that one car in three different colors so that people would think it was in production," Fred Gamble said.[31]

Gamble had retired from racing the previous year after driving the same Birdcage Maserati that Shelby had run in his final race. The two of them happened to sit together at an industry luncheon in New York, and Shelby offered him a job as advertising director. "He wanted me to jump in my Volkswagen Beetle and drive it across the country," Gamble said. "And I did."[32] That was the effect that Shelby had on people. Gamble spent about a year in California before joining Goodyear and becoming the founding director of its international race tire division, where he helped support Shelby's European aspirations.

By mid-1962, Shelby was at an impasse. Alchemy had gotten him this far. But without actual cash money, he couldn't hire a crew or rent and outfit a space large enough to put the Cobra into production. Enter Ed Hugus, a man who had for many years been erased from the Cobra story, much like Trotskyites were written out of official histories of the Soviet Union. A World War II paratrooper who'd seen combat during the island-hopping campaigns in the Pacific, Hugus opened European Cars in downtown Pittsburgh in 1952 and Continental Cars next door three years later. At those two dealerships, he sold everything from Jaguars and Porsches to Maseratis and Alfa Romeos. He was an accomplished club racer who competed regularly at Sebring and Le Mans, and he helped found the local chapter of the SCCA. He'd known Shelby casually for years. When they ran into each other at the New York Auto Show, Shelby explained the challenges he faced getting the Cobra into production, and Hugus volunteered to help.

What was announced at the time was that Hugus would become the Cobra's first dealer, with exclusive distribution rights east of the Mississippi. Although this was true, it was only part of the story. Hugus also offered to take on Shelby's AC debt and finish the cars coming from England in his shop. This was a generous arrangement not only financially but also in terms of labor, which was substantial, since AC supplied only rolling chassis, and plenty of tedious finish work had to be done in addition to installing the engine and the four-speed Borg-Warner T-10 transmission. Shelby latched onto Hugus's offer as eagerly as a drowning man grabbing a life preserver. Hugus, a stand-up businessman, agreed to the deal on the basis of a handshake. And so it happened that six of the first seven production Cobras were built not in the heart of SoCal hot-rod country but in downtown Pittsburgh with absolutely no input from Shelby and his skeleton crew. Altogether, more than two dozen early Cobras were invoiced to Hugus at European Cars. Needless to say, this inconvenient truth was expunged from official company histories.

A few months down the road, Hugus and Shelby had a bitter falling out, and although it was patched up after some bruised feelings, their relationship was never the same. Shelby was often generous with his praise, but he also knew how to hold a grudge. Whether consciously or not, he omitted Hugus from his version of the Cobra saga. (Unbelievably, Hugus doesn't rate a single mention in Shelby's memoir.) Hugus, for opaque reasons, minimized his role in bringing the Cobra to market—or at least he did for the better part of fifty years. But after a half century of self-imposed silence, he finally decided to speak out. He provided all the gory details of his troubled association with Shelby to his biographer, Robert Walker, and stated flatly, "I alone was the person financially responsible for those first Cobras, and my job was to complete them as quickly as possible and try and make a profit."[33]

Although Shelby churlishly refused to give Hugus the credit he deserved, Joan Sherman acknowledged the debt she and Shelby owed him. "Ed Hugus really saved our program in the beginning, and we owe him a lot," she said. "Without him, our lives could have been miserable."[34] Would the Cobra adventure have ended in purgatory without his help? Although it's possible, it doesn't seem likely. The car made too much sense, and Shelby was too cunning a salesman. If Hugus hadn't stepped up, Shelby would have redoubled his efforts to find another sugar daddy to prevent the project from cratering. Anyway, by the summer, he had locked in a more pliable and reliable source of funding, which allowed him to ease Hugus out of the picture.

Ford was finally warming to the project. Over the past decade, the company had lost market share to GM because its cars were perceived by younger buyers as dull and dreary. Iacocca was determined to bring them back into the fold through a program called Total Performance, which used racing as a marketing tool. Besides developing a new engine to conquer the Indianapolis 500, Ford was also sinking massive resources into NASCAR, drag racing, muscle cars, and even international rallying. The Cobra, designed to outrun the Corvette, seemed like a logical and economical addition to the Total Performance portfolio. A formal contract with Shelby was negotiated. Not only would he get engines for free, but chassis purchased from AC would be billed directly to Ford Motor Credit. Geddes also scrounged up $20,000 to pay for a new shop so Shelby could finally move out of the cramped space he was renting from Moon. Coincidentally, Shelby heard that Lance Reventlow, the wealthy Woolworth heir who'd funded construction of the Scarab sports racers and Formula 1 cars, was shutting down his operation in Venice. Shelby thought it would be perfect for his new company.

Reventlow's shop, at 1042 Princeton Drive, was nestled between bustling commercial storefronts on Lincoln Boulevard and a sedate, blue-collar residential neighborhood farther east. (A few blocks from the ocean, it later became part of Marina del Rey.) It was housed in a red-brick building with a mezzanine level for offices cantilevered over the front wall. With eight thousand square feet of floor space, the shop was a state-of-the-art facility equipped with a Heenan & Froude engine dynamometer, lathes, mills, drill presses, sheet-metal brakes, and just about anything else needed to build a car from scratch. Equally, if not more, important were the human assets that came with the shop. The two most prominent were the people who ran it—general manager Warren Olson and his wife, Simone, who was in charge of the office.

Warren was a fixture on LA's road-racing scene, and hiring him gave Shelby's start-up instant credibility. Simone also played a critical role in Shelby American's early days. Although the company was rooted in the *Mad Men* era of male domination and racing was—and still is—very much a boy's club, women were critical to its success. Besides keeping the books, Simone also provided adult supervision. And Sherman, though often thought of as nothing more than Shelby's girlfriend, handled a lot of the hiring early on and drummed up new business that helped keep the doors open. She was so well trusted, in fact, that she signed company checks as "Joan Shelby."

Still, it was the third ex-Reventlow employee who turned out to be the most valuable. Phil Remington is the Paul Bunyan of American motorsports, except that most of the folklore that's sprung up about him was absolutely true. Dan Gurney worked with him for the better part of fifty years, and he never ceased to be amazed by Remington's skills and accomplishments. "Rem is a remnant of an age of American ingenuity," he said. "He's the kind of guy who can *do* things. It doesn't matter what you're talking about; he can do it. If you're stuck out in the middle of nowhere, he's the guy you want with you. He's a walking encyclopedia, and he's a one-man band. He's just like a tornado—a great, unstoppable force of nature."[35]

Remington could beat out a dent in a fender, and he could tune an obstinate Weber carburetor. He could rig a spring latch for a door, and he could fabricate a cross-ram intake manifold so complicated and elegant that it would make grown men weep with envy. "Phil was probably the greatest race car builder in the world,"[36] Brock said. "We had some really good guys in the shop—*really* good. And some of them could do some things as well as Phil. But he could do *everything* well, and he was unbelievably fast. He'd be working on something of his own, and if he happened to look up and see somebody doing something wrong on the other side of the shop, he'd walk over, shove the guy out of the way, get it done in half the time, and walk away without saying a word. He set such a high standard that it was difficult to work with him."[37]

He was known as "STP," for "Super Twitchy Phil," because he was always busy, busy, busy. Several of the guys who worked with him tell the same story—that he was at the shop when they left at night and he was there when they arrived in the morning, and they weren't willing to swear under oath that he'd left at any point in between. "Phil is a human generator," fabricator Bill Eaton said.[38] "I've never seen him get tired mentally or physically. And there doesn't seem to be any bottom to his ability. You work with most people on a project, and you eventually reach a point where they can't go any further. Phil just keeps on going."

Of course, someone has to be the best. Someone has to be the fastest. Someone has to work the longest hours. What made Remington more than a mere all-time great were two qualities that verged on super-powers. First, he was able to examine a broken component and almost immediately suss out why it had failed. Second, and even more extraordinary, he had the rare ability to come up with solutions on the spot, in the heat of battle, while the clock was running. As Carroll Smith, one of Shelby's longtime employees, once put it: "When there is a problem, by the time other people realize it, he's already made six fixes."[39]

Remington grew up steeped in the SoCal go-fast car world. He belonged to the Santa Monica Low Flyers, the legendary hot-rod club whose members included Phil Hill, fuel-injection pioneer Stu Hilborn, noted cam grinder Jack Engle, and Jim Travers and Frank Coon, founders of the famed Traco engine dynasty. After seeing action as a B-24 flight engineer in World War II, Remington set speed records with a flathead Ford on the dry lakes of the Mojave Desert. He later scratch-built the fiberglass-bodied special that Sterling Edwards use to win the first major sports car race in California, then worked on several Indy 500-winning cars and was a core component in the team behind Reventlow's Formula 1 Scarab. He'd just finished his last project for Reventlow, almost single-handedly building the final Scarab, a mid-engine precursor to the Can-Am cars, when Shelby offered him a job. "I just changed payrolls, I guess you could say," Remington remembered.[40]

Shortly after moving into the new shop in Venice, Shelby finally received a second chassis from AC. From the start, CSX2002 was

Virtuoso fabricator and quick-fix genius Phil Remington had done everything from dry lakes racing to the Indy 500 to Formula 1 before he was hired by Shelby in 1962. Thereafter, with the exception of Shelby himself, nobody meant more to Shelby American than this fabled master of all trades. According to company lore, blueprints bore the legend: "Draftsman: Remington. Designer: Remington. Engineer: Remington. Approved: Remington." *Revs Institute / Jean Charles Martha Photograph Collection*

meant to be a race car, but there was a ton of work to be done before it was ready to be tracked. What especially irked Remington was the cheap hardware that AC preferred. By this time, all the serious builders in Southern California used aircraft-grade fasteners, but early Cobra chassis arrived from England with the kind of nuts and bolts typically found in American hardware stores. "The car was an absolute shitbox when we got it," Remington said.[41] "The way [the cars] came over, they wouldn't go two laps." Shelby was equally scathing. "Everything broke on it for the first three months," he said. "Everything."[42]

Although Shelby had been out of the cockpit for only two years, he was never tempted to seriously test, much less race, the Cobra. Instead, he got Gurney, who was coming off his first F1 win in France, to shake down the car at Riverside. Gurney thought the camber settings were out of whack, leading to persistent understeer. "It was still a little bit short of the Corvette," he recalled. "I talked to Rem and said, 'You need to do this, this, and that.' Within no time at all, we went back to Riverside, and the car was faster than the Corvette."[43]

Shelby quickly filed homologation papers with the Fédération Internationale de l'Automobile (FIA). Approval would entitle the car to race in the GT class in international competition. To be honest, Shelby had no immediate intention to enter any FIA races. But the homologation document got two critical points on the record. First, the form established that the car wasn't an AC Cobra; it was a Cobra, period, and was therefore entirely independent from the British roadster on which it was based. Second, the manufacturer was listed not as AC Cars but as Shelby American, a brand-new company that Shelby recently had incorporated to build, race, and sell Cobras. It wouldn't be long before Shelby American was the eight hundred-pound gorilla of American road racing.

The buzz was building. Although only one car was available, it made the rounds of *Car Life, Cars, Hot Rod,* and *Sports Car Graphic,* which called the Cobra the fastest production car it had ever tested. "The upper limit is such that it takes practice and a double handful of brave

"Tall, skinny, wearing striped overalls, always with a pretty girl, and always enjoying himself hugely, he was the very essence of what a race driver ought to be," James T. Crow wrote in *Road & Track.* Wearing his signature duds, Shelby celebrates with his then-wife, actress Jan Harrison, after scoring his last win as a driver, squiring a Scarab around Continental Divide Raceway in 1960. *Dave Friedman*

pills to find the point where adhesion ends and sliding begins," Christy reported. *Road & Track* put the car on the cover of its October 1962 issue, with an instrumented test inside. The magazine listed the specs as 260 horsepower at 5800 rpm and 269 lb-ft of torque at 4500 rpm. The dragstrip numbers were 0-to-60 in 4.2 seconds, with the quarter mile covered in 13.8 seconds and a trap speed of 112 mph. (*Sports Car Graphic* got slightly better numbers.) Top speed was 153 mph. None of the magazines were quite sure what to call the car. AC Cobra? AC Ford Cobra? Shelby AC Cobra? In later years, Shelby insisted that Cobra, plain and simple, was the proper name. But in the company's own ad copy, it was AC/Cobra, so confusion reigned.

Shelby was planning to make a splash by debuting the racing Cobra at the big *Los Angeles Times* Grand Prix at Riverside in October. But at the end of August, he was annoyed to learn that Hugus had beaten him to the punch by entering a Cobra with an ungainly roll bar in a puny SCCA event at Connellsville Airport near Pittsburgh. Even worse, the car had performed dismally. Hugus had been so busy building cars that he hadn't had time to thoroughly test them, so he didn't realize until he got onto the track that the stock Delaney Gallay radiator was hopelessly inadequate. (Remington would switch to a more efficient aluminum Harrison unit, used in Corvettes, for CSX2002.) Hugus managed only a handful of slow laps at the back of the field before the car overheated. *Competition Press* reported: "The biggest disappointment of the day was when the Ford-powered Shelby Cobra failed to equal the time of its Bristol-powered counterpart—even with the driving finesse of international hero Ed Hugus at work."[44]

Shelby was incensed, and the incident further soured his relationship with Hugus. Fortunately, the story was buried and went largely unnoticed for more than fifty years, until Walker published his biography of Hugus. Meanwhile, Remington kept developing CSX2002. Most of the testing was handled by Brock at Riverside. But when it came time to select a driver to race the car, Shelby chose Billy Krause, a hard-nosed ex-midget ace who'd won the *Times* Grand Prix in a Birdcage Maserati the previous year, beating Moss and Gurney. At the time, Brock—who'd lapped Riverside just as quickly as Krause—felt he'd been shafted. But he later realized that Shelby, with only two cars to his name and one chance to make a first impression, had to go with a proven commodity rather than taking a flier on a neophyte.

Attending one of the last test sessions at Riverside was a young, bespectacled would-be racer from Chicago by the name of John Morton, who was taking a class, with Brock serving as his instructor, at Shelby's high-performance driving school. In fact, Morton had spent $500 extra dollars that had been earmarked for his college education to rent the school's Cobra. This, amazingly, was the prototype, CSX2000, which had by then been transformed by school duty and countless magazine tests into a clapped-out piece of junk. After Brock introduced him to Shelby, the diffident Morton screwed up enough courage to ask for a job. Morton was thrilled when Shelby told him to come to the shop on Monday. Morton arrived at the appointed hour, and Shelby loudly gave him his marching orders. "I want these things painted and the floors and bathrooms kept clean," he said as he gave Morton a shop tour and showed him the brooms and mops. "I want the floors swept every morning, huh? Do you understand?"[45] Morton understood. The wannabe racer was being hired as a janitor.

At that point, the Shelby American team could almost be counted on the fingers of two hands. Shelby. Remington. Joan Sherman. Ex-racer Fred Gamble. Warren and Simone Olson along with two additional Reventlow holdovers, mechanic Frank Schmidt and parts manager Gordon Goring. Engine guru Bill Likes, the former machine shop manager at Edelbrock and a prominent lakes racer. Garry Koike, known as "Foreign Intrigue" because he was the in-house philosopher and had spent several years at the Manzanar internment camp during the war. Don Pike, handsome as a matinee idol, who'd signed on to work on prototype cars for Ford before transitioning to the race car. The crew was so sparse that, come the Riverside race weekend, Remington, Pike, and Likes were the only Shelby American mechanics assigned to the car. To lend a hand, Pike's younger brother, Gary, was picked up en route as they towed the Cobra on an open trailer to the track. Morton, meanwhile, made his own way to Riverside and slept on the floor in the motel room being shared by Remington and Pike. This was racing on the cheap, even by the standards of 1962.

The Cobra was entered not in the big-money main event for pure-bred race cars but in the three-hour preliminary for production-based

GT cars. Leading up to the race, the big news had been another debut—four stunning split-window Corvette Sting Rays outfitted with a high-performance Z06 package that Arkus-Duntov had engineered specifically for SCCA racing. Three of them were being driven by West Coast Corvette studs who would later become Shelby American factory drivers—Dave MacDonald, Bob Bondurant, and Jerry Grant—while Corvette stalwart Doug Hooper was in a Mickey Thompson entry benefitting from back-door support from GM. "It's our little ol' Cobra against General Motors," Shelby poor-mouthed to an *LA Times* reporter before the race.[46]

Although this outing at Riverside looms large in Shelby American lore, the Cobra was treated more like a footnote at the time. Painted red, with no graphics other than large race numbers, it looked like a standard AC Ace with louvers cut into the hood (by Remington to help cool the engine) and slightly bigger wire wheels shod with tall Goodyear tires as hard as quartz. Nothing to see here, was the general prerace consensus, just a lightly modded British antique with a lump of Detroit iron under the hood. "It was archaic," Shelby admitted, "but it was light. It was so limber, and it bent so much, that the wheels stayed on the ground."[47]

By this time, the Cobra was packing a high-performance 260 with a big Holley center-pivot four-barrel carb and an upgraded intake and exhaust. With a curb weight of less than two thousand pounds, the car was lightning quick under acceleration and braking, even if the handling was still a bit wayward. The race commenced with a Le Mans-style start on the back straight. MacDonald, who'd started off as a drag racer, got away first and was already leading by half a lap by the time he reached the start-finish line. Krause, driving cautiously, was twentieth at the start, but he effortlessly scythed through the field. After dogging MacDonald for a few laps, Krause breezed into the lead on lap nine. Seven laps later, he was ahead by seven seconds. Coming around Turn Nine, the high-speed sweeper leading onto the front straight, he felt the rear end lurch. In the pits, the Cobra crew saw one of Krause's wheels bouncing into the air. "Goddamned son of a bitch!" Sherman shouted, sounding decidedly unladylike.[48]

The left rear hub had broken. Remington took one look at it and realized that the stock piece simply wasn't strong enough for the loads the Cobra was putting on it. After the race, he got some 4340 forging blanks from his old friend Ted Halibrand and machined a beefier set of hubs with a wider radius. AC Cars prepared new drawings to Remington's specifications. Although later Cobras would go much, much faster, the hubs never broke again.

By this time, Shelby American had started taking orders for cars, and an assembly line had been set up in Venice. Actually, "assembly line" is very much a euphemism. The operation was so casual that customers would come in and kibbitz as they watched their cars slowly taking shape. Overflow cars were stored in a vacant lot across the street, like beaters in an open-air used-car emporium. Reventlow still had a skeleton crew and a couple of Scarabs in a small area off to the side. It wasn't until mid-November, after many delays big and small, that the first production Cobra assembled in Venice finally went out the door. As Robert and Sylvia Neville drove off, Shelby and Sherman stood in the parking lot with their fingers crossed, silently praying that nothing would fall off the car before the new owners reached their home in Malibu.

At the same time, two new race cars were also under construction. One was being built for John Everly, a wealthy Midwesterner who planned to race a Cobra in the Bahamas during the year-end Caribbean races-cum-bacchanal staged by promoter Red Crise. The second had been commissioned by Ford for Holman & Moody, the powerhouse behind the company's high-flying NASCAR program. Ford motorsports execs Jacque Passino and John Cowley suspected that Holman & Moody could do a better job than Shelby American since it already had a fully staffed motorsports factory cranking out race-winning cars in Charlotte. The races in Nassau would serve as an unofficial bake-off between the West Coast and East Coast racing outfits.

Oakes Fields was a tight, bumpy racecourse, and the point-and-squirt nature of the circuit suited the Cobra better than the long-legged Ferrari 250 GTOs that were the odds-on favorites in the Tourist Trophy race for GT cars. The steering in Krause's car broke in the prelim when he was running second to Roger Penske's GTO, but in the final, he set sail and left the Ferraris trailing in his wake. When Krause pitted for fuel, Don Pike popped the hood to check the engine while Shelby himself manned the dump cans. The instant Pike dropped the hood,

In October 1962, the prototype Cobra race car, CSX2002, made its debut at Riverside, where Billy Krause was leading when the left rear hub broke. Two months later, here at Nassau, Krause was handily outrunning a quartet of Ferrari 250 GTOs when he ran out of fuel. Later, Shelby sheepishly admitted that he hadn't filled the tank. Oops! Next time out, the Cobra would drive into Victory Lane. *Revs Institute / Karl Ludvigsen Photograph Collection*

Shelby stopped fueling the car. Krause was still leading despite the pit stop—until he ran out of gas. Oops!

After the race, Shelby gritted his teeth and admitted that he'd screwed up. But at least his Cobra had showed the pace to humble the 250 GTOs, which had been, before Nassau, considered the fastest GT cars in the world. Better still, the Holman & Moody entry had been an unmitigated disaster. It covered only nine laps total in three races, and during the rare occasions when it was moving under its own power, driver Augie Pabst described the handling as "terrible."[49] To be fair, the pitiful performance reflected the shortcomings of the stock Cobra more than the weaknesses of the Holman & Moody organization. But this nuance was lost in the postmortems after Nassau.

At year's end, Shelby looked back with satisfaction upon all he'd accomplished during 1962. The Cobra race car had bared its fangs, and Shelby American had decisively beaten Holman & Moody in the undeclared battle to become Ford's factory road-racing team. About sixty chassis had been delivered from AC, and nearly thirty street cars had been completed in Venice. Car magazines were publishing wildly enthusiastic reviews. Hugus was being nudged out of the picture. Ford had skin in the game. Against all odds, Shelby had deftly maneuvered all of the pieces of the puzzle into place.

The Year of the Cobra was about to begin.

CHAPTER TWO

THE YEAR OF THE COBRA

1963

The Help Wanted sign was out at Shelby American as 1963 dawned. With production of street Cobras ramping up, Phil Remington was looking for adaptable and resourceful young men willing to work long hours doing everything from fabricating sway bar brackets to installing Borg-Warner T-10 transmissions. And with plans to create an armada of race Cobras to rout the Corvettes on the track, he was also in the market for mechanics accustomed to working in the crucible of motorsports, where the pace was relentless and where there was no margin for error. But despite the pressing need for reinforcements, Remington could afford to be picky. Only the best and brightest would do. Fortunately, he was working with a deep pool of candidates.

Southern California had been the American epicenter of professional racing ever since Harry Miller set up shop in downtown Los Angeles in 1912. Although Indianapolis, Charlotte, and Daytona Beach were emerging as rivals to LA, local mechanics had worked on practically every type of race car on the planet—Indy cars, sprint cars, midgets, stock cars, sports cars, dragsters, land-speed-record cars, you name it. Southern California was also the capital of the aerospace industry, which had flourished while companies like Lockheed, Douglas, Northrop, and North American built airplanes during World War II and was now benefiting from lucrative cost-plus government projects funded by the Space Race. So there were plenty of highly skilled machinists, welders, and metalworkers to choose from, and the racing community was able to draw upon the aerospace world for new (to motorsports) materials such as titanium, new components such as AN fittings, even new tools such as tin snips.

Another factor made LA an especially appropriate home for the Cobra: Southern California was the cradle of hot-rod civilization. Cleverly modified homebuilts, often powered by hopped-up flathead Ford V-8s, began speeding along the dry lakes of the Mojave Desert in the 1930s under the auspices of the Southern California Timing Association, which pioneered racing on the Bonneville Salt Flats in Utah after the war. The first "official" drag race was held on an out-of-commission air base in Santa Ana, California, in 1950, and the National Hot Rod Association was founded the next year by Wally Parks, the editor of *Hot Rod*, which had started publishing—in LA, naturally—in 1948. There were pockets of hot-rod culture all over the county, of course, but Los Angeles was the undisputed mecca of the hobby.

In later years, it was customary to refer to the crew at Shelby American as Southern California hot-rodders, as if the phrase were a badge of honor. This annoyed Shelby to no end, and he would stomp around his office and angrily point out that the race shop had also employed mechanics from England, Australia, New Zealand, and Switzerland. There were times, in fact, when foreigners outnumbered the Americans on the race team. But there's was no denying that Shelby American prized the can-do, DIY ethic that was the foundation of hot rodding. And it was no coincidence that two of the acknowledged chiefs in the shop, Remington and original engine man Bill Likes, were lakes legends. As race engineer Carroll Smith put it, "Carroll wasn't the type to sit around and wait for things to happen. He made things happen, and he hired the kind of people who made things happen. That's why we were so successful."[1]

There was a handful of old-timers in the mix, from veteran fabricator Red Rose to virtuoso machinist Mahlon Lamoureux, a genial cynic who ate lunch by himself in his VW Kombi and inevitably returned to the shop with a wine-fortified smile on his face. But most of the new hires were much younger, and many of them had no prior interest in road racing. Shop foreman Donn Allen had worked on Indy cars. So had Louis Unser, the older brother of Bobby and Al, who'd also been the crew chief on a championship-winning USAC stock car. Wally Peat and Wayne "Red" Pierce had been running a sprint car on the dirt. George Boskoff, Bruce Burness, and Jim Culleton gravitated to Venice from sports cars. Allen Grant was a husky, blond-haired college student who'd won a bunch of Northern California SCCA races in his AC Bristol—the pre-Cobra, so to speak. He made a pilgrimage to Shelby American during a break between semesters at Fresno State College and wrangled an audience with Shelby. Grant exuberantly gave Shelby chapter and verse about his racing exploits and suggested that he be given a shot racing a Cobra.

"Well, Allen," Shelby said, "I don't need drivers right now. I've got Phil Hill and Dan Gurney and Dave MacDonald. I'm looking for welders. Can you weld?"[2]

Quick on his feet, Grant said he could, and he was hired to work on street Cobras. Later, he would do a stint as a fabricator in the race shop before being moved upstairs to sell cars. Eventually, he would become a team driver alongside Hill and Gurney.

The most notable new face was a twenty-year veteran of the Coast Guard, who showed up for his job interview with a crappy little toolbox that prompted snickers around the shop. Shelby American was a meritocracy where there was a profound appreciation for fine craftsmanship and no patience for amateurs. This didn't mean polishing or plating components so they'd be ready for a concours d'elegance, but edges were expected to be radiused and welding beads were supposed to be elegant enough that they didn't require filing or grinding. It was the kind of place where Joe Fukushima could climb to the top of the totem pole because he was so adept at welding "boxed" components in tight spaces. (He was nicknamed "Two Gun" because he could lay a perfect welding bead with either hand.)

Tools, in this environment, were more than mere implements. Most of the guys owned rollaway toolboxes, and on Friday—payday—they lined up outside the Craftsman truck to supplement their inventory. The toolbox carried by the Coast Guard vet was too small to be taken seriously. While he was being interviewed upstairs, somebody flipped open the lid to see what was inside, and the guys were aghast to find a haphazard collection of pipe wrenches, hammers, and other blunt instruments—a faux pas that was every bit as inappropriate as smuggling a porno magazine into a monastery. So they were stunned when the toolbox's owner was hired. But they thought it only fitting that he should be given the lowliest job in the shop, positioning Cobras on jack stands, then spraying them with solvent and cleaning them with a bucket.

This was Al Dowd. With a debonair mustache, a shiny pompadour, a notorious reputation as a skirt chaser, and a faultless ability to work the system, he was dubbed "Greasy Slick," often shortened to "Greasy." Dowd wasn't much of a mechanic, but Shelby quickly recognized his many other skills. After a couple of weeks, Dowd was promoted off the shop floor, and before too long, he was managing the race team.

"Al Dowd was a logistical genius,"[3] said race secretary Susan Schafran, who's now known as Susan Warne and who was instrumental in running the motorsports department. "He organized the parts, engines, spares and other equipment, team members, drivers, and, of course, the race cars. For international shipments, he had to generate Carnets de Passages or other legally required documents that were needed in that particular country. He also arranged transport, hotels, and food for the crew and drivers, and storage for the cars—and made sure the crew was prepared to travel. Think for a moment: How do you get everything and everyone safely to Sicily for the Targa Florio? Al could organize."

Shelby American also needed new drivers. After Nassau, Billy Krause left the team to drive for Mickey Thompson. In retrospect, Krause admitted that this was a huge mistake. But the decision seemed like a no-brainer at the time. Thompson was a protean figure who'd already built one car that raced in the Indy 500 and another that was clocked at 406.60 miles per hour at Bonneville. Plus, he had an in at GM and plans to race everywhere from Daytona to Le Mans in 1963.

Al Dowd, wearing sunglasses and working a toothpick, was the logistical genius who ran Shelby American on an organizational level. Here, at Sebring in 1964, he plots strategy with Remington and general manager Peyton Cramer. Behind them is the original 427 Cobra, better known as The Turd, that Miles and John Morton flogged unhappily in the race after Miles wrecked it during practice.
Revs Institute / Jean Charles Martha Photograph Collection

By comparison, Shelby seemed like a minor leaguer. Hardly any Cobras had been built, and it wasn't clear how solid his relationship with Ford really was. So Krause bailed, and nobody thought he was making the wrong call.

To replace him, and to hobble the opposition, Shelby poached the most spectacular and successful of the Corvette drivers, twenty-six-year-old Dave MacDonald. Crew-cut, with grease under his fingernails, MacDonald was working as a line mechanic at a Chevy dealership when he started drag racing, and he soon segued into running solid-axle Corvettes in SCCA competition. He was the master of oversteer; most photos of him show his car cranked sideways, with smoke wisping off the rear tires. "He had this tremendous ability to jump in anything and go like hell," said Joe Freitas, a rival Corvette driver and, later, another Shelby American employee.[4] "He could have raced at the beginning of the century, and he could have raced today. I think he would have raced a Sherman tank. Come to think of it, he would have driven a soapbox derby car if it looked like it had potential." What Shelby appreciated about him was the fire in his belly. "Davey was a lot like that Gilles Villeneuve," Shelby said. "He was going to win a lot of races, or he was going to get killed trying." Prophetic words, as it turned out.

The second driver was the antithesis of the all-American Mac-Donald. Ken Miles was very much an English dude with a 'tude. He'd apprenticed at Wolseley Motors before the war and served as a tank mechanic in France after D-Day. Dismayed by his prospects in drab postwar Great Britain, he immigrated to sunny Southern California in 1951 to become the service manager of an MG dealership in Los Angeles. He immediately started winning races in a series of home-built MG-based specials, then moved up the food chain to bigger, more exotic machinery and became a pooh-bah in the California Sports Car Club. He opened his own service shop, first in North Hollywood and then in Hollywood. Although his clientele included celebrities such as Steve McQueen, Natalie Wood, Gregory Peck, and Walt Disney, he was an indifferent businessman. At one point, shortly before Shelby called him, his shop was padlocked by the IRS for nonpayment of taxes.

At forty-four, Miles was older that most of the guys at Shelby American. When he wasn't driving, he wore ties and tweed jackets, and he was more likely to read a book than a car magazine. He was almost cadaverously thin, with a sharp, angular face and beaked nose that inspired the nickname "The Hawk." Because he traveled with a portable stove and insisted on brewing a "cuppa" in the morning before test sessions, he was also known as "Teddy the Teabagger." But the name that best captured his personality was "Side Bite," for his penchant for delivering caustic commentary out the side of his mouth. He was a famously polarizing personality, with admirers and detractors in roughly equal proportions. Fiercely intelligent and defiantly independent, he was also brutally sarcastic and notoriously unwilling to suffer fools gladly. Love him or hate him—he couldn't have cared less.

Although he would later assume the role of competition manager, Miles was hired as a racer. As the team's principal test driver, he played a critical role in developing the Cobra. "After a test session at Riverside,"

With a hawkish visage that mirrored his sharp-edged personality, Ken Miles was a polarizing English racer best known for driving Porsches and MG specials before being hired by Shelby. He turned out to be not only the winningest driver in Shelby American history but also a test driver par excellence. Most of the cars—street or race—that came out of the shops in Venice and LAX were developed by Miles. *Ford Motor Company*

said Lew Spencer, another sports car racer who joined the team a bit later, "you could ask him what his oil pressure was in Turn Six, and he'd say, 'Which part? The beginning, the middle or the end?' He was *that* good."[5] Or as Smith put it: "He could tell you exactly what the car was doing, he could drive the car at the limit almost endlessly, and he had the ability to analyze the effect of changes very quickly, in two or three laps. That's so important during a test session. You can't afford to waste an hour out there while the driver tries to sort things out."[6]

With Miles on board, Shelby American was ready for prime time. Shelby provided the vision, secured the funding, and served as the public face of the team. Remington was the engineer/fabricator/mechanic par excellence who ran the technical side of the operation with machine-like precision. Miles was the man behind the wheel and an integral part of the feedback loop that produced better race cars and faster lap times. Dowd kept the trains running on time. Later on, after Miles was killed in a testing accident, the team's letterhead stationery would have three names across the top—Shelby, Remington, and Dowd, the triumvirate who ruled American road racing for the next five years.

Even with the additional manpower, Shelby American was still so small that everybody had to do a little bit of everything. When a truck driver quit on short notice, Joan Sherman came down to the shop floor to complain that she had three Cobras sitting on the dock in New York. "How am I going to get them here?" she asked.[7]

"Well, I'll go get them," mechanic Red Pierce said.

She stared at him. "Can you drive a truck?"

"What could be so difficult about driving a bloody truck?"

Pierce and his friend, engineer Wally Peat, took off with day-old commercial driver's licenses and no directions or training. They didn't even figure out how to shift the truck's transmission properly until they reached Flagstaff, Arizona. Somehow, they found the docks, picked up the cars, and hauled them back to California. The next time Sherman needed a truck driver, Pierce volunteered for that assignment too. "I wanted to go to the races," he explained, "and I come to find out that as long as I drove that transporter, I got to go to every race while the guys in the shop had to stay and work on the cars. So that's how I became the transport guy."

The road racing landscape was a lot easier to navigate in the 1960s than it is now. The most popular category was the production class, which was open to street-type cars built in large enough numbers (usually one hundred) to be homologated for racing. Street cars that had been customized too thoroughly—with bigger engines, for example, or disc brakes instead of drums—were bumped up to the modified class. The modified class was also the home of purpose-built race cars, which were often referred to as prototypes in international racing. All of these classes were further subdivided based on engine capacity. Open-wheel cars competed in classes of their own.

Road racing circa 1963 was governed by two major sanctioning bodies—the FIA internationally and the SCCA here in the States. Founded in 1944, SCCA had always focused on amateur competition, known generically as club racing. But this year, it was inaugurating a professional series called the US Road Racing Championship (USRRC).

Shelby planned to race in all three arenas. First, he intended to contest the FIA's three stateside races in the World Sportscar Championship—Daytona, Sebring, and Bridgehampton. Second, he was going to compete in the USRRC. Third, he was determined to emasculate the Corvettes in SCCA A Production racing from coast to coast. Over the course of the year, eight team cars with incremental upgrades would be built. To be honest, they weren't much more than street Cobras with roll bars, flared fenders, wider wheels and tires, hood scoops, and bigger openings for the oil cooler. But that was more than enough to do the job.

SCCA's club racing season opened at Riverside in February. Fans were expecting a battle royal between the two Cobras—MacDonald in a new car and Miles in the one Krause had driven the previous year—and a bevy of Corvettes. Instead, they saw a lions-versus-Christians massacre. MacDonald and Miles finished one-two. They were so much faster than the Corvettes that the cynics theorized that Miles had pitted unnecessarily just to rub it in. (Actually, he stopped to check to see if his car had been damaged when the driver's door swung open during an off-course excursion.) "They beat them off the line, were quicker through the turns and, outsped them down the backstretch," *Competition Press* reported of the lopsided contest between Cobras and Corvettes.[8] After the race, Shelby American ran a brash magazine ad:

"ATTENTION CORVETTE OWNERS! To get rid of that foul taste in your mouth (Cobra exhaust) order a COBRA 'RIVERSIDE REPLICA.'" Only one Riverside Replica ended up being sold, but plenty of other Cobras terrorized Corvettes on and off the track.

Next up were the FIA races at Daytona and Sebring. There, the competition would be a lot tougher—quasi-works Ferrari 250 GTOs shepherded by world-class drivers. Shelby knew he had to raise his game to play in this sandbox. Ford agreed to supply him with an experimental 255-cubic-inch aluminum engine that was being developed for Indy. This prompted him to ask Remington, "Why don't we have a manifold?"[9] Meaning that Remington should create an aluminum intake manifold for the 48-millimeter downdraft Weber carburetors that Shelby wanted to use at Sebring.

This was easier said than done. First of all, neither the as-yet-unbuilt intake nor the carbs had been homologated. Shelby American had to apply ASAP for an amendment to the original homologation document. Second, and more problematic, Remington had to design and fabricate the manifold, and this would involve at least a week's worth of bending, wedging, and hammering aluminum into shape. With the clock ticking, Remington worked with a patternmaker to rough out the unit in wood, then painted it silver to look like metal. And this is what was photographed for the homologation amendment that was approved by the FIA just before Sebring. It wasn't strictly kosher, but, hey, it wasn't cheating if nobody noticed.

Shelby American hauled three Cobras to Daytona on an automobile transporter—the two cars that had raced at Riverside two weeks earlier and a third one that had just been built. In the three-hour Daytona Continental for GT cars, MacDonald would be joined by Gurney and West Coast racer Skip Hudson. Their race was what *Road & Track* described as "a vast comedy of errors."[10] The freeze plug in Gurney's experimental engine blew out during the final practice session, and Remington frantically swapped in a new engine with the help of Bill Gay, the chief engineer in charge of Ford's Engine & Foundry Division, who was working in his tie and button-down shirt, with a cigar stuck in his mouth. Even so, Gurney was nearly two laps down when he started the race from the pits, and before too long, his ignition failed. MacDonald, meanwhile, was hamstrung by a broken water hose. Hudson fared even worse. His hood hadn't been latched, and it flew open on the pace lap. Contorting like a gymnast, Hudson wriggled halfway out of the cockpit while the car was on the banking to secure one latch. Despite starting last—well, except for Gurney, who was still in the pits—Hudson fought his way into the lead. Then his flywheel exploded coming off the Turn Four banking, and he broke his ankle when he crashed nose-first into a makeshift fence fashioned out of palm tree logs. *Road & Track* reported: "The Cobra has more bugs than a flophouse mattress, but it has great potential."[11]

When the team returned to California to lick its wounds, it got some good news on the mechanical front. Ford had enlarged the bore of its small-block V-8 yet again so that it now displaced 289 cubic inches, and several Hi-Performance versions had been delivered to Venice. In the 289 Cobra's first outing, MacDonald and Miles were first and second at the SCCA race on a tight but scary course laid out in the parking lot of

Dodger Stadium. Nowadays, Cobras with 427-cubic-inch engines tend to be more valuable, and most modern Cobras—including the many copies—use styling cues from the big-block cars. But the 289 roadster was the car that won the most races, and it, far more than the 427, was the one that established the Cobra mystique.

Thanks to Peter Brock, the team was starting to develop a distinctive look. The first Cobra had been shipped from England wearing standard AC Cars badges on the hood and trunk lid. Shelby immediately junked them and metaphorically marked his territory by having "Shelby" painted in freehand script on the nose. The next batch of cars arrived bearing crude white emblems with "Shelby" in red block type, "AC" in script on a field of blue and "Cobra" in black block letters. Shelby hated them because (a) they looked lame, (b) they didn't say "American," and (c) they *did* say "AC." The badges had to go. But removing them left rivet holes in the bodywork. Rather than fill them and repaint the hood and trunk, Shelby commissioned the design of replacements, apparently from a die-cast company he plucked at random out of the Yellow Pages. The result was what's now known as the "flat head" insignia. When Brock—who'd been trained as a car designer—stumbled across a carton filled with them, he was appalled.

"Carroll," he said, "I can't let you put these badges on the car. They're just too ugly. You can't cheapen up the car like that."[12]

"Goddammit, Brock!" Shelby yelled. "You just have to say every god-damned thing around here is wrong."

"Let me redo it. I just want to change the graphics."

Shelby and Brock had many shouting matches over the years, generally over the relative merits of better looks versus less money. This particular argument ended with Brock finally wearing Shelby down. "Goddammit, just do it the way you want," Shelby grumbled. "But make sure it's got a snake on the front, and it says, 'Cobra.'"

Brock redrew the snake, chose a more striking font and created a red-white-and-blue color scheme. These revisions made the emblem bolder, sharper, and exponentially more memorable—an enduring symbol that looks as arresting today as it did nearly six decades ago.

Meanwhile, AC Cars had been busy developing a much-anticipated rack-and-pinion steering unit. While testing a street prototype, Miles had been 1.5 seconds faster around Riverside than he was in a worm-and-sector car, so this was obviously the way to go. A few days after the race at Dodger Stadium, AC buttoned up two Cobras with a newly developed rack-and-pinion steering and shipped them on an airplane at Heathrow. They arrived in Venice just in time to be loaded on transporters and hauled to Sebring, never having turned a wheel.

Sebring was a thrash. It was also a fiasco. The crew subsisted on greasy hamburgers and pep pills while humping to prep the two rack-and-pinion cars, along with a pair of older models. All the hard work seemed to be worth it at the start, when Phil Hill, grinning maniacally, outdragged everybody down to Turn One. At the end of the first lap, he was leading the entire field, including the Ferrari prototypes. But Sebring was a twelve-hour race, not a thirty-minute sprint. Although Gurney was leading the Ferrari GTOs in the GT class halfway through, the junky hardware store-quality bolts securing the steering rack failed, and the rest of the Cobras ran into troubles of their own. But as badly as things were going on the track, they looked even worse in the pits.

The Shelby American team was dressed clownishly in striped bib overalls with bright red shirts. Although they were designed to evoke Shelby's old driving uniforms, the outfits had the unfortunate effect of making the mechanics look like a 4-H team competing in a Future Farmers of America livestock show—not the image Shelby American was trying to project. Most of the team blamed the apparel on Joan Sherman, but she insisted later that it was Shelby's idea. Considering Shelby's well-documented determination to pinch pennies, he's surely the one who opted for cheesy knockoffs rather than spending the money on authentic Carhartt gear. As Cobras were breaking on the track, the overalls were disintegrating in the pits. They were also cut so tight and short that Grant ripped the crotch out of his outfit when he bent over to change a tire. "I'm amazed that no one in our pits went up in flames," Sherman said.[13]

Some people were convinced that Warren and Simone Olson quit Shelby American rather than wear the undignified overalls. Others say they were uncomfortable with Shelby's business practices. In any event, the shambles in Sebring inspired the team to issue white T-shirts with the dramatic "CS" or "Cobra" logos that Brock had created. Later, he

Hope springs eternal during the hours before a race begins. Then, reality sets in. The Cobras wouldn't be the only thing to fall apart at Sebring in 1963. Before the twelve-hour enduro was over, the team's cheesy bib overalls were equally trashed. Looking self-conscious in their "stylish" team gear are, (from right) Ole Olsen, Al Dowd, Don Pike, Shelby—with "Shel" on his overalls—Bruce Burness, and an unidentified crewman. *Ford Motor Company*

designed the powder blue "COBRA" jackets that eventually became the team's signature.

After dark, as Lew Spencer was about to rejoin the race in the last surviving Cobra, Shelby spoke urgently to him. "Where it finishes is not material—that it does finish is," Shelby said.[14] Spencer was surprised. He was nearly fifty miles behind the class-leading GTO and still losing ground, so what did it matter? But he was told later that Ford would have shut down the program if at least one Cobra hadn't made it to the checkered flag. Spencer soldiered on and finished eleventh overall, and Shelby American lived to fight another day. Would Ford really have pulled the plug if the last Cobra had DNFed? It's hard to believe. But despite his outward confidence and all the publicity he'd generated over the past year, Shelby himself wasn't sure. Which just goes to show how precarious the whole project was. And how close the Cobra came to joining the ranks of Cunningham and Muntz and all the other small sports car companies that briefly left the ground with elaborate flight plans before crashing and burning.

The Cobra team looks surprisingly upbeat after getting steamrolled by the Ferrari 250 GTOs in the 12 Hours of Sebring in 1963. But all Shelby cared about was making sure that one car finished the race, which was enough to persuade Ford Motor Company to continue backing the race program. Beaming at the camera are, (from left) Miles, Lew Spencer, Phil Hill, Dan Gurney, Dave MacDonald, Shelby, and Peter Brock. *Ford Motor Company*

Money was always a concern. Even before building the first Cobra, Shelby had created an entity called Shelby Enterprises. This was the umbrella company under which all of his other businesses operated—Shelby American, the Carroll Shelby School of High Performance Driving, and his deals with Koni and Champion. But the most profitable, by far, was the Goodyear racing tire distributorship. Toward the end of 1963, Shelby hired the man who would become his longest-serving employee, J. L. Henderson. (He remained on the job until retiring in 2011.) Besides being universally regarded as one of the nicest guys in the racing fraternity, Henderson was also one of the most astute. After his first month running the Goodyear operation, he told Shelby that the company had earned $40,000. Shelby was pleasantly surprised. "Man, that's great," he said. "It looks like you're probably gonna double that next month. So I'm gonna take eighty thousand dollars out of the company right now."[15] This became Shelby's standard operating procedure, Henderson generating tidy profits and Shelby siphoning them off for other projects. "If it hadn't been for Enterprises," Henderson said, "I really don't think he could have paid for the Cobra."

Shelby was forever looking for ways to bring in extra income. One of the most lucrative gigs was a deal Sherman negotiated with Ford to prepare hand-built prototypes of new models that were photographed and filmed for advertising purposes. The Pike brothers, Gary and Don, worked virtually 24/7 on these projects, which generated enough money to keep the rest of the shop going. "They'd bring cars in at night, and we'd mask off the chrome and glass and shoot the things with strip paint, which was a latex coat, and then a coat of enamel," Remington recalled.[16] "They'd get up real early the next morning and shoot pictures of the car in this particular color, and then they'd bring it back at night, and we'd take a razor blade and cut through the lines of the chrome and blow all the paint off and then paint it a different color for the next day. For a while, we did this in the shop at the same time we were building Cobras. It was a real mess. The whole shop was filled with overspray."

The company soon needed room to grow. Shelby leased space about a block away from the Princeton Drive shop and moved the assembly of Cobra street cars—and the painting of Ford prototypes—to the new facility at 3219 Carter Street. The company also needed to improve the product. "The Cobra I drove at Sebring is essentially a hot rod," Miles told *Car and Driver.*[17] "It's a rather archaic English chassis, into which an extremely good Ford engine and transmission have been inserted. Frankly, at the moment we have more engine than we have chassis, a situation which we have to remedy during the coming years."

Street cars were upgraded on almost a monthly basis. Rack-and-pinion steering was one example. Wheels were enlarged from 5.5 to 6.0 inches by 15 inches, which necessitated a taller final-drive ratio. Chronic cooling issues were addressed by cutting vents in the fenders and installing a McCord radiator sourced from Ford. The Prince of Darkness electrics from Lucas—allegedly the inventor of the short circuit—were scrapped in favor of more reliable Ford units, and Smiths gauges gave way to Stewart Warner instrumentation. But the biggest and most important change was the move to the 289-cubic-inch engine. And not just any 289.

The Cobra was an early recipient of Ford's Hi-Performance 289, also known as the K-Code engine, which was reserved for the hottest cars in the company's portfolio. It benefitted from a host of upgrades ranging from larger two-bolt main caps to heavier-duty connecting rods to flat-top pistons that allowed for a high compression ratio. In street car form, fed by a four-barrel Autolite carburetor, the Hi-Po engine was officially rated at 271 horsepower at 6000 rpm and 312 lb-ft of torque at 3400 rpm. Still more upgrades (Webers, dual-coil valve springs, et cetera) went into the race version, which was developed over the next two years to routinely produce 385 to 390 horsepower—404 horses was the highest number seen in 1964—while safely being spun to 7000 rpm. In a car that weighed a mere 2,000 pounds, the 289 was a motor that turned the Cobra into a genuine monster.

By the fall of 1963, about two hundred cars had been built, and the package was reasonably standardized, which translated into better quality control. But despite all the development, the Cobra remained raw and rough-edged, very much a barely civilized race car. "We'd like to say that this car is one in which you could blast through a 600-mile day with no ill effects, but we can't," *Motor Trend* wrote in a piece that called the car the Ford-Shelby-AC-Cobra.[18] "We found the combination of severe wind buffeting (without the top or without the side curtain) excessive. Engine heat in the cockpit (even on mild days) plus high wind, road, and engine noise level, and a driver's seat that's not nearly as comfortable as it should be became fatiguing after as little as 150 to 200 miles. There's a limit to our enthusiasm."

Of course, *Motor Trend* was one of the stodgiest of the car magazines. For *Sports Car Graphic*, the very challenges posed by driving what it called "Carroll Shelby's pet snake" were an essential element of its appeal. "The Cobra is a sports car of the traditional variety, perhaps the last of the big, hairy, fast wind-in-your-face cars," John Christy wrote after his first test of the 289.[19] Despite the additional power, the extra weight and longer gearing produced slower test times—0-to-60 mph in 6.7 seconds and the quarter mile in 14.9 seconds at 93 mph. *Motor Trend* got slightly better numbers—0-to-60 mph in 5.8 seconds and the quarter mile in 13.8 seconds at 104 mph—but the car ran out of steam at 130 mph.

The pace of production increased as the year passed. Peyton Cramer, who had been working under Ray Geddes in Dearborn, moved to Southern California to become Shelby American's general manager, and he brought with him a higher level of financial discipline. But production was still a piecemeal process rather than a true assembly line. Cars rolled up ramps and were secured there while mechanics moved from car to car, performing assigned tasks. Production manager Leonard Parsons, trained as a helicopter mechanic at Hughes, ran the facility with a light and friendly touch. But most of his employees were so young and inexperienced that he functioned more like a scoutmaster than a taskmaster, and the Carter Street operation was sometimes referred to as "Father Flanagan's Boys Town."

Strictly as a lark, Shelby had ordered the race shop to lever a Hi-Po 289 into a Ford Fairlane 500. This piqued the curiosity of three young would-be racers working on the production line—Randy Shaw, his friend Tony Stoer, and production foreman Jere Kirkpatrick. "Every time we would see Carroll, we'd ask him if we could take his Fairlane out to the drag strip," Kirkpatrick says. "He finally got tired of it, and he gave Leonard six thousand dollars and an old Cobra that was way too old and no good for anything anymore."[20]

The donor car, CSX2019, had been ridden hard and put away wet after a grueling tour of duty that included promotional shoots, magazine tests, and a role in the Elvis Presley flick *Viva Las Vegas*. Shaw, Stoer, and Kirkpatrick worked after hours to upgrade the old Cobra with re-arched front leaf springs and longer ones at the rear, Koni 90/10 drag shocks, a stump-puller gear, performance headers, six-spoke Halibrand magnesium wheels, drag slicks, and a hardtop designed to improve the aerodynamics. Then it was painted Sun Gleam Viking Blue, a brilliant metal flake. Stoer, who'd amassed plenty of experience street-racing a '34 Ford Coupe in the Napa Valley, became the principal driver. "I used to launch it at about three thousand rpm, dump the clutch, and go," he said.[21] "I'd leave my foot on the floor and just power-shift it—BAM! I got so good at it that I could do it without the clutch. I just flogged the hell out of it."

Although the National Hot Rod Association refused to let the car compete in a stock class because the engine was equipped with twin four-barrels—and Chevy valves!—Stoer cleaned up against modified Corvettes and set an American Hot Rod Association record at 12.86 seconds at 108.95 mph in the quarter mile. (He later lowered the ET to 12.06.) But the other mechanics in the shop weren't very impressed.

"I was probably the only guy in the whole place who was interested in drag racing," Stoer said.[22] "The road racers used to say, 'You don't have to drive that thing. You just have to *aim* it.'" Parsons impishly added a fresh line of paint to the door: "Aimer Tony Stoer."

Stoer's quick-shifting talent aside, the key to the car's success was its Ford V-8. To pump up the performance for all the racing Cobras, camshafts were sent out to the preeminent hot-rod grinders in town—Engle, Racer Brown, Iskenderian, and, later, Sig Erson, who had been Isky's shop foreman. The engine dyno at Princeton Drive ran almost constantly as Jack Hoare, Ole Olsen, Cecil "Old Folks" Bowman, and Jim O'Leary vied to achieve the best combination of power and longevity. As race weekends approached, the pace inside the engine shop would reach a delirious level of intensity. On at least one occasion, an infuriated resident of a nearby trailer park showed up late at night with a shotgun and told the guys to shut down the dyno—or else.

The race shop got an injection of new blood in the form of a British invasion. No, not John, Paul, George, and Ringo, who played to a sold-out throng of maniacal teenyboppers at the Hollywood Bowl during the summer. New faces included Englishmen John Collins, called "Granny" because he was so finicky, and master fabricator Bill Eaton, who'd apprenticed at Rolls-Royce before working at Hilborn. Eaton was known as "Big Five" in honor of his huge hands. According to shop lore, he'd once ended an argument by brandishing his fist and demanding, "Do you want to talk to 'Big Five'?" At the other end of the size spectrum was Charlie Agapiou, a twenty-one-year-old Cockney live wire who'd talked his way into a job as a mechanic at Miles's service shop in North Hollywood after leaving London. A month after Miles moved to Shelby American, he offered Agapiou a job.

"But I don't know anything about race cars or Cobras," Agapiou said.[23]

"You bluffed me," Miles said. "You can bluff them."

<hr />

After Sebring, comp Cobras fanned out all over the country on a search-and-destroy mission to conquer every Corvette, E-Jag, and Ferrari that dared to face off against them. Cars were upgraded with quad 48 IDA

Webers, bigger Halibrand mag wheels on pin-drive hubs, reworked exhaust manifolds with side pipes, quick-jack pads, reprofiled fenders, and sway bars front and rear. As if MacDonald and Miles didn't bring enough firepower to the racetrack, Shelby added East Coast Porsche ace Bob Holbert, a four-time SCCA national champion, to the mix. But it was seriously quick privateer Bob Johnson who notched the Cobra's first victories in SCCA national competition, with back-to-back wins at Cumberland and Bridgehampton.

Steamrolling over the competition in SCCA races was good for the corporate ego, but the real prize for Shelby American was the US Road Racing Championship. The team missed the season opener at Daytona, then laid an egg on a bumpy airport circuit in Pensacola. Though they were fastest by far, all three Cobras broiled their differentials. At Laguna Seca Raceway two weeks later, the Cobras walked away and hid in the prelim but ended the race with smoking rear ends. No problem. Differential coolers were fitted before the feature, and Holbert, Mac-Donald, and Miles finished one-two-four. Three weeks later, the team went one-two-three at Watkins Glen. No shock there. The surprise was that Johnson finished ahead of Miles and MacDonald. Afterward, Shelby told him, "You're coming to work for us."[24]

During the summer, the Cobras marauded from coast to coast like western desperadoes on a bank-robbing spree. On the way back from Watkins Glen, the whole team stopped at Lake Garnett in Kansas to support Johnson's campaign for the A Production championship. The Corvette drivers protested the rear-axle coolers, which were legal in USRRC but not in A Production. After the Shelby American guys dutifully disconnected them, the Cobras ran one-two-three. Then Miles reconnected his and won the Modified race to rub it in. The hits kept coming—Pomona, Kent, Continental Divide, Road America. The Cobras didn't just win. They won in formation, swapping places to entertain the crowd while never being challenged, turning races into high-speed parades celebrating the might of Shelby American. The Corvettes were no longer rivals; they were fodder. "Chevrolet," the guys joked, "breakfast of champions."

Shelby American only occasionally deigned to enter smaller SCCA club races. This opened up an opportunity for Grant, who brazenly promoted himself a ride in an ex-team car. At the time, Grant was working as a Cobra salesman. He got a call from Jay Brown, an owner of Coventry Motors, a Northern California dealership that was one of Grant's biggest customers. Brown was interested in buying a used race Cobra.

"I've only got one rebuilt factory race car," Grant told him, "and I'll sell it to you under one condition."[25]

"What's that?" Brown asked.

"I drive it."

Long pause. "Have you ever raced before?"

This was the cue for the supremely self-confident Grant to provide details of every race he'd ever run. Before Brown could get a word in edgewise, Grant clinched the deal by adding, "Furthermore, you need to put in five hundred bucks extra because I want to build a special engine to blow off the factory team."

After Brown agreed, Grant commissioned a motor with a hotter cam from his friend Ole Olsen. To create an attention-grabbing paint scheme, Grant sought out the advice of a fellow member of the Ecurie AWOL car club in Modesto, a young film student by the name of George Lucas. Yes, that George Lucas. The design they came up with showcased what Grant described as "the yellowest yellow in the world," with two black stripes running from fender to fender.[26]

Shelby made the trip out to Santa Barbara to watch Grant's debut in a lowly SCCA regional. Grant was mortified to be mid-pack after being outqualified by a dozen Corvettes. Only after the session was over did he discover that they were running gummy recaps. Grant procured a set of his own retreaded tires for the race. Still, Shelby told him, "I recommend you cool it a bit, you know, pick those guys off on the back straight."[27] Grant vowed to follow this advice. Then the red mist descended. He was second going into Turn One, leading by Turn Three and in another time zone by the time the race ended. There's a famous photo of him in the yellow Cobra, with Lucas holding a checkered flag, beaming in the passenger seat. (Fun footnote: Grant was the inspiration for the John Milner character in Lucas's feature film *American Graffiti*.)

In September, on the sandy up-and-down circuit at Bridgehampton, New York, Gurney became the first American to drive an American car

The sentence structure needed a little work, but driver Dan Gurney got the message anyway en route to scoring the Cobra's first victory in FIA competition, at Bridgehampton in 1963. That's crew chief Jim Culleton holding the "Time" pit board and driver Bob Holbert—whose Cobra broke—brandishing the "Beer" sign. Behind them (from left) are truck driver Red Piece, Shelby, and driver Bob Johnson, in white, who also DNFed. *Revs Institute / Albert R. Bochroch Photograph Collection*

to victory in an FIA race since a Briggs Cunningham Hemi-powered C4-R co-driven by John Fitch and Phil Walters won the 12 Hours of Sebring ten years earlier. As Gurney and Miles casually lapped the field, Holbert—whose car had broken—and crew chief Jim Culleton held out pit boards reading "Beer" and "Time." The cars they beat, ironically, were E-type Jags entered by Cunningham. But none of the foreign factory teams were there, and Shelby knew he'd be in for a much tougher tussle if and when he took the fight to Ferrari on its home turf in Europe. He had Brock working on a controversial skunkworks project to skin the roadster in more aerodynamic bodywork just in case.

First, though, Shelby was determined to score a big payday at the prestigious pro races held on the West Coast in the fall. Ever since the inaugural event in 1958, the *Los Angeles Times* Grand Prix had been the most lucrative sports car race in the world. It was now the centerpiece of an informal month-long schedule of races—the Fall Series—that included Laguna Seca in Northern California and Pacific Raceways, in Kent, Washington. Other than a prohibition against open-wheel cars and single seaters, pretty much anything went. Because the races were scheduled after the European season had concluded, they attracted several F1 drivers enjoying busman's holidays in everything from Le Mans prototypes to precursors of the Can-Am cars of the not-too-distant future.

The Cobras weren't fast enough to compete in this league, so Shelby ordered a couple of mid-engine Cooper Monaco T61s, which repurposed the marque's space-frame single-seater architecture as sports racers with full-width bodywork. Like the Cobra, the Cooper was built around a last-gen chassis, but Shelby figured that he could perk it right up by fitting it with a 4.7-liter V-8 instead of the four-cylinder 2.5-liter Coventry Climax it had originally been designed to accommodate. Installing the 289 required myriad chassis modifications, not just to fit the bigger engine but also to support the additional weight and torque.

The first Monaco arrived during the summer. The job of converting it to V-8 power was entrusted to MacDonald's close friend Wally Peat, a GM engineer who moonlighted at Shelby American. Helping him were MacDonald himself, Joe Freitas, and Craig Lang, a young, affluent club racer from Hawaii who would later buy a Cooper Monaco of his own. Remington put Peat in a corner and told him to have at it. "I didn't like the suspension, so I changed the roll centers," Peat said.[28] "I set the seat differently. I changed the windshield. I moved the radiator and changed the flow of the water. There were a lot of little things that people don't know about."

Mid-engine sports racers were still relatively rare, and transaxles—which combine transmissions and differentials in a single unit—were in short supply. Shelby had planned to use Colotti T.37s, which had been developed for the Lotus-Ford Indy car effort, but they didn't arrive in time. Instead, MacDonald's car was fitted with a Huffaker transaxle that married a Halibrand quick-change rear end to a synchromesh Corvette gear cluster. Meanwhile, the second Monaco, earmarked for Holbert, arrived even later, so it didn't get all the TLC—and canny

Wally Peat spearheaded the transformation of a Cooper Monaco into a King Cobra, but he had plenty of help. Working in rudimentary conditions in Venice, the crew includes, (from left) Frank Lance, Jeff Schoolfield, Dave Peat (Wally's brother), MacDonald—the designated driver—and Sherman Falconer, the brother of Ryan and Ralph. Not pictured are Wally Peat, Joe Freitas, and Craig Lang, who also played important roles. *Dave Friedman*

modifications—that Peat had lavished on MacDonald's car. Also, this car was completed with a McKee transaxle, which was basically an upside-down Corvette four-speed with parts scavenged from other gearboxes inside a custom-cast differential case. There was time for only a single shakedown at Riverside before the cars were towed up the coast. MacDonald broke the track record during the session, but he didn't have a chance to do any serious durability testing, and this omission would come back to bite the team in the ass.

Although Shelby stubbornly insisted on calling the cars Cooper-Fords, the press immediately dubbed them King Cobras, and the name stuck. The cars looked pretty ratty when they arrived in Kent—a function of the rush to get them finished—but they were wicked quick. Holbert was easily fastest during qualifying on the picturesque tree-lined circuit. Lamentably, that was the highlight of the weekend. In the first of two heat races, both his and MacDonald's cars overheated. Holbert was done for the weekend. After starting the second heat dead last, MacDonald wrestled the lead away from Gurney's Ford-powered Genie on lap four. He was in front by half a lap when he cut a tire on debris on the track. After a tire change, he spun, nearly hit a boulder, and abandoned the car before walking glumly back to the pits. "We came here against my better judgment," Shelby said. "The cars are new. It was too early to run them."[29]

The problems with the King Cobras weren't limited to individual components. The entire *car* was falling apart. "For some reason, the welding that had been done in England wasn't worth a shit, and if we hadn't rewelded everything, the frame would have come apart as soon as we'd gone testing," Peat said.[30] "The chassis tubes were always the weak point of those cars, and I never quit having to weld them up at the races. No matter what we did, they broke; those chassis just weren't made for the amount of stress we put on them or the speeds we were running."

Two weeks later, the circus moved to Riverside. This gave the team enough time to properly paint and prep the King Cobras. MacDonald and Holbert qualified on the front row. But the pole was claimed by Jim Hall in his revolutionary Chaparral 2, which was built around a fiber-glass tub and featured a snowplow front splitter that pointed the way to the future. In front of more than eighty thousand spectators who braved scorching one hundred-degree heat, Hall pulled away by a second a lap until breaking early. MacDonald inherited the lead and said, "See ya." Holbert's engine overheated again, blowing the head gasket. But MacDonald lapped the entire field while putting on a four-wheel-drift car-control clinic that thrilled fans and captivated photographers. Those who saw it never forgot the spectacle of watching him dance through Turn Six in glorious power-slides, with the 289 bellowing.

Riverside also gave Grant another chance to impress Shelby. Besides his yellow roadster, three factory Cobras were entered for Gurney, Spencer, and Bob Bondurant in the one-hour GT race before the grand prix. Grant had never raced at Riverside before, and a lower radiator hose blew off during practice, which left him mired in fifth. But he blew past Bondurant and Spencer at the start and was running second to Gurney halfway through the first lap. "Bondurant was pissed that I passed him," Grant said.[31] "So going into Six, he tapped me and spun me out, and I had to wait for all thirty cars to go by." (For the record, Bondurant denied that he hit Grant, and the two continued to spar over who did what to whom for the next fifty-plus years.)

After the spin, Grant was the fastest man on the track. Driving "like a constipated bull,"[32] according to a press account, he sliced through the pack, got by Gurney, repassed Spencer, and was catching Bondurant when he ran out of time. "Had the race lasted one more lap, I would have won," Grant said.[33] Although he was disappointed, Grant's performance helped convince Shelby to use him as a factory driver in Europe in 1965, where his partner was none other than—wait for it—Bob Bondurant.

The next weekend found almost all the Riverside entrants up at Laguna Seca, on the Monterey Peninsula, for the final race on the West Coast pro swing. While Holbert qualified on the pole, MacDonald's engine swallowed a valve and imploded. Then, during last-chance qualifying, he lost the rear end of his Cobra coming over the brow of the hill on the front straight. In those days, Turn Two was a scary fast left-hand sweeper rather than the 180-degree Andretti Hairpin that's there now. So instead of spinning harmlessly into a runoff area, he crunched heavily into a dirt embankment and bent the frame like a pretzel. Peat was accustomed to welding cracks in the chassis tubes after most sessions, but this level of damage called for sterner measures—and an indispensable porta power hydraulic jack. "We put a chain around the frame, put a block of wood on the hydraulic jack and pushed [the frame rails] back into place," Peat said.[34] "Then we took the frame rails off the trailer, and we put them alongside the car. Fortunately, they were straight and longer than the car. I measured from side to side, and I used that distance to align the wheels." Shade-tree engineering at its best.

Holbert was the class of the field, and he would have gone flag to flag if he hadn't tangled with a back marker—or maybe that should be back markers, plural. Some articles about the race say he hit Masten Gregory's Elva-Porsche. Others say he clobbered Lloyd Ruby's Lotus-Ford Harrison Special. One story said he hit both of them. Whatever happened, a collision pinched the bodywork and closed up the radiator grille, causing his engine to overheat for the third race in a row. After he dove into the pits, the crew yanked the bodywork up and away to allow air to flow to the front-mounted radiator. The repairs left the King Cobra resembling a largemouth bass. Pretty soon, it looked like a beached whale. After a second stop, Holbert freewheeled down the hill leading to the pits with a geyser of steam shooting twenty feet in the air, and he retired the car.

MacDonald was progressing through the field—slowly. Besides the underpowered engine and less-than-ideal suspension geometry, he also had to deal with a pesky gearbox issue. The lever wouldn't stay in third gear, which was the ratio used for many of the corners at Laguna Seca, so he had to hold it in gear with his right hand even as he was arcing through the turns. Despite these problems, MacDonald took the lead just after the halfway point, and by the time the race was over, the only other driver on the lead lap was A. J. Foyt, in the last of the Scarabs built at the Princeton Drive shop now occupied by Shelby American. When MacDonald took off his black leather driving gloves, his right hand looked like bloody ground beef.

With the win at Laguna Seca, MacDonald had scored back-to-back victories in the two most profitable sports car races in the world. In the process, he'd outrun F1 aces such as Jim Clark, Graham Hill, and Richie Ginther as well as sports car champs including Roger Penske, Walt Hansgen, and Augie Pabst. It was a star-is-born moment for an introverted mechanic who'd been doing brake jobs on Chevrolet Bel Air station wagons only two years earlier, and it raised Shelby American's profile immeasurably from a small-time sports car company that had won a lot of races on provincial stages to a team with international motorsports aspirations. For both MacDonald and Shelby, the sky seemed to be the limit. It was hard to believe that barely a year had passed since the Cobra had debuted at Riverside in the hands of Billy Krause.

Shelby American came back to earth with a thud two months later at Nassau. Young Houston oil tycoon John Mecom Jr. showed up with a fleet of cars powered by suspiciously stout Chevy engines. Although Mecom enjoyed no official support from GM, several Chevrolet engineers had decided to take vacations in the Bahamas—purely by coincidence, it was said—and they just happened to show up at the track for the races. The King Cobras were outpaced by both Mecom's Scarab, driven by Foyt, and a Cooper Monaco T61, in Penske's hands. Holbert and MacDonald both suffered suspension failures and went home empty-handed.

The GT races were even more humiliating. Miles was racing a Cobra prepared to the specs that had been virtually unbeatable in the States. But in Nassau, he ran into a buzz saw called the Corvette Grand Sport. Zora Arkus-Duntov's latest creation was just as light as the Cobra but sported at least 100 more horsepower, thanks to a no-horses-left-behind aluminum-block V-8 punched out to 377 cubes. The Grand Sports obliterated the competition in the Bahamas. Miles returned to Venice with his tail between his legs—but also with an idea that would allow the Cobra to regain its rightful throne.

MacDonald captured in a characteristic opposite-lock attitude during the USRRC race at Laguna Seca in 1963. He finished second to Holbert's Cobra in the GT class, with Miles fourth in the third team car. Shelby American Cobras raced anywhere and everywhere during 1963 as they not only crushed the Corvettes but rendered them irrelevant. MacDonald alone ran sixteen race weekends from coast to coast between February and August. *Revs Institute / Duke Q. Manor Photograph Collection*

Miles knew that Ford was successfully racing 427-cubic-inch motors in NASCAR. Obviously, they would have to be modified for road racing, but he wanted to stick one of them into a strengthened Cobra chassis. When Jacque Passino at Ford got wind of Miles's idea, he laughed. No way, Passino scoffed, that Miles could shoehorn a big block into a car that size.

"You send me a 427, and come back in a month," Miles told him, "and you'll see it in this car."[35]

It would take more than a month, and it would be in a different chassis. But a 427 Cobra was on its way, and Miles planned to use it to go after bigger game.

At year's end, Shelby American ran a large win ad titled "Champions!" featuring a dramatic overhead photo of Shelby standing next to three team Cobras in front of the shop on Princeton Drive. In addition to the successes of the King Cobra, Shelby American had won the USRRC title by scoring more points than Ferrari, Chevrolet, and Jaguar combined, and Johnson had nailed down the A Production title in his roadster. "In an unprecedented display of engineering perfection," the ad copy read, "the Cobra Sports Car has risen in one short year of production to the pinnacle of road racing success."

This was truth in advertising. But it was just the beginning. In 1964, Shelby American aspired to nothing less than world domination.

CHAPTER THREE

TAKING ON THE WORLD

1964

The backstory behind the greatest achievement in the Cobra's illustrious competition history began in 1957 in the General Motors Styling Section in Warren, Michigan. This magnificent technical complex, created by car design czar Harley Earl and celebrated architect Eero Saarinen, dedicated a small space to an automotive design library. Here, young car designer Peter Brock would satisfy his boundless curiosity by rummaging aimlessly through the stacks. Brock had been attending the Art Center School in Los Angeles when, at nineteen, he was headhunted by GM Styling. An after-hours conversation with Earl led to Brock conceptualizing and styling a tiny rear-engine commuter car that would later take shape as the Corvair. At the direction of Earl's successor, Bill Mitchell, Brock also drew the initial sketch for what eventually went into production as the Corvette Sting Ray. Now, killing time during lunch hour, he stumbled across a fascinating document written by German aerodynamicist Reinhard Freiherr von Koenig-Fachsenfeld in the 1930s and confiscated by US troops after World War II.

"There were six or eight mimeographed pages, purple on gelatin," Brock recalled.[1] "All the writing was in German, and the drawings were super crude, like little hen scratches. But the coefficient of drag numbers were there. And I thought, 'Hmm. That's kind of interesting.' The drawings showed that the roof couldn't slope down more than seven degrees or you'd get turbulence off the back end. There were examples of conventional cars versus their ideal form. It was strange looking. I took their stuff, and I modified it a little bit and changed the window pattern around so that it didn't look like a giant lump of clay."

Brock showed his sketch to Mitchell. "That's the ugliest shit I've ever seen," Mitchell told him, and Brock shelved the idea for future reference.[2] Fast-forward to 1963. While continuing to work at Shelby's driving school, Brock was also handling most of Shelby American's design work—badges, logos, apparel, even letterhead stationery. But racing was still his thing, and he stayed abreast of developments in the world of motorsports. He knew, for example, that a loophole in Appendix J of the FIA rulebook allowed GT cars that had already been homologated to be fitted with a new body. If ever there was a race car that would benefit from updated bodywork, he realized, it was the Cobra.

With its blunt nose and open cockpit, the Cobra was saddled with the aerodynamic qualities of a one-ton two-by-four. "The windshield acted like a huge air brake," Dan Gurney explained.[3] "At Daytona, we angled it so much that we would look *over* the windscreen." Even with a 289 that put out 385 honest horsepower at the flywheel, the car hit a figurative brick wall at about 165 miles per hour. That was high cotton for a roadster, and not an issue in the States, where races were run on purpose-built tracks with relatively short straightaways whose length limited top speed no matter how powerful the engine or slippery the bodywork. But many of the classic circuits in Europe were fashioned out of public roads or designed to mimic them—places like Spa-Francorchamps, Reims, Monza, the Nürburgring, and, most important of all, Le Mans, which were full of endlessly long straights and daunting high-speed sweepers. Here in America, Cobras had been able to use their superior acceleration and braking to outrun Ferrari 250 GTOs. But at Le Mans and the other continental racetracks, the roadsters would be gobbled up on the straights by the more aerodynamically efficient Italian coupes.

Brock saw an opportunity to use the aerodynamic insights he'd discovered in the German documents in the GM library six years earlier as the basis for a sleek new skin transforming the Cobra into a coupe. Shelby was skeptical. The previous year, Ed Hugus and AC Cars had raced a couple of roadsters with rudimentary hardtops at Le Mans, and they hadn't set the world on fire. Also, for a variety of reasons, Remington wasn't interested in devoting shop resources to such a speculative project, and Shelby usually took his advice on technical matters. But Ken Miles immediately recognized the possibilities a brand-new body offered, and he persuaded Shelby to take a flier on building a coupe.

Now, for the record, the notion that Shelby created the Cobra to settle a score with Enzo is revisionist history, if not outright bullshit. "I had no idea about beating Ferrari," Shelby said.[4] "All I wanted to do was build one hundred cars so that the Cobra would be a production car." And as a production car, the Cobra could then compete against—and shellac—the Corvette, which was the principal selling point in his pitch to Ford. But Shelby was a racer, which is to say competitive as hell, and as he put it, "Who wouldn't want to kick Number One in the ass if he had the chance?"[5] Despite his misgivings, he gave Brock his marching orders.

"How much money and how much time [do we have]?" Brock asked him.[6]

"No money and no time," Shelby said.

"I'm going to build this thing like an airplane. It's going to be functional first and beautiful second."

"I don't care what the hell it looks like as long as it goes fast."

This was music to Brock's ears. "I didn't have a drawing board," Brock said later.[7] "I didn't have anything. There was no room in the shop. So I taped butcher paper to the floor in the accounting office, and that's where I made all the drawings for the wooden buck. I drew the thing up in quarter scale. Then, I took 35mm photographs, and, to blow it up full size, I projected the slides onto the wall. AC wouldn't give Carroll the engineering drawings. I guess they were afraid that he was going to start making the chassis over here. So we had to reverse-engineer the chassis, which was no big deal since it was just two parallel tubes. Then we put Ken in the bare chassis in his personal seat, and with some masking tape and string and stuff, I figured out the basic dimensions and hard points that would tell me how big the windscreen would be. So even before I designed the car, I designed the windscreen and sent that off to PPG. I knew that I couldn't change the glass, but I could change the aluminum to fit it."

Brock took the buck to nearby California Metal Shaping, a prestigious SoCal coachbuilder whose corpus of work stretched from hot rods to Indy cars. In a week, the artisans there had hammered out an aluminum body. To modern eyes, Brock's coupe looks like the avatar of the all-American sports car, purposeful and pugnacious but far more sophisticated and graceful than the roadster. But at the time, to men raised on statuesque Indy roadsters and sleek Ferrari prototypes, the flat rear deck and chopped-off Kamm tail seemed perverse and ungainly. Remington, especially, thought it looked goofy, and considering his standing in the shop, his opinion quickly became conventional wisdom. "Brock's Folly," the guys called it, and none of them volunteered to work on it. "If John Ohlsen hadn't come on board, it never would have gotten built," Brock admitted.[8]

Ohlsen was the new guy. A Kiwi by birth, he'd been working as a mechanic for a British race team that competed in the fall pro races at Riverside and Laguna Seca, and he'd signed on with Shelby American to avoid returning to England during the winter. He turned out to be the perfect choice for Brock's coupe. Like a lot of residents of New Zealand, where the remote location cultivated self-reliance as a national trait, Ohlsen was an accomplished jack-of-all-trades. He and Brock began working on the Cobra chassis that Skip Hudson had wrecked at Daytona the previous January. The car was literally built around Miles, who saw the coupe as a chance to play with something more exotic than a plain-Jane roadster. Later on, Granny Collins also began helping out, and his fastidiousness—he insisted, for example, that rivets be perfectly spaced—was a useful asset. Another major player was shop foreman Donn Allen, whose experience with Indy cars made him sensitive to the demands that higher sustained speeds placed on a chassis. Most of the welding was done by Jack Lane, who'd recently joined Shelby American after leaving John Mecom Jr.'s team in Houston.

On February 1, 1964, Ohlsen and Collins climbed into the shop's F-250 pickup and towed the bare aluminum coupe to Riverside on a single-axle open trailer. Although Miles arrived after the car had been unloaded and warmed up, he insisted on brewing a civilized cup of tea before getting to work. As soon as he donned his helmet and took to the track, he felt two huge improvements. First, the extra torsional rigidity of the chassis—dramatically stiffened with a triangulated subframe over the transmission—produced higher cornering speeds. Second, the coupe bodywork also translated into more top-end velocity, though Miles wasn't sure how much because he suspected the tachometer wasn't working properly. Still, the stopwatch didn't lie. Lap times showed the car was 3.5 seconds—3.5 seconds!—faster than a Cobra roadster. "This thing's a rocket ship!" Miles told Shelby on a phone call from the track.[9]

Racing tends to be an incremental business. Even when revolutionary changes are introduced—wings, ground effects, slick tires—the advantages are usually measured in tenths of a second. To find a full second in a test session is cause for boisterous celebration. To find 3.5 seconds? "It was just mind-blowing," Brock remembered.[10] "Nobody could believe that the car was that much better." Miles immediately grasped the ramifications of the implausible lap times. Before returning to Venice, Miles told Collins and Ohlsen, "We'll put a full crew on that thing and have it ready for Sebring! I think it can win the 12 Hour."[11]

That same afternoon, by Shelby's command, space was carved out so that Brock's Folly could be moved from the corner where it had been ignored for the past few months to a prime spot in the center of the shop. "All of a sudden, Pete Brock was the new sweetheart in town," mechanic Ted Sutton said.[12] Miles told Sutton to drain the diff and pull the cover off so he could count the teeth in the ring and pinion gears. At the track the day before, the numbers Miles had seen on the tach were so hard to believe that he doubted that the car was running a long "Riverside gear"—a final-drive ratio of 3.73:1. Even a test using a crayon to mark a full revolution of the tires in the pits hadn't convinced him. "They're bloody wrong," he'd said.[13] "They must be 3.91s." A shorter gear, he thought, would explain the rpm numbers. But Ohlsen physically counted the teeth and confirmed that it was a 3.73. When Miles used his cardboard "dream wheel" to translate rpm into mph, he realized that he'd been doing 183 mph down the backstraight at Riverside. The coupe was nearly 20 mph faster than the roadster. With a longer final-drive ratio, Brock thought, the car could go 200 mph at Le Mans and compete for an overall win in the twenty-four-hour race.

A folly no longer, Brock's coupe became the focus of an all-hands-on-deck effort that energized the shop. Miles had said he thought the car could win Sebring. But Shelby wanted to run it in the season opener at Daytona, and the race was less than two weeks away. Miles insisted that the car needed a wider rear tire. A call was placed to Goodyear, but Tony Webner said there wasn't enough time to create a new mold. Instead, he overnighted new front tires that had just been developed for NASCAR. A second test at Riverside showed the extra rubber made the car even better.

Shortly before the car was loaded up for the trip to Florida, Miles was informed that he wasn't going to be racing the car at Daytona. He was mystified; at that point, he was the only person who'd even driven the car, which had been designed around his dimensions. He was also enraged. "I'm gonna quit," he told Brock.[14] But he'd been around long enough not to make any rash decisions. After reconsidering overnight, he swallowed his anger and decided to be a team player. Miles ended up racing virtually every car that came out of the Shelby American shop. But he never raced Brock's coupe, a car that wouldn't have existed if Miles hadn't pushed Shelby into building it.

Initially, the car didn't have a name. For lack of anything better, the crew started calling it the "Daytona car." Before too long, this morphed into the "Daytona Coupe." The name stuck.

The coupe wasn't the only car that got its baptism of fire that Saturday morning at Riverside. Miles also had made good on his boast to Jacque Passino a few months earlier and equipped a Cobra with a big-block 427-cubic-inch Ford V-8. Crewmen Jerry Bondio, Sherman Falconer, and Wally Peat had driven up from Venice so Miles and Bob Bondurant could test the car, and driver Richie Ginther and artist George Bartell had tagged along to observe. Naturally, Dave Friedman was there to document the occasion.

A self-taught photographer with deep roots in the feature-film industry, Friedman had been hired a few times by Shelby on an ad hoc basis.

Brock wore many hats at Shelby American, from serving as the first driving instructor at his school at Riverside to creating the graphics for the original GT350. But his most enduring claim to fame was designing the Daytona Coupe. By clothing the clunky roadster in sleek, aerodynamic bodywork, Brock transformed the Cobra into a car able to beat the Ferrari 250 GTO at Le Mans— and everywhere else. *Peter Brock Collection*

When the first Cobra was being built in Santa Fe Springs, Friedman was brought in to shoot the car while it was in bare aluminum. The following year, Friedman joined the Shelby American staff full time, which meant that he was able to photograph not only the major races but also the construction of race cars and action behind the scenes. Shelby, who understood better than anybody the potency of a memorable image, often joined Friedman in his darkroom at the Carter Street facility. "He came in my darkroom all the time. I had to throw him out," Friedman recalled.[15] "He was mesmerized by me putting a piece of paper in what he called 'water,' and watching the image come up. But he hated the smell.[16] He always said, 'This fucking place smells like sheep shit.' And he was right. Smelled worse."

Photos from the day show a grungy red Cobra that didn't look much different from a stock 289 other than the bare-metal nosepiece, which had been reworked to accommodate a larger grille. The car betrayed none of the swagger that would become the signature of the big-block Cobra—no brawny fender flares, no wide-track chassis, no scoops or

A rare photo of the man behind the camera. This is Dave Friedman, the best-known and most prolific chronicler of the Shelby American years, standing next to the Daytona Coupe at Daytona in 1964. Shelby commissioned him to document the Cobra as it was being assembled in Dean Moon's shop. Later, Friedman worked full time as the team photographer, covering everything from races to behind-the-scenes action in the shops in Venice and at LAX. *Dave Friedman*

louvers. At this point, it was still running on dainty wire wheels and street tires. The car was very much a pet project being pushed by Miles, and only one mechanic had been assigned to work on it.

Sutton was another example of the resourceful young men whom Remington had plucked from obscurity. After graduating from high school in Indiana, Sutton had moved to LA and retrofitted an Austin-Healey 3000 with a K-Code Ford V-8. In the summer of 1963, he swung by the Shelby American operation in Venice to pick up a clutch slave cylinder and some other parts. When the car was finished, Sutton returned to Venice to show it off. Although he wasn't looking for work, the Healey served as both his résumé and his job interview. After walking outside to examine the car, Remington hired Sutton on the spot.

Not long after joining the team, Sutton was assigned to another conversion—squeezing a big-block V-8 into a box-stock Cobra, chassis CSX2196. The original plan had been to use one of Ford's highly touted aluminum-block 390s, but this engine turned out to be something of a unicorn. Instead, he was told to work with a wood mockup of the about-to-be-introduced single-overhead-cam 427, popularly known as the Cammer and destined for great things in drag racing. The model had been fastidiously painted to look like the real thing. But as Sutton pointed out, the wood mockup wasn't strong enough to support the bell housing of the massive T-10 transmission. It wasn't until he got his hands on a 427 side-oiler that he was able to make any serious progress.

The 427 was the king of the hill of Ford's FE lineup of big-block motors. Originally designed for heavy-duty applications, the 427 became the weapon of choice for high-performance models competing everywhere from Woodward Avenue in Detroit to the high banks of Daytona International Speedway. Early versions used a conventional top-oiling system, where lubricant bathed the camshaft and valvetrain before draining down to the crankshaft. But cranks suffered from oil starvation while running at high rpm for long stretches on oval tracks. So an alternate oiling system was developed on the left side of the block to get oil directly to the crank, hence the name side-oiler.

Despite thin-wall casting, the big block was a *huge* mass of iron. But Sutton didn't run into any structural showstoppers, and he made the changes necessary to fit the engine inside the Cobra's engine compartment. When he finished the conversion, he couldn't resist the temptation to take a test hop in his new hot rod. Sutton raced around the neighborhood in full hooligan mode, and he returned to the shop feeling proud of himself. Then he heard that Shelby wanted to see him. Uh-oh. Sutton figured he was about to get fired. Instead, Shelby took him for a hair-raising spin around the neighborhood near the shop. When Shelby parked the car in front of 1042 Princeton Drive, he pronounced himself satisfied with what Sutton had fashioned.

Miles and Bondurant were less impressed when they tested the car at Riverside. Yes, the 427 Cobra accelerated hard enough to pull the spokes out of the wire wheels. But the handling was mushy, which is exactly what you'd expect of a ponderously nose-heavy car. And the hybrid looked very much like a work in progress. Shelby American wit Garry Koike came up with a moniker that reflected the car's flaws and the shop's sensibilities: "The Turd." When a magazine writer asked him about the name, a publicity-conscious Miles gave it a positive spin, saying it referred to the car's ability to shit on the competition. But the guys who worked on it knew better. "We called it The Turd," John Morton explained, "because it was."[17]

Full disclosure: Sutton, who had a proprietary interest in the car, preferred to call it "The Beast." And Miles couldn't wait to race it, whatever it was called. But there was no chance that it could be readied soon enough to run at Daytona. The guys in the race shop were still testing and modifying Brock's coupe almost on a daily basis. "We spent hours and hours on that car," Collins said.[18] "John Ohlsen and I went out to Riverside with it nearly every day, testing. Then we'd come back at night and work on it until maybe eleven o'clock or twelve o'clock. Then we'd go home and come back early in the morning and leave for the track at about six a.m."

And that wasn't the only thing the team was working on. Also being prepped were a pair of the latest—and greatest—of the small-block Cobras, known as the FIA roadsters.

The earliest Cobra race cars had been street cars modded for the track. Over time, various racing-specific components were incorporated at the AC factory in Thames Ditton. For the 1964 season, a batch of five FIA-legal roadsters was planned with about three dozen upgrades ranging from a 12:1 compression ratio, Weber 48 IDA carbs, and straight side pipes to a 37-gallon gas tank, 9-quart oil sump, and quick-jack pads to anti-roll bars, modified rack-and-pinion steering, and pin-drive hubs for Halibrand cast-magnesium wheels. Front and rear fenders were flared to cover the 6.5- and 8.5-inch wheels, and so-called cutback doors were installed to follow the radii of the more shapely contours. Other than minor changes made to meet slightly different regulations, the FIA roadsters served as the template for the Cobras raced by Shelby American and assorted privateers in USRRC and SCCA competition.

Unlike previous Cobras, the FIA roadsters arrived from England in bare aluminum. The necessity of painting the car gave Shelby the opportunity to adopt a team color. He selected a silvery blue metallic Ford factory color known as Viking Blue. To distinguish team cars, each one was painted with a horizontal stripe in a contrasting color across the nose. Brock also created a team uniform consisting of a darker blue button-down shirt with white stripes at the shoulders and "COBRA" emblazoned across the back. The crewman's name was embroidered over the front pocket. (Charlie Agapiou chose "Who" because nobody could pronounce his name.). Tucked into crisp white pants, the shirts gave the crew the smart look of a crack Indy car team.

But despite the snazzy new uniforms and the team's dominant domestic campaign in 1963, Shelby American wasn't yet a well-oiled machine ready to compete on the world stage. Racing, especially endurance racing, magnifies the smallest flaws in cars, drivers, and teams, and so it proved at Daytona. In 1964, for the first time, the race was being contested as a two-thousand-kilometer enduro open only to GT cars, which meant prototypes weren't eligible. Besides the new coupe, Shelby American was also debuting a pair of FIA roadsters. But the entry list featured no fewer than eight Ferrari 250 GTOs, which promised to be the Cobra's main rival for the FIA championship.

The Gran Turismo Omologato was the pinnacle of the storied 250 series of Ferraris and the ultimate road-race sports car. Designed by engineer Giotto Bizzarrini and refined by Mauro Forghieri around a Columbo V-12 with six downdraft Weber carburetors, it sported a voluptuous Scaglietti body that remains a high-water mark of front-engine coupe styling. In theory, it could be driven to and from the track, though anybody planning to do this on a regular basis would have been wise to keep a masseuse, hearing-aid specialist, insurance adjuster, and traffic-law attorney on call. The 250 GTO had ruled GT-class racing since its introduction in 1962, and an upgraded version had been developed for 1964. Phil Hill and Pedro Rodriguez, neither one a slouch, were in a factory-supported model at Daytona, so the enduro would be a good barometer to measure Shelby American's progress.

The early returns were promising. "New coupe really flies," Dave MacDonald's wife, Sherry, wrote in her calendar after the first practice session.[19] As a bonus, it also got 20 percent better fuel economy than the roadster. Shelby paired MacDonald with Bob Holbert, the wise old head. (Holbert described MacDonald as "terribly fast yet not consistently fast.") MacDonald planted the car on the pole without pushing.[20] Holbert, who hadn't even sat in the coupe before arriving at Daytona, diced with Rodriguez for the lead early on before steadily pulling clear. The two FIA roadsters were both hamstrung by burnt pistons—the product, it turned out, of substandard gasoline at the track. But the coupe ran like a dream despite being brutally hot inside the cockpit. Holbert was in front by four-and-a-half laps when he made a routine pit stop at two-thirds distance.

When Agapiou changed the right rear tire, he spotted some oil inside the wheel. Not enough to concern him, but noticeable. Shelby, standing behind him, was less blasé. "What's that?" he demanded. Agapiou said it was probably fluid seeping out of the differential. "Tell [crew chief Jim] Culleton we might need some more [diff] oil," Shelby said.

"There's no point," Agapiou said. "We don't have any [diff] oil in the pits." This lack of preparation was Mistake Number One.

"Goddammit!" Shelby snapped. "Tell Culleton."[21]

The team had rigged a pump with a long syringe so the oil sump of the engine could be filled quickly during a pit stop. When Culleton heard Shelby browbeating Agapiou, he used the pump to shoot light-weight engine oil into the differential instead of the much heavier gear lube that was recommended. Mistake Number Two. Predictably, Holbert returned to the pits a few laps later, trailing smoke like a tramp steamer. By this time, the crew had located the missing diff fluid. It also seemed likely that the electric rear-end cooling pump must have failed, allowing the diff to overheat and the seals to leak. As soon as the car came to a stop, Ohlsen slid underneath it to undo a section of the belly pan and allow more air to flow around the differential. Meanwhile, Shelby ordered mechanic Tom Greatorex to refuel the car even though the tank had just been filled a few laps earlier. That was Mistake Number Three. Pressurized fuel sloshed out the overflow vent on the right rear fender. When it hit the superheated brake rotor, there was a gigantic *WHUMP!*, and the car was engulfed in flames. Ohlsen slithered out from underneath the Cobra, burning like one of those Buddhist priests who'd set themselves on fire to protest the Vietnam War. Even as the flames were being extinguished, he could be heard yelling, "Get my wallet! Get my wallet!"[22]

Ohlsen's burns weren't life-threatening, and a new differential could have been swapped in in less than an hour. But Shelby was so dispirited by the debacle (and, presumably, his role in it) that he overruled his crew and retired the car. This was yet another mistake since it prevented Shelby American from earning points that would have come in handy at the end of the year. Ferrari 250 GTOs finished one-two-three, with the first Cobra—an FIA roadster flogged home on seven cylinders by Gurney and Bob Johnson—a distant fourth. Still, the mood at Shelby American was upbeat. If nothing else, Brock's baby had shown that it could outrun Ferrari.

Shelby decided to build five more coupes. The chassis would be modified in Venice. But he realized that the fastest and most efficient way to build the bodies would be to farm out the work to a firm that specialized in handmade sports racers. Shelby called his friend Alejandro de Tomaso, a wealthy Argentine expatriate who ran a prototype car company in Modena, looking for a recommendation for an Italian coachbuilder. De Tomaso suggested a small firm named Carrozzeria Gransport. The price and the timing turned out to be right. Shelby also savored the idea of having the work done in Ferrari's backyard. The message he was sending to Enzo was clear: *We're coming to get you.*

The next race on the World Sportscar Championship schedule was Sebring, five weeks away. This gave the team time to iron out some of the kinks in the coupe. The two FIA roadsters that had raced at Daytona were refreshed, and a third car, recently arrived from AC, was prepped for the 12 Hour. The fifth and final car in the Shelby American stable would be The Turd, which Miles planned to use as his entrée into FIA racing. But when Jean Guichet abandoned his ride in a Cobra for what he felt was a better one in a 250 GTO, Miles was left without a co-driver.

Meanwhile, Morton—the one-time janitor who was working his way up through the SCCA club-racing ranks—was on the road to Sebring. He and fellow mechanics Jeff Schoolfield and John Shoup were so desperate to attend the race that they'd agreed to drive to and from Florida on their own nickel in return for a twenty-five-dollar-a-day gig at the track to work as night watchmen. Ah, to be twentysomething again! Crammed in a Karmann Ghia, they endured fifty-four consecutive hours on the road, stopping only for food and gas, before collapsing in a dumpy motel at four in the morning. A few hours later, at tech inspection, Morton ran into Miles.

"Do you have an FIA license?" Miles asked him.[23]

Morton stared incredulously at him. Of course, he didn't have an FIA license. All he had was an SCCA regional license, which was the motorsports equivalent of a high school diploma, and he didn't have it with him. But Miles wanted Morton in reserve just in case he needed a co-driver. On the spot, Miles wrote out a brief letter of recommendation. To Morton's amazement, he was given a license, no questions asked. Like Miles, he figured the odds of him actually getting to race were infinitesimal. Not counting Miles, there were eight other drivers on the Shelby American team, and one of them surely would be available if and when Miles felt he had to get out of the car. But just in case, Morton bought a race suit from a trackside vendor for fifteen dollars and arranged to borrow a helmet from a motorcycle racer.

Unlike Daytona, Sebring was open to prototypes as well as GT cars, and Ferrari had shown up with its latest 330 Ps. Still, Miles was third-fastest in the 427 Cobra—which was itself classified as a prototype since it hadn't been homologated—during the early stages of the first practice session. Then, he skidded off the track. Sebring was a bland airport circuit without much to hit. Except that he happened to be headed directly for what everybody later delighted in describing as the only tree for miles in any direction. "There's no way I'm going to hit that tree," Miles thought—right up until the moment of hard impact.[24] His nickname instantly changed to Teddy the Treebagger. Looking at the wreckage, Hill said, "Looks like you got a little behind in your steering."[25]

The crash destroyed The Turd's right front suspension, bent the frame and the headers, and knocked the hell out of the body, which hadn't looked that great to begin with. It also badly bruised or broke several of Miles's ribs. (He refused to see a doctor for fear that he'd be denied permission to race.) Still in his race suit, he, Morton, Schoolfield, Culleton, Sutton, and Koike pulled an all-nighter bending, hammering, and otherwise whipping the car back into shape. The next morning, Shelby, still recuperating from knee surgery, rolled up in a wheelchair and introduced Sutton to a big, burly man with a round face.

"This is John Holman," Shelby said. "He would like you to put one of his new engines in the car."[26] Sutton and his exhausted crew used an airplane crane designed for pulling engines out of DC-3s to manhandle a

The wages of sin, or at least an off-course excursion. Miles, with the torch, John Morton, wearing glasses, and fellow mechanic Schoolfield (along with unpictured crew chief Ted Sutton and crewmen Culleton and Garry Koike) repair the prototype 427 Cobra that Miles had wrecked when he hit a tree during practice at Sebring in 1964. Amazingly, Miles and Morton would run it in the 12 Hour, though it puked just before nightfall. *Dave Friedman*

full-on NASCAR 427 into the hastily repaired Turd. Miles never posted a time in qualifying, and he started the race in sixty-first position.

Things were going better for the rest of the team, except for Mac-Donald briefly being thrown in jail after getting into an argument with an overly officious policeman over where to park the Daytona Coupe. Holbert had no trouble claiming the GT pole, light-years ahead of the GTOs. But the bumpy, twisty nature of the Sebring circuit didn't play to the strengths of the coupe. Also, in the swampy Florida humidity, it was like a steam bath inside the cockpit as heat radiated from the aluminum transmission tunnel and the side pipes. During a pit stop, Remington deftly used a pair of shears to cut an air scoop into the roof. But the pedals got so hot that they melted the soles of MacDonald's high-top sneakers. After his stint, he soaked his feet in a bucket of water and walked barefoot around the pits. By the time he got back behind the wheel, he was wearing borrowed shoes and had taped newspapers around his lower legs as insulation against the heat.

Miles had nothing but trouble with The Turd—first, brake problems, then a blocked fuel line, not to mention a frustrating disinclination to head in the direction it was pointed. But the car refused to die, and since all the other Cobras were still running, it looked like Morton might have to drive after all. Shelby called him over. "John," he said, "do you know this track?"[27]

Moment-of-truth time. "Yes," Morton said. "I've been here several times." As a spectator, that is, but never as a driver. There were parts of the track he'd never even seen.

"If Miles needs relief when he comes in, you be ready, huh?"

Morton was ready. He was also terrified. When Miles pitted, about three hours into the race, Morton approached him in his brand-new race suit and borrowed helmet. "Do you want relief?" he asked tentatively.

Miles gave him a long, withering look connoting . . . what? Disbelief? Amusement? Resignation? After three hours wrestling The Turd around Sebring with a set of broken ribs, he damn well was ready for relief, no matter who provided it. "Yes," he said.

It was a be-careful-what-you-wish-for moment for Morton. Holding down the heavy clutch, his left foot started shaking so violently that his whole body was vibrating. When he finally eased out of the pits, he was stunned by how badly the car wallowed. "It felt more like a '49 Buick than a race car," he recalled.[28] On his out lap, he spun at the hairpin, largely because he didn't know it existed until he was driving around it. He then spun a second time on the same lap at another turn he'd never seen before. But nobody in the pits noticed. Nobody was even paying attention. Morton survived a brake failure, then a clutch failure and was clicking off respectable lap times when the engine grenaded shortly before dark. The Turd was well and truly dead.

Ironically, the GT race was being dominated not by the highly touted Daytona Coupe but by an FIA roadster in the hands of Gurney and Johnson. But the racing gods evidently wanted the newer car to grab the glory. With less than an hour to go and while holding what seemed to be an unassailable lead, Johnson rear-ended a tiny Alfa Romeo that was puttering down the front straight with barely visible taillights. It was a hellacious hit. The Cobra was doing 140 mph when it smacked the Alfa and then flew high in the air. The Alfa driver survived the accident only because he was heroically yanked out of the burning wreckage by a driver who'd been watching from the pits. Johnson suffered a black eye and broken nose in the course of cartwheeling like a demented Olympic gymnast doing a tumbling pass. The car was so thoroughly wadded up that it was tossed in a dumpster.

The Holbert/MacDonald Daytona Coupe won the GT class, with the remaining Cobra roadsters second and third. The crew partied heartily after the race in Shelby's hotel room, where liquor flowed and the team indulged its passion for fireworks. Except for the unlucky Johnson and Gurney, it was the best possible result for Shelby American, since it confirmed the ability of the coupe to beat the Ferraris. Up until now, no money had been earmarked to send the Cobras to Europe. Instead, Ford was sinking a small fortune—and, later, a large fortune—into an effort to develop a new-from-the-ground-up prototype, the GT40, designed to win Le Mans overall. But that looked like it was going to be a long-term proposition. After the GT-class victory at Sebring, Ray Geddes was able to sweet-talk Ford into providing a modest budget to fund a European assault led by the Daytona Coupe *right now.*

The FIA World Championship effort was obviously a big deal. The stakes would be higher, the competition fiercer. Logistics alone promised to be a nightmare. But what people often forget is that, by 1964, Shelby American had grown into a large and complicated machine with hundreds of moving parts. Even as the coupes were being readied for the European campaign, work was continuing on the 427. King Cobras and roadsters were racing in the US Road Racing Championship. A Cobra fitted with a hardtop was burning up drag strips on the West Coast. A one-off Sunbeam was waiting for its debut. Plans to transform the humdrum Mustang into a take-no-prisoners sports car were being kicked around. Raoul "Sonny" Balcaen, who'd briefly worked for Carroll Shelby Sport (singular) Car in Dallas, was given an office next to Brock's to handle marketing and catalog work. (He also doubled as a company pilot.) Before long, the company was doing a lively business selling "trinkets and trash," from three-inch decals (25 cents) to lapel pins ($1.25). Celebrities ranging from Mort Sahl to Elvis Presley dropped in. Steve McQueen would swing by in the Cobra that Shelby had given him, often with a spent joint in the ashtray. One day, Morton saw a very tall Black man in the shop. "He was looking inside a Cobra, and his ass was as high as the top of the car," he recalled. "It was Wilt Chamberlain."[29]

By this time, more than fifty people were working at the Princeton Drive and Carter Street facilities. The hourly pay was competitive, especially compared with the going rate in the UK, which was one of the benefits that attracted so many Brits to Southern California. Better still, Shelby American paid overtime, and lots of it, which was virtually unheard of at race shops of the day. Shelby could afford to be so generous because Ford was paying the freight. The more hours he billed, the more he got paid, so mechanics would accumulate twenty, thirty, forty, fifty, even sixty hours of overtime as race weekends approached. And there was no shortage of applicants.

Jim Marietta was seventeen when he dropped out of high school in suburban Cleveland to work in a garage. On weekends, he flew all over the country to follow the Cobras at USRRC races. "I would buy a general-admission ticket, and then I'd jump the fence and hang out in the Shelby pit," he said.[30] "After I did that for a couple of races in different parts of the country, Al Dowd finally said to me, 'I'm gonna make a deal. I'm not gonna pay your way to the races. But if you get here, you can sign on for our pit deal so you don't have to jump fences anymore. And we'll find you a place, and we'll feed you. But we're not paying you. Is that okay with you?'"

Marietta gladly agreed. After volunteering for several months, he moved to Southern California and joined the team as a full-time mechanic. "They had me fill out some paperwork—which was pretty rudimentary, I can tell you," he said.[31] "Al said, 'We're going to pay you ten hours day, six days a week, with time-and-a-half over eight hours. Some weeks you're only gonna work forty hours, and some weeks you're going to work eighty. But if it's okay with you, we're just going to pay you for sixty,'" Marietta recalled. "Today, they'd put you in jail for that. But back then, it was fine."

Working at Shelby American was a job, of course, and guys some-times called one another "donkeys"—overworked pack animals. But for many employees, it was also a calling, and they took more pride in what they were doing than the faceless drones manning an assembly line knocking out widgets. Generally speaking, the "Snake Pit" was a cheer-ful workplace. The shop spaces were wide-open, which encouraged mingling and camaraderie. Hijinks were tolerated. For the Christmas party, the water cooler was spiked with moonshine. Dowd kept a pet snake—a cobra, naturally—named Herman in a glass enclosure on the second floor. One morning, when the shop opened, the enclosure was empty. Muy macho mechanics locked their toolboxes and loitered across the street until Herman was found. Or so the story goes.

Other than Dowd, Herman didn't have many fans around the shop. One winter morning, Dowd arrived in his office to find the cobra coiled lifelessly in its glass cage. According to scuttlebutt around the shop, somebody with a snake phobia had turned off the heat the previous evening, and Herman had frozen to death overnight. A stuffed cobra was imported as a replacement. Of course, the substitute wasn't nearly as entertaining as the real thing. For a while, Shelby amused himself by ambushing people, often miniskirted women with exposed thighs, with a cattle prod that produced a mild but unpleasant electrical shock when the trigger was pulled. This was not, as you might imagine, appreciated by the recipients. Legend has it that an anonymous do-gooder reversed the polarity of the device so that when Shelby pulled the trigger, he shocked himself instead of his unsuspecting victim. That was the end of the cattle prod.

Most of the grunt work was done by young men who hadn't out-grown their boyhood fascination with explosions, the bigger the better. The gas from acetylene torches could be rigged to blow things up in dramatic fashion. Morton was the culprit behind one blast that caused his ears to ring for days. Agapiou was the master of sneak firecracker attacks. Dowd was the cherry bomb king. Whenever trucker Red Pierce returned from a trip that took him through the South, he replenished the shop inventory of M-80s, which were a cross between firecrackers and sticks of dynamite. Pierce's specialty was removing the gunpowder and then terrifying his victims by lighting what they didn't realize was a dud. He outsmarted himself once during breakfast at a hotel back east, when he lit off what he thought was a blank—but wasn't.

"Needless to say, it blew that table and everything else into a million pieces, and we were asked to leave," Pierce said.[32] "I used to wonder how much money Al Dowd paid to keep us guys out of jail. We wanted to win races and we did, so we worked hard and we worked seriously. But we played just as hard as we worked."

They worked hard because there was more than enough work to go around. But what made Shelby American so unusual was that everybody wasn't working together toward a single goal. There was so much happening simultaneously that it was sometimes hard to tell who was doing what and why. "The coupe was just one of thirty-five projects Shelby had going on at the shop," Brock explained.[33] "Guys would work on something for six months, and he'd just forget about it. He was ruthless about choosing what to go ahead with. But he usually chose wisely."

A rare outside project undertaken by Shelby produced what was later named the Sunbeam Tiger. Ian Garrad, the West Coast general manager of the Rootes Group, which owned Sunbeam and several other small British car companies, had been wowed by the Cobra's debut at Riverside in 1962. Garrad wanted to goose sales of the Sunbean Alpine, a cute but criminally underpowered two-seat sports car, by fitting it with a 260-cubic-inch Ford V-8. At the time, Miles still owned his own shop, so Garrad paid him $600 to do a fast-and-dirty conversion. Working with Agapiou and Jean Stucki, another mechanic who would later move to Shelby American, Miles did the job in less than a week. The result was rude, crude, and quickly forgotten. The moral of the story? You get what you pay for.

Even as Miles was busy with his Alpine, Garrad sent a second car to Shelby, who was to be paid $10,000 for a much more refined conversion. The project was assigned to George Boskoff, a meticulous craftsman with fabrication skills on par with Remington's. Boskoff approached the project more holistically than Miles. He realized that the bigger, heavier engine would put too much weight on the nose, so he relocated it lower and farther back in the chassis. Among other changes, this entailed upgrading the Alpine to rack-and-pinion steering, modifying the firewall, and adjusting the suspension geometry. Working largely by himself in a semi-secret room near the dyno, Boskoff used parts scrounged from hot-rod hero Doane Spencer to fashion what was, in effect, the Son of Cobra.

Thanks to its most-favored-nation status with Shelby, *Sports Car Graphic* was allowed to drive the car, though strictly on an off-the-record basis. The magazine was underwhelmed. "It went alright—almost as fast as a well-optioned Sting Ray. But anything but a straight line was Panicsville," read a story published a year after a "secret hop" in the prototype.[34] "The engine sat high and not very far back, promoting body-walk and horrible understeering."

Undaunted, Garrad took the car back to England, where it received glowing reviews from Rootes management. Boskoff's hot rod was put into production with only minor changes as the Sunbeam Tiger. Come

Although the program shows a Cobra winning the race, the USRRC event at Riverside in 1964 turned out to be a bust for Shelby American. The King Cobras of MacDonald and Holbert failed to finish, and Miles was fourth overall in a 289 roadster. *John Gabrial Collection*

79

April 1964, the car was ready for its racetrack debut. Boskoff was gone by this time, so crew chief duties passed to Sutton, while Jim O'Leary looked after the engine and Lew Spencer was named the driver. Besides being a longtime acquaintance of Shelby's, Spencer had won countless SCCA races with a series of Morgans he called Baby Dolls, so he knew how to go quickly in a British roadster. But he couldn't get past the foibles of the pale yellow Tiger. In his first outing, at an SCCA regional in Tucson, he detoured into a gravel runoff area, blew a tire, spun, got a new tire, then locked up the brakes at the end of the front straight and spun again in spectacular fashion. He finished a disappointing fourth in B Production, happy merely to have made it to the finish in one piece. A few weeks later, he won a dinky race at Willow Springs, but that did nothing to change his opinion of the car.

"We could never get the car to handle," Spencer said.[35] "It was too short in the wheelbase, had too much weight on the nose, and always wanted to go backwards, not forwards."[36] He proved the point not once but twice later that year at Laguna Seca. During practice, he badly pranged the car after losing the rear end blasting over the hill just past the start-finish line, just as MacDonald had done in the King Cobra a few months earlier. It took eight hours for Sutton and O'Leary to repair the damage. The same thing happened again during the race, only this time Spencer took evasive action to avoid the dirt embankment—and ran into a ditch he hadn't noticed.

"I hit the nose on the concrete culvert, and the car rose up into the air, and there was another dirt road that went across by a dirt bank," he said.[37] "I slid across that road and buried the car's nose into the bank. An absolute dead stop. The car fell back down, and the impact knocked my goggles off. I knew I had bounced my feet around in there because I could already feel a kind of numbness. The car was destroyed clear back to the windshield." Spencer remained in the car for several minutes, and when he finally managed to climb out, he was so unsteady on his feet that he had to lie down on the ground. It took him six weeks to recover.

Spencer washed his hands of the car after that. In September, Miles scored an improbable class win at Road America, where the Tiger shocked everybody by overcoming chronic overheating problems and lasting for two hundred miles. After that, Shelby wisely declared vic-

Driving the Shelby American-built prototype of the Sunbeam Tiger, Spencer drifts out of Turn Nine—now Turn Eleven—at Laguna Seca. As he powered over the crest just past the start-finish line, he lost the rear end of the ill-handling roadster and crashed awkwardly into a culvert. Spencer never raced the car again. After Miles scored an unlikely win at Road America, Shelby wisely left the Tiger in Sunbeam's hands. *Dave Friedman*

tory and left the Tiger to Sunbeam. The car turned out to be a surprise success; more than seven thousand Tigers were sold over the next four years, proving that there was a market for a poor man's Cobra.

But Shelby American wasn't quite done with the prototype. Before sending the car back to England, production manager Leonard Parsons ordered Cobra drag racer Jere Kirkpatrick to replace the 260 with a Hi-Po 289. With skinny tires and hardly any weight on the rear, the car spun its wheels virtually on demand—a sweet hot rod, perhaps, but not a proper sports car. After sampling the car, the folks at Sunbeam sent Shelby a telegram: "You bloody Americans are fucking nuts."[38]

Shelby American now had a Drag Racing Division, called Department "R," for some inexplicable reason. Working under the titular direction of Parsons, Stoer continued to set quarter-mile records with CSX2019 into 1964. Then Stoer came into work one Monday morning in April and discovered that the drag-racing Cobra he'd developed with Kirkpatrick and Randy Shaw had been sold. "I started yelling and screaming," Stoer recalled.[39] "So Leonard said, 'Calm down. Just pick another car and build a brand-new one.'" Stoer went to the back of the building, where unfinished rollers were lined up awaiting drivetrains. He grabbed CSX2357 at random and started assembling it in his spare time. He finished the car at ten o'clock on a Saturday night and called Parsons.

"I got it running," Stoer told him.[40]

"Take it out and put some miles on it," Parsons said.

Stoer didn't have to be told twice. He threw some dealer plates on the car and headed out with the exhaust blasting. Not to nearby Lincoln Boulevard for a quick shakedown. Not to the Wich Stand or the A&W in Hawthorn to line up a street race. No, Stoer made a beeline for the Sunset Strip in Hollywood, the most glamorous automotive see-and-be-seen territory in LA. Blipping the throttle, he rumbled past the Whisky a Go Go, where headliner Johnny Rivers sang hits like "Memphis" and "Maybelline" while the line of would-be patrons snaked around the corner. "We were thinking, 'Man, the girls are really gonna like this!'" Stoer said.[41] "They didn't pay a bit of attention. But all the guys were going ape shit. I pulled onto one of the freeways, I forget which one, and I got it up to 7000 in fourth gear. That son of a bitch was faster than shit."

Much to his chagrin, Stoer was drafted before he could race the car. After Stoer left for basic training, Shaw came up with a memorable name for the new Cobra: Dragonsnake. An artist was commissioned to design and paint a bold logo on the rear fender—a coiled cobra riding on a pair of smoking drag slicks. Kirkpatrick was designated the new aimer. He modified the shifter and adjusted his shifting technique to make seamless gear changes. "We had a [Borg-Warner] T-10L in it, and I was bending shift levers all the time," he said.[42] "So I got two sets of levers, cut the buds off them, and arc-welded them together. At Half Moon Bay, I was interviewed after the race, and the guy said, 'I wasn't aware that the Cobras had an automatic transmission.' And I told them, 'They don't.' It was that quick."

Fitted with a Weber carb so it qualified for a stock class, Kirkpatrick set a record of 12.00 seconds at 114.83 mph at Riverside, then bettered it at Fremont with a fast time of 11.81 seconds at 116.27 mph. "We didn't have much competition," he said, "so we'd let the other guys leave the starting line first, and then we'd come from behind and bury them at the finish."[43]

Ford started to promote the car, and Shelby belatedly realized he had a marketable product. Ads started appearing in hot-rod magazines: "RECORD HOLDER! The Drag Racing Division of Shelby American's famous competition department has been working for months on the strips of Southern California developing the fastest production sports car to ever hit the quarter mile lights! These special new 'Dragon Snakes' are now in limited production and available to qualified serious competitors." Although only three turnkey Dragonsnakes were sold to customers, privateers fashioned several other cars into drag kings. And many a Cobra found its way to local drag strips over the years.

In addition to the original crew, Shelby American sales manager Don McCain raced the car on several occasions. At the 1964 National

The first Shelby American drag car was a beater Cobra retrofitted for quarter-mile racing. Version 2.0 was a newbie earmarked from birth as a dragster. Tony Stoer did most of the mechanical mods, and Randy Shaw came up with the Dragonsnake name. But in 1964, Jere Kirkpatrick was the chief driver—or maybe that should be chief aimer, according to the legend on the hardtop—and he was virtually unbeatable. *Dave Friedman*

Championship Drag Races in Indianapolis, the mega-event popularly known as the Big Go, Ford put factory driver Ed Terry behind the wheel of the Shelby American Dragonsnake against four privately owned Cobras and fourteen Corvettes. Ralph Falconer, one of three Falconer brothers who worked for Shelby, was looking for an edge at the track. "I ended up putting one-inch-thick risers from an old Chevy truck underneath the carburetors," he said.[44] "They were about the right bolt spacing for the Webers, but the bore was about a quarter inch too small, so I opened them up with a rat tail file. Imagine how long that took! That isolated the carburetors from the manifolds, so there was a little less heat going into the carburetor. And it seemed to run better." Terry won A/Sports with a run of 12.06 seconds at 113.45 mph.

Still, road racing was Shelby American's raison d'être, and in terms of shop resources in Venice, the USRRC program remained its main focus. At most races, Shelby American fielded three roadsters in the GT class along with a pair of King Cobras for Holbert and MacDonald competing for overall wins. Besides being long in the tooth, the King Cobras were technically overmatched by Jim Hall's Chaparral 2A. MacDonald managed a somewhat fortunate win in the season opener at Augusta when Hall spun late in the race. Two months later, while practicing in MacDonald's car at Kent, Holbert aquaplaned on a damp track and gyrated into the pits. Three cars were wrecked, and three people were injured. It was a ghastly scene. Holbert announced his retirement shortly afterward.

Now racing in Holbert's King Cobra, MacDonald lucked into another win when Hall broke while leading with two laps to go. He then headed to Indianapolis to qualify for the 500. On the strength of MacDonald's high-fly act in 1963, Mickey Thompson had offered him a ride at the Speedway. This was a double-edged sword; several experienced drivers had already backed away from Thompson's strangely streamlined cars, which looked—and handled, some said—sort of like roller skates. But after years in the minor leagues, MacDonald was eager to take a shot at the big time, and he drew upon his otherworldly car-control skills to put the car in the show. Despite qualifying a respectable fourteenth,

MacDonald privately admitted that he was spooked by the car. Friends and teammates begged him to walk away and come back to race another day. "I tried and tried and tried," said Wally Peat, who accompanied him to Indianapolis. "But Dave was the type of guy who, when he said something, that was it. He wouldn't quit."[45]

MacDonald started the 500 like he'd been shot out of a cannon. He passed six cars on the first lap. Coming out of Turn Four to start the second lap, he started to go underneath Walt Hansgen, another road racer making his Indy debut. Just then, Hansgen decided to pull the same move on Jim Hurtubise. As MacDonald juked left to avoid Hansgen, the front end of his roller skate lifted up, and the rear end got away from him, and he slewed nose first at almost undiminished speed into the inside wall protecting pit lane. The fuel tank split, and forty-five gallons of gasoline ignited. His car careened across the track, trailing a curtain of fire. With nowhere else to go, Eddie Sachs tried to squeeze through the quickly closing gap between MacDonald's car and the outside wall. He didn't make it. Sachs died instantly. MacDonald succumbed to gruesome burns a few hours later. He was twenty-seven years old. The race was halted for nearly two hours as dense clouds of black smoke billowed over the grandstands. It was the worst accident in the history of Indianapolis Motor Speedway, and it ended MacDonald's meteoric rise almost as quickly as it had started.

The guys in the shop were devastated by MacDonald's death. During the span of three weeks, the team had lost its two most successful drivers. MacDonald, in particular, had occupied a special place in the Shelby American family. Unlike Holbert or Gurney or Hill, he didn't just show up at the track to race cars prepared by other people. He was a mechanic who worked tirelessly on his own car. From humble blue-collar roots, he'd achieved the dream of graduating from wrenching on cars to driving them professionally. In an instant, because of misguided loyalty and one small mistake on track, the dream had shape-shifted into a nightmare. It was a grim reminder of just how cruel the sport of racing could be.

With MacDonald and Holbert gone, Shelby American redoubled its efforts in GT racing. The USRRC versions of the Cobra were virtually identical to the FIA roadsters that had raced at Daytona and Sebring.

They were driven by members of what Dowd called the Old Folks Racing Team—Miles, Johnson, and former combat aviator Ed Leslie, all over forty. (Leslie had driven a privately owned Cobra to the SCCA's A Production championship the previous year.) Although the fit and finish of the cars left something to be desired, the team was so far superior to the competition that it was like watching the Harlem Globetrotters barnstorming across the country, dunking on the hapless locals. Miles, Leslie, and Johnson finished one-two-three in four of five races. At one point, they started flipping coins to determine the finishing order. At Elkhart Lake, near the end of the USRRC season, two new names snuck into Victory Lane after the Road America 500—Morton and Skip Scott, whose Cobra survived when the other two Shelby American entries failed to finish. (Morton acknowledged that he and Scott probably wouldn't have won the race if Miles hadn't driven the final stint in their car.) Leslie and Johnson put a bow on the season by going one-two in the American Road Race of Champions at Riverside, thereby claiming the Cobra's second consecutive A Production championship.

Still, the Cobra was a big fish in a small pond here in the States. It was in Europe, competing against Ferrari for the GT World Championship, where Shelby American's mettle would be tested more seriously. Along with Dowd and Remington, four crewmen were assigned to the program—Culleton, Stucki, Jack Hoare, and relative newcomer Mark Popov-Dadiani. They would be based in England at Ford Advanced Vehicles, the wholly owned subsidiary that had been created to build and campaign the GT40s that were just about ready to make their debut.

Ohlsen, now recovered from his burns at Sebring, was working temporarily in England for John Willment, who was building his own version of Brock's Daytona coupe. Ohlsen would join the Shelby American guys at Le Mans, where Shelby planned to spring a wicked surprise on Ferrari. After Sebring, Shelby told *Competition Press*, "Ferrari beat us here today for the overall prize with a prototype. So now I'm going into the prototype business. At Le Mans, we'll have a prototype car with a new-type, bigger engine that's going to be a big surprise to Ferrari."[46] Translation: Shelby intended to put a much more powerful motor in one

This is what American road racing looked like circa 1964, when Cobras eviscerated the competition in the GT class while competing on bucolic circuits carved out of natural terrain. Here, at Bridgehampton, Ed Leslie leads Charlie Hayes in two of the six Shelby American entries in the Double 500. Even though both of these cars broke, Miles led Ronnie Bucknum and Johnson home as the Cobras romped. *Revs Institute / Albert R. Bochroch Photograph Collection*

of the coupes being built at Carrozzeria Gransport in Modena. Back in Southern California, Bill Eaton went to work stretching a chassis to accommodate a big block V-8.

The European season began with the Targa Florio in Sicily—Mafia country. Dowd left the States with $15,000 in cash stuffed in a money belt he wore around his waist. During a reconnaissance run the week before the race, three gangsters stopped him and waved a submachine gun in his direction. Dowd, no stranger to tense situations, made peace by offering them some Shelby American swag, then hired them as security guards. Wearing bandoliers and Carroll Shelby T-shirts, they amused themselves after leisurely lunches by blasting empty wine bottles with shotgun shells. Shelby American had four cars, including one co-entered by Ford of Italy. The fans loved the Cobras' fierce acceleration, truculent exhaust note, and propensity for being pointed in every direction except straight. That said, the stiffly sprung roadsters were the wrong horse for the course, which ran along 44.7 miles of gnarly two-lane roads carved through mountain villages. By the time the drivers finished practice, the cars were toast. Gurney was the only driver to finish, and that was after lurching home with a shattered rear suspension.

"Even though we didn't do well at the Targa Florio, it was really fun," he said.[47] "The Cobra was just a hot rod, really. It was a throwback with cart springs and big mag wheels and the 289 engine. The Ferrari was technically far and away more advanced, so people didn't expect the Cobra to be as successful as it was. But for me, the most enjoyable part of the experience was the camaraderie of being part of a group of Americans."

Of course, that was Gurney speaking thirty years after the fact. At the time, he was mystified, then frustrated, and ultimately enraged when he finally straggled to the finish line and realized that the team had already packed up and left. He found Shelby and John Wyer drinking at the bar in the chi-chi Villa Igiea. Too angry to speak, he glared at them for a few seconds and left without saying a word. In fact, he refused to speak to anybody on the team until they left Sicily.

While he was in Italy, Shelby negotiated the purchase of the double-deck Bartoletti transporter that Lance Reventlow had commissioned to haul his Scarab F1 cars around Europe. There was room for three Cobras and a ton of spares. Ohlsen was dispatched from England to overhaul the rig, along with its diesel flat-12, and paint it in Ford's Viking Blue (called Princess Blue in Europe). On the nose of a cab-over was a bold legend: "Powered by Cobra Ford." It would later serve as a prop in the John Frankenheimer movie *Grand Prix*, painted red as the Ferrari 512 transporter and then powder blue to hold the Porsche 917s.

The next race on the schedule was Spa-Francorchamps in Belgium, whose long straights and high-speed corners promised to be ideal for the coupe. Not so, as it turned out. Hill reported that the car was terrifyingly loose through corners like Stavelot, Burnenville, and Eau Rouge. This didn't come as a surprise to Brock. He'd originally designed the coupe with an adjustable "ring" spoiler—an integrated rear wing attached to a cable that would allow the driver to raise or lower the angle of attack. Remington had said there wasn't time to fabricate the unit during the scramble to get the car ready for its debut at Daytona, and it hadn't been an issue until Spa. Now, working feverishly in the paddock, Remington fashioned a primitive spoiler from a flat sheet of aluminum and pop-riveted it to the tail. Hill reported that this eliminated the oversteer. Instead, the car *understeered*. Remington then penciled a horizontal line one inch below the top of the spoiler and used tin snips to cut it down to size. Voila! Hill qualified second, two-tenths off of Mike Parkes's 250 GTO. During the race, he went 4.5 seconds faster, repeatedly shattering the lap record—but only after losing three laps and any chance of a decent finish at the start due to a fuel filter clogged with cotton. Afterward, there was dark muttering about industrial sabotage, but nothing was ever proved.

Next up was the Nürburgring, with 188 turns, many of them blind, and a host of jumps. One of them catapulted gentleman driver Vito Coco so high into a tree that Hoare, standing on tiptoe, couldn't quite reach the scar on the trunk made by the flying Ford of Italy Cobra. "Fortunately," Culleton said, "Coco wasn't wearing any seat belts, and that saved his ass."[48] But he still broke his jaw and two ribs. Bondurant, even then a student of driving technique, prepped for the race by going through the driving school and paying two deutsche marks per lap for practice, then drawing a circuit map from memory. But at the first turn of the race, Peter Lindner, a German driving a lightweight Jaguar E-type, drove him into a signpost, puncturing a tire, caving in the right rear fender, and forcing Bondurant to do an entire fourteen-mile lap in limp-home mode. "I was really pissed when I got to the pits," he said.[49] "I thought, 'Man, if I ever see that son of a bitch, I'm gonna run him right off the road.' Well, I caught him eventually, but he blew his engine before I could hit him. So I thought, 'Thank you, God. You took him out for me.'"

Divine intervention or not, Bondurant didn't make it to the finish either, and the other Cobra was way back. The GTOs, meanwhile, were first and second in the GT class, beaten only by prototypes. Shelby American was now 0-for-3 in Europe, and Shelby's grand plan to dethrone Enzo was looking like a naive pipe dream.

Remington and Ohlsen headed to Modena to check on the progress of the new coupes. What they found at Carrozzeria Gransport was a disaster unfolding in slow motion. Rather than shaping aluminum panels on an English wheel, for example, the Old World metalcrafters beat it against a tree trunk. To be fair, the workmanship was superlative, but the pace of production was glacial, and the Italians were more concerned with aesthetics than slavishly following blueprints. It soon became apparent that the car with the chassis lengthened to accommodate the big-block motor wasn't going to be finished in time for Le Mans. The other car was further along, but it didn't look quite right. Turned out that there'd been some confusion resulting from discrepancies between the dimensions of the wooden buck and the engineering drawings provided by Brock. When the various hand-formed pieces of bodywork were put together, the roofline was several inches higher than it was supposed to be. Back in the States, Brock was mortified. But there was no time to do anything about it. At the last possible date, the car was shipped to a garage near Le Mans, where Remington, Ohlsen, Stucki, and Hoare worked nearly nonstop for four days to prep the car. (Popov-Dadiani had been drafted, and Culleton had been fired after a disagreement with Remington.) The first time it turned a wheel under power was when it was driven to scrutineering. This was *not* how things were drawn up in the *How to Win Motor Races* handbook.

Technically, this wasn't the first time that Cobras had raced at Le Mans. The previous June, Ed Hugus had persuaded AC Cars to enter a pair of roadsters fitted with ungainly hardtops. (Remington had been there at Ford's request, looking after not only the Cobras but also the brand-new Ford-powered Lola GT, which later served as the development mule for the Ford GT40.) Although Hugus's car had been disqualified for illegally added oil, the Cobra shared by Ninian Sanderson and Peter Bolton finished seventh overall and fourth in GT. Still, neither car had posed a serious threat to the Ferrari dynasty. This year, Shelby intended to go mano a mano with Enzo himself.

The Circuit de la Sarthe was tailor-made for the Daytona Coupes. Gurney, uncommonly tall by racing standards, chose to co-drive the just-completed car with Bondurant because the higher roofline gave him more head room (well, helmet room). Despite giving away some top-end velocity on the Mulsanne straight, the Gurney/Bondurant entry was the fastest GT car, while Chris Amon and Jochen Neerpasch were several seconds behind in the original coupe. The sleek blue Cobras easily outpaced the Ferraris, with their 289s spitting flames and snarling through the night. The Amon/Neerpasch car was DQed because the crew didn't realize that an external battery couldn't be used to restart the car after the alternator failed. Gurney broke the GT lap record over and over and was catching the Ferrari prototypes as dawn approached. The team was starting to fantasize about winning the race overall when Gurney pitted at 5 a.m. with the oil pressure dropping alarmingly.

The oil cooler had developed a small leak. The rules required that cars had to complete twenty-five laps before adding more oil. In contrast with later expeditions, this year's run at Le Mans was a shoestring effort. So instead of installing a new oil cooler—which he didn't have—Remington came up with a quick fix, jury-rigging a bypass connecting the inlet and outlet hoses of the oil cooler. This stopped the leak but compromised oil cooling. Even running at reduced revs, the oil temperature in the Cobra hovered above three hundred degrees. "Man, I never thought it'd finish," Shelby admitted.[50] The coupe gradually gave back the laps it had earned earlier. Then, with an hour to go, Bondurant pitted with a misfire. One of the points in the distributor had failed. Remington reset the ignition to operate as a single-point system and sent Bondurant back onto the track.

"This was my first time to Le Mans. No one told me that when you go across the finish line, you go slow because the fans jump over the wall and come onto the track," Bondurant said.[51] "Fifteen minutes before the finish, I saw the lead Ferrari [prototype] pull off. Then, I saw the second Ferrari pull off, and then the third. I couldn't believe it! I thought, 'This thing better not quit because we might have a shot at the overall win!' Then, about five minutes before the end of the race, they restarted the Ferraris, and they crossed the finish line side by side."

Bondurant held on to win the GT class and finish a remarkable fourth overall, a lap ahead of the highest-placed 250 GTO. The Daytona Coupe had justified Shelby's faith in Brock's vision. By winning Le Mans, Shelby American had scored the biggest American road-racing victory on foreign soil since Jimmy Murphy won the 1921 French Grand Prix—at Le Mans, coincidentally—in a straight-8 Duesenberg. Shelby American would win a lot of races over the years, but none was sweeter than this one.

The rest of the European season was up and down. "Reims was a fucking disaster," Innes Ireland said about his lone outing in a Cobra Daytona Coupe.[52] During practice, his steering wheel came loose at 180 mph. In the race, flagged off at midnight, he accidentally turned on the windshield wipers and turned off the engine while trying to find the light switch. "I reckon I did half a lap before I found the bloody thing," he said. Figuring discretion was the better part of valor, he spent the rest of the continental season driving 250 GTOs.

On the other hand, Bondurant shocked everybody by racing an FIA roadster to class wins ahead of Ferraris in a pair of daunting hill climbs. "The roadster had a lot of understeer and oversteer, and you were in a four-wheel drift most of the time," he said.[53] "If you tried to drive it smooth and quick, then it would understeer—the front end would plow. To compensate for that, you had to either stand on the gas harder and get the back end out or ease off and go through the corner slow. It was a pretty hairy car to drive, but once you knew how it worked, you could just stand on the gas and go."

The Tourist Trophy at Goodwood was another good day for the Americans. Gurney and Hill qualified one-two. Gurney was content to hold station behind Hill until his teammate pitted after a rock holed his oil cooler. Shelby told Hoare to give Gurney the "GO" signal. Gurney immediately went. "The coupe was a car that you could really get down to business in. You could do things that were pretty damn amazing with that car," Gurney said.[54] "You could take that car to the limits and then some without it getting you into trouble. It was a lot of fun to drive. It made that great noise, had an American flavor to it, and had great people driving and working on it." Gurney was barely a lap down to the Ferrari prototypes, and he left the GTOs for dead.

Humiliated by the beatdown, the Ferrari team petulantly protested Gurney's car. "They took everything apart," Remington said.[55] "They even checked the intermediate gear ratios, valve diameters, port sizes, throttle bodies, every damn thing on it." The coupe passed inspection. Now that it was clear that the GTO couldn't beat the Cobra on the track, Enzo Ferrari had to dig deep into his bag of tricks to find a stratagem to beat them *off* the track. And that's just what he did.

There were three major races left on the calendar. The Tour de France was an oddball nine-day stage event mixing road rallies and sprint races.

Ferrari was a virtual lock for this one. (The Scuderia had won it eight years running.) Shelby figured to win the five-hundred-kilometer race in the States at Bridgehampton, where six roadsters would be entered. The tiebreaker would probably be at Monza, held in a city park near Milan, and with the high-speed banking being used and so many other fast sections, it was leaning toward the Shelby American column. Advantage: Cobra. At the eleventh hour, Enzo threw a stage-managed hissy fit.

Ferrari threatened to boycott the rest of the season if the FIA didn't immediately homologate the 250 LM, a mid-engine racer that didn't even come close to meeting the standards for being classified as a GT car. The FIA refused since there were only a handful of LMs in existence, and Ferrari was more likely to open a pasta factory on Mars than he was to build one hundred of these ultra-expensive, mid-engined beauties. So Enzo took his ball and went home. In theory, this should have sunk Ferrari's chances for the championship. But in practice, the organizers at Monza understood where their ciabatta was buttered: No Ferrari, they realized, no *tifosi*. Rather than cancel the race altogether, they came up with an appropriately Machiavellian solution: They limited entries to GT cars displacing fewer than 2.0 liters. Porsches and Alfa Romeos ruled, the Cobras were left outside looking in, and the points Shelby American likely would have won evaporated into the Milanese atmosphere.

Predictably, Cobra roadsters dominated the GT class at Bridgehampton, with Miles at the head of a one-two-three-four-five-six train. But Ferrari still ended up winning the GT title by a score of 84.6 points to 78.3. Shelby was gutted by Enzo's chicanery. "We had six cars ready to go at Monza and the old son of a bitch got the race canceled. It was pure politics. He knew he was going to get his ass beat," he said.[56] "He'd do anything to win races. I admired him for that. But when he was doing it to me, that was a different thing."

─────────────

Although Bridgehampton marked the end of the World Sportscar Championship season, there was still plenty of money left on the table, and Shelby wanted to pocket some of it at the big pro West Coast races in the fall. With a lack of any other options, he ordered three new (though already obsolete) 61M Monacos from Cooper and converted them into King Cobras (which he continued to call Cooper-Fords). At Riverside, during the *LA Times* Grand Prix, they were to be raced by Bondurant, Ginther, and Indy 500 winner Parnelli Jones, while a refurbished 1963 chassis was entrusted to Ronnie Bucknum. Leslie was in a fifth Monaco with unusual Brock-designed bodywork that had been commissioned by Cobra enthusiast Craig Lang. The team couldn't get a handle on the aerodynamics, and Leslie endured a dreadful weekend in the so-called Lang Cooper.

Ford had suggested that Shelby hire Jones, and Shelby had reluctantly agreed. Although Rufus (Parnelli's given name) was a titan on oval tracks, most of his road-racing experience had come in a midget and a stock car at Riverside. Another sticking point was commercial: Jones was a Firestone dealer while Shelby was a Goodyear distributor. "What are we going to do about tires?" Jones asked Shelby.[57]

"You run whatever's fastest," Shelby said.

That was fine with Jones. He was even happier when he discovered that the Firestones were, in fact, quicker than the Goodyears. This didn't sit well with Dowd and Peyton Cramer, who were managing the team in Shelby's absence. Before qualifying, they told Jones, "We had a meeting last night and decided we're going to run the Goodyear tires."[58] Stone-faced, Jones stared at them with his ice-blue eyes and said, "Well, I just had a meeting and decided that I'm not going to drive it." And he walked away. A half hour later, Dowd and Cramer diplomatically asked Jones if he'd consider qualifying the car for them. "On Firestones?" he asked. They agreed. And after he qualified third, they decided to let him race on Firestones after all.

No matter what kind of car he was in or what type of course he was on, Jones was one of the fastest drivers around. He was also one of the toughest on equipment—a driver of whom it was said, "He could break an anvil with a rubber mallet." During practice and qualifying, he'd survived several on-track altercations and off-course excursions that left his King Cobra with a bashed-in nose and a missing headlight even before the race began. "I said to myself, 'Shit, if I could just keep from spinning this sucker out, I could win this race,'" Jones said.[59] "I was overdriving the car, so I slowed down on race day. The car puked gas on

The King Cobra's swan song. The previous week, Parnelli Jones had humbled an international field, not to mention his own impressive teammates—Bob Bondurant, Richie Ginther, and Bucknum—as he drove a Shelby American–modified Cooper Monaco to victory in the *Los Angeles Times* Grand Prix at Riverside in 1964. But here at Laguna Seca, he crashed in a qualifying heat, ending the reign of the King Cobra. *Revs Institute / William Hewitt Photograph Collection*

me, and I had absolutely no clutch. It was engaged all the time. How it lasted was a miracle." Jones took the lead on lap four and outran Roger Penske's far more sophisticated Chaparral to the checkered flag. It was the last win a King Cobra would ever record. And the only one Jones ever scored while driving for Shelby.

The following weekend, Shelby American was at Laguna Seca with three King Cobras and the Lang Cooper, but the magic was gone. On a track that *Sports Car Graphic* described as "slick as bear grease," Jones slithered between a pair of Monterey pine trees, then broke the right-rear wheel in Turn Two.[60] The gas tank split when he slammed into the hay bales, and the fire burned for three-and-a-half hours. Jones's only injury was a cut on his leg, incurred when he escaped from the cockpit. Bondurant and Bucknum finished a distant third and fourth, two laps behind the leaders.

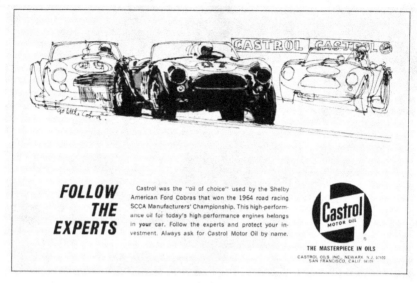

This Castrol ad depicting three Cobras running in typical formation celebrates Shelby American's USRRC manufacturers' title. *John Gabrial Collection*

The mighty King Cobra dynasty ended with a whimper. No matter. Shelby was already looking ahead to new challenges—a 427 Cobra, a hotted-up Mustang and a prototype racing program aimed at winning Le Mans. But what was still foremost in his mind was the FIA World Championship that had slipped out of his grasp.

"Next year," he growled, "Ferrari's ass is mine."

CHAPTER FOUR

NEW HORIZONS

1965

The New York World's Fair of 1964 was a sprawling, glamorous, proudly capitalistic paean to progress featuring 140 pavilions ranging from the House of Formica to the Enchanted Forest of Paper Products. But none of the dozens of corporations with exhibits at the fair boasted a larger footprint than Ford Motor Company. Visitors strolled through the soaring, seven-story spires of the Wonder Rotunda before passing into the Ford Pavilion, where they queued up at the Magic Skyway—designed by Disney Imagineer Bob Gurr—and rode in various Ford models along a half-mile track past dioramas depicting dinosaurs and cavemen and the Space City of the future. There was always a line to get in. Not only because the skyway was such a popular attraction but because so many visitors insisted on waiting for one particular car:

The brand-new Ford Mustang.

The brainchild of Ford Division general manager Lee Iacocca, the Mustang debuted at the Wonder Rotunda on Friday, April 17, 1964. Ford dealers took twenty-two thousand orders before the day was over and racked up 418,000 sales that first year. Although Iacocca was thrilled by the numbers, he knew that the Mustang was little more than a tarted-up Ford Falcon with an anemic six-cylinder engine. To pump up the car's image, he planned to take a page out of the company's Total Performance playbook and create a racing version of the Mustang. But when Ford tried to strong-arm the SCCA into approving the car for competition, executive director John Bishop got his back up. It was, after all, the *Sports Car* Club of America, and the prosaic four-seat Mustang didn't pass the sniff test.

Iacocca called Shelby and asked him to intercede. Shelby and Bishop spoke the same language, so there was no need for sweet talk. "Okay, it's very simple," Bishop told Shelby.[1] "Make it a two-seater, beef up the suspension, give it larger brakes and more horsepower so we can put it in the same class with the [B Production] Corvette." The kicker, of course, was that Shelby would have to build one hundred of these heavily modified Mustangs to get the car homologated. From Iacocca's perspective, this wasn't a big deal; Ford produced nearly two million cars a year. But for Shelby, the ramifications would be huge, and he was a reluctant partner.

Shelby's reservations were well-founded. The AC Ace hadn't been a ball of fire when he adapted it into the Cobra. But at least it had been a sports car. The Mustang, on the other hand, was what he derisively called "a secretary's car."[2] Transforming it into something capable of winning races was going to take tons of time and money. And that was the easy part. Putting the car into even limited production was also going to require more space, more manpower, and more input from Ford, which would fundamentally change the scale and character of Shelby American. "Shelby wasn't too enamored with the idea of having to find a much bigger place and have a bigger organization. He was happy with what he had and with the Cobras," said Chuck Cantwell, who was about to become the project engineer for the Mustang program.[3] "It was really more than he wanted to tackle, but Iacocca said, 'You owe me one.'" It was, in other words, a deal Shelby couldn't refuse.

On the other hand, the team had already amassed some experience with the Mustang. Even before the car's official debut, Ken Miles and Phil Remington had helped Ford evaluate an independent-rear-suspension version developed by Ford's in-house suspension wizard, Klaus Arning. (It was deemed too expensive.) During the summer, two stock notchback Mustangs were delivered to Shelby American, and Miles and Bob Bondurant tested them at Willow Springs. They needed work. When Miles returned to Venice, he started poring over Ford's parts catalog and was pleased to find plenty of components that would help bring the Mustang up to speed. But Miles and Remington were already overloaded with responsibilities for other projects. Shelby needed an infusion of fresh blood to launch the Mustang program. The unflappable Jack Khoury, an ex-GM production manager, was hired to run the production line, industrial engineer Bruce Junor was brought in to oversee facilities and Cantwell was named project engineer. Cantwell was a young, mild-mannered General Motors Institute graduate who was working as a mechanical engineer at GM Styling when he applied for a job at Shelby American. He was also an accomplished club racer who was in the process of driving an MGB to the D Production championship in the SCCA's Central Division. So he knew something about the corporate world, he knew something about racing, and he knew a lot about engineering. At Shelby American, he would operate as a cross between Miles and Remington—a particularly useful hybrid because the Mustang program would be operating more or less on its own.

Two fastbacks had been delivered to Venice by the time Cantwell started in September 1964. They were referred to generically around the shop as Shelby Mustangs, but Ford executives thought—not without justification—that this name put the cart before the horse. Many fruitless brainstorming sessions were convened to choose a name. After yet another meeting failed to pick a winner, a frustrated Shelby asked Remington how far it was from the shop on Princeton Drive to the one on Carter Street. "About three hundred fifty feet," Remington said.

And the GT350 was born. Or so the origin story goes.

From the beginning, there were going to be two models—a street car and a race car, which was later unofficially dubbed the R-Model. This wasn't because Ford had a burning desire to put a Shelby hot rod into production next to the standard Mustang. It was simply to satisfy the SCCA's homologation requirements. Or as Cantwell put it, "Iacocca wanted a car to beat the Corvettes, and this was how you got there."[4]

Although the two models shared many of the same components, the race car was the mo' better version of the street machine. Both would start as plain-Jane Mustangs at the massive 1.4-million-square-foot Ford factory in San Jose. Cantwell's job was to figure out not only how the cars were going to be spec'd but also how they were going to be built. Components that were already in the San Jose parts bin could be fitted to the cars as they rolled down the assembly line—the heavy-duty 9-inch rear end, for example. Another useful addition was a so-called export brace, a V-shaped strut that tied the shock towers to the firewall—a handy option in countries with primitive road systems. On the other hand, unnecessary components could be deleted on the line, like the hood, which would be replaced later with a fiberglass substitute. But cars had to be drivable when they left San Jose. So the stock intake, exhaust, and carburetor couldn't be removed even though they were going to be swapped out for a Cobra-spec aluminum high-rise manifold, Tri-Y exhaust, and 715 CFM Holley when they got to Venice.

A year earlier, in April 1964, the original Ford Mustang had debuted here, in Ford's Wonder Rotunda pavilion at the New York World's Fair. To goose interest in the 1965 models, Ford displayed its brand-new GT350, a factory-blessed hot rod developed by Shelby American. Although it didn't look much different from the stock Mustang it was based on, the GT350 was really a race car for the street. *Ford Motor Company*

Mechanically, the GT350 was an order of magnitude more exotic than even the sportiest of Mustangs—a GT model equipped with a Hi-Po K-Code V-8. Performance goodies included a close-ratio Borg-Warner T-10M with an aluminum case and tailshaft, a baffled aluminum high-capacity oil pan, a longer idler and Pitman arm steering, and a Detroit Automotive Products NoSPIN Differential, aka a Detroit Locker. Another beneficial add-on was a stout metal tube called a Monte Carlo bar, previously used on Falcons that had been rallied overseas. Coupled with the export brace, the bar provided triangulation that did wonders for torsional rigidity.

The race car got all this and less—no bumpers, no sound-deadening material, no glass other than the windshield. (The side and rear windows were lighter plexiglass.) Standard racing upgrades such as porting, polishing, matching, stronger reciprocating parts, and so on were allowed on R-Models. The race car also got a thirty-two-gallon gas tank, which was essentially two stock tanks welded together. While the standard K-Code 289 was rated at 271 horsepower, the street GT350 made 306 horses, thanks to the racier intake, carb, and exhaust, and the race car pumped out between 325 and 370. The idea was that, if the Hi-Po version of the Mustang was good, the GT350 was better, and the R-Model was best.

All of the cars shipped from San Jose were Wimbledon White. Boring. Peter Brock was charged with embellishing the GT350 with some visual panache. He drew up plans for a new front valance artfully integrating an opening for the radiator and the oil cooler, brake scoops grafted onto the rear fenders, and rear quarter windows instead of the louvered C-pillar of the fastback Mustang. Ford bean counters nixed all three ideas because, they said, they would cost too much and take too long to implement. As an alternative, Brock suggested a pair of blue racing stripes running the length of the hood, roof, and trunk—a simple but handsome graphics package that paid homage to the cars Briggs Cunningham had raced in American national colors during his many expeditions to Le Mans. Ford execs didn't like that idea either. "Nobody's going to buy a car that looks like a skunk," they complained.[5] Wiser heads prevailed, fortunately, and the stripes stayed as an option. To further dress up the cars, Brock added another set of stripes and

"G.T. 350" lettering in Microgramma Bold Extended on the rocker panels. Brock himself wasn't crazy about these graphics, but Shelby insisted that the car be instantly identifiable from the side, and the side stripes became one of the car's signature elements.

By the way, the precise name of the car was—and remains—a source of constant confusion. The rocker panel graphics read "G.T. 350," but the Shelby American chassis plate said "MUSTANG G.T. 350," and the Manufacturer's Statement of Origin said "GT-350." But advertisements and internal documents from the 1960s refer alternately to the "Shelby GT," "Shelby G.T.," "Shelby Cobra GT," "Cobra GT," and "GT 350." Today, GT350 seems to be the most popular construction, but that doesn't necessarily make it "correct."

Although the GT350 would be sold in Ford showrooms, the car reflected its SoCal hot-rod heritage in ways that would never be apparent to customers. Berry Plasti-Glass in Long Beach provided the early fiberglass hoods; Buddy Bar Casting in South Gate, the aluminum intake manifold; Traction Master in Burbank, the torque-control arms; Cyclone Automotive in North Hollywood, the headers; Ray Brown Automotive in Pacoima, the seat belts. The race car also got several performance upgrades in local shops, from heads ported and polished by Valley Head Service in Northridge to machining done by Offenhauser in Los Angeles.

Shelby American placed its initial Mustang order in September. Three fastbacks arrived from San Jose just after Halloween. Peter Bryant, who'd come to Shelby American after a stint as a Formula 1 mechanic/engineer, was assigned to work on them. He soon was joined by Jerry Schwarz, a Midwestern drag racer who'd been working in a local body shop. At his job interview, race shop foreman Jack Balch handed him an air hammer and ordered him to flare a fender of a Mustang. "It was taking one man about four days, working not at a fast pace but not at a leisurely pace, just working along, to re-radius one rear fender," Schwarz said.[6] "I wanted the job so bad I just really hit it, and I finished one fender and about a third of the other side in a day. That impressed them enough that they wanted me to start the next day." Those who were there still remember the racket that Schwarz produced. And they're still grateful that he came up with a quicker method of flaring fenders that

GT 350 STREET VERSION	DIMENSIONS	
Two-place fast back coupe; Shelby American prepared 289 cubic inch O.H.V. Cobra V-8 engine equipped with special high riser aluminum manifold, center pivot float four barrel carburetor, specially designed hand built tubular "tuned" exhaust system featuring straight through glass packed mufflers, finned Cobra aluminum valve covers, extra capacity finned and baffled aluminum oil pan; fully synchronized Borg Warner special Sebring close ratio four speed transmission with lightweight all alloy case; computer designed competition suspension geometry; one inch diameter front anti-roll bar; fully stabilized, torque controlled rear axle equipped with "No-Spin" limited slip differential; 15" diameter wide base steel wheels mounted with 130 m.p.h. rated, Goodyear "High Performance-Blue Dot" tires; Kelsey Hayes front disc brakes with ventilated disc and special full competition pads; wide drum rear brakes with metallic linings; Koni adjustable shock absorbers; trunk mounted Cobra battery for optimum weight distribution; light weight fibreglass hood with integrally-designed functional air scoop; all black interior with bucket type seats and Shelby approved competition "quick release" seat belts; special instrument cluster with tachometer and oil pressure gauge in addition to speedometer, fuel gauge, and water temperature gauge; two speed electric windshield wipers and washers; woodrim racing steering wheel; 19:1 quick ratio steering; spare wheel cover; heater; 350 competition side stripe.	Wheelbase, In.	108
	Tread Front and Rear, In.	57
	Length, Overall, In.	181.6
	Width, In.	68.2
	Height, In.	55
	Turning Circle, ft.	38
	Ground Clearance, In.	6
	SPECIFICATIONS	
	Curb Weight, Lbs.	2800
	Tire Size	7.75 x 15
	Front Brakes	Disc
	Rear Brakes	Special Drum
	Engine Type and Size, Cu. In., OHV-V8 289	
	Compression Ratio	10-1
	BHP 6000 RPM	306
	Torque 4200 RPM	329 ft/lbs
	Weight Distribution %	53/47
Complete With Above Standard Equipment $4547.00		
FACTORY INSTALLED OPTIONAL EQUIPMENT	GEAR RATIOS	
Shelby Aluminum Wheels $ 273.00	Differential	3.89
GT 350 COMPETITION PREPARED VERSION	4th	1.00
Additions to street version include: Fibreglass front lower apron panel; engine oil cooler; large capacity water radiator; front and rear brake cooling assemblies; 34 gallon fuel tank, 3½ inch quick fill cap; electric fuel pump; large diameter exhaust pipes, no muffler; five magnesium bolt-on 7" x 15" wheels, revised wheel openings; interior safety group—roll bar, shoulder harness, fire extinguisher, flame resistant interior, plastic rear window, aluminum-framed sliding plastic side windows; complete instrumentation—tachometer, speedometer, oil pressure and temperature, water temperature, fuel pressure; full Shelby American competition prepared and dyno-tuned engine; special final track test and adjustments. Note: This version is for competition only.	3rd	1.20
	2nd	1.62
	1st	2.36
	PERFORMANCE	
	0-60	5.7
	0-100	14.9
	Standing ¼ Mile, Sec.	14.5
	Standing ¼ Mile, Speed	98
	Top Speed, MPH	133
Complete With Above Standard Equipment $5950.00	Prices and Specifications Subject to Change without Notice.	

MUSTANG G.T. 350
SHELBY AMERICAN, INC. ● 6501 W. IMPERIAL HWY., LOS ANGELES, CALIF. 90045

Spec sheet for the all-new 1965 GT350. Such a deal! *John Gabrial Collection*

didn't require the use of the air hammer. Before long, Mike Sangster was added to the build team.

The first GT350s were assembled in a glorified hallway near the entrance on Princeton Drive. To move other cars into or out of the shop, the Mustangs had to be dropped off jack stands and shifted out of the way—a royal pain. Even after a more suitable space was located, it took a solid forty hours to transform a Mustang into a GT350 after it arrived in Venice. Besides all the bolt-on tasks, fenders were flared to accommodate wider tires. Two additional holes were drilled into each side of the frame to lower the front control arms by an inch, which dramatically improved the suspension geometry. A far more time-consuming—and obnoxious—task was cutting out sections of the wheel well and creating new mounts in the interior to install longitudinal torque control arms, popularly known as traction bars, to reduce axle tramp on acceleration.

The first car, finished in November, was the street car prototype, later tagged as 5S003. (The "5" stood for 1965, the "S" for street—as opposed to "R" for race—and the "003" for the internal reference number. Confusingly, the first three cars were numbered out of sequence because they were built before the numbering system was established.) The other two were completed shortly thereafter as race cars, 5R001 and 5R002. During the week before Christmas, 110 additional cars arrived, and Shelby began amassing a dedicated crew of "Mustangers" to work on them. Bishop visited the shop and officially blessed the GT350 with its homologation papers, and testing at Riverside and Willow Springs commenced in January.

The GT350 was the cover story in the March issue of *Sports Car Graphic*. "Except for braking IN a turn, it is an embarrassingly easy car to drive at competition speeds," wrote Jerry Titus, who would go on to become Shelby American's most successful GT350 driver.[7] "At full power, it uses all of the road—a real drifter—but it gets a surprising amount of bite when cornered in a neutral or closed-throttle attitude."

Despite the rave, most of the guys in the shop still didn't think much of the GT350, which they dismissed as a measly Mustang—until Shelby dispatched Miles and 5R002 in February to Green Valley Raceway near Dallas for an SCCA regional. This was the low minors of road racing, so nobody was surprised that the GT350 crushed the competition in B Production, but Miles scored a PR coup by getting the car airborne lap after lap as he crested a hump on the front straight. Photos of the GT350 flying with all four wheels off the ground were published across the country. And even though the race was small potatoes, Max Muhleman issued a press release quoting Shelby. "This is exactly what we were aiming for with this machine—a true dual-purpose sports car that is a top performer on and off the track," he said.[8]

The race program for the 1965 Daytona Continental showcases the Daytona Coupe that led the race the previous year before going up in flames during a pit stop. In 1965, Daytona Coupes would finish one-two-three in class. *John Gabrial Collection*

DAYTONA INTERNATIONAL SPEEDWAY

Fourth Annual DAYTONA CONTINENTAL

2000-Kilometer Race For Grand Touring, Sports and Prototype Cars.

"America's Longest and Most Outstanding Race"

SUNDAY FEB. 28 – 10 am

1965 DAYTONA SPEEDWEEKS · PROGRAM NO. 2, FEB. 15-28 · $1.00

But even as the sun was rising on the GT350, it was setting on the first-generation Cobra. The last leaf-spring 289 model—equipped with an automatic transmission!—was shipped to Shelby American on October 23, 1964. (Shelby owned it until he died in 2012.) When all was said and done, 655 small-block cars had been built during a two-year period. For the sake of comparison, Ferrari produced 654 cars in the 1964 calendar year. In later years, other Shelby creations would accrue far more prestige and generate much higher prices on the collector-car market than their predecessors. But the 289 Cobra, with its buggy-spring suspension and 289-cubic-inch motor, was where the Shelby American story started, and everything that followed was predicated on its success.

Still, nothing lasts forever, and it was time for the Next Big Thing. Although The Turd had stunk up the joint when Miles raced it at Sebring the previous March, Ford executives were intrigued by the potential of the 427-powered Cobra—especially since rumor had it that Chevrolet was planning to stuff a 427 into the Sting Ray, and there were no horses in the Blue Oval stable that could match up with that combination. It was decided to begin work on what AC Cars called the Mark II Cobra and Shelby American referred to as the Cobra II. Bob Negstad, a crackerjack but contrarian Ford engineer, was ordered to draw up plans for a Cobra designed around a big-block engine. And while he couldn't start with a clean sheet of paper, he gave the car a thorough rethink.

Negstad realized that this was the obvious time to junk the antiquated leaf-spring suspension in favor of adjustable coil springs. He'd already worked with Arning—and software engineer Chuck Carrig, who used a main-frame computer to run a suspension-simulation program he'd written in FORTRAN—to develop a state-of-the-art four-link independent suspension for the GT40, so he simply adapted this system to the Cobra. To accommodate the bigger motor and provide more room in the cramped cockpit, he also planned to lengthen the wheelbase by three inches and widen the track by seven inches.

Negstad traveled to Thames Ditton during the summer of 1964 and proudly presented the Hurlocks with his painstakingly produced blueprints. They were unimpressed. They walked him over to a warehouse full of parts and said, "These are the spindles, these are the steering gears, these are the ball joints, these are the rotors, brakes. This is what you are going to use. You're not designing all new parts."[9] Disheartened, Negstad junked all his drawings and started over.

Before long, Negstad was hit with more bad news: The lightweight aluminum 390 that he'd built his design around wasn't available. Instead, he was told to use an iron-block 427, which would add at least two hundred pounds to the car, all of it on the nose. It was too late for Negstad to reposition the engine to alter the weight distribution. On the other hand, all parties were now thankful that they'd agreed to build new chassis from scratch with four-inch-wide tubing instead of the three-inch tubes of the 289 Cobra. Naturally, there were a lot of similarities between the old and new car—the 90-inch wheelbase, windshield, hood, trunk, doors, and various trim pieces. But the 427 was seven inches wider and improved in almost every way imaginable.

To clear the bigger wheels and tires, the chassis was covered in exaggerated, almost cartoonish bodywork that made the big-block car look far more menacing that its little brother. Today, when most people conjure up an image of a Cobra, the bulked-up 427 is the car they picture.

When the FIA season concluded and the Daytona Coupes returned to the States, Remington and John Ohlsen made a detour to AC Cars to support Negstad. By October 20, the Cobra II was ready for a test session at Silverstone, with Chris Amon at the wheel. Amon didn't think the car was appreciably faster than the 289. But these were early days, of course. The car was shipped to Shelby American, where Miles started developing it. After numerous changes large and small, from bronze bushings to a magnesium intake manifold, he chopped a few seconds off the small block's time at Riverside. But like Amon, he wasn't totally sold on the car.

Miles was placing his money on his own big-block Cobra—a new-and-improved version of The Turd that he and Morton had flogged at

Although Shelby American raced the 427 Cobra on only a handful of occasions, privateers spread the big-block gospel far and wide. This car, CSX3009, was the first one sold, and it amassed the longest racing history. Johnson didn't fare well here at Nassau in 1965, but Sam Feinstein earned an A Production national championship—beating a bevy of Corvettes—by winning the American Road Race of Champions in 1973. *Ford Motor Company*

Sebring. Joe Fukushima had reworked the battle-scarred chassis while Red Rose fabricated brand-new, much more attractive bodywork. To reduce weight, thin aluminum panels had been welded into two large sections hinged at the front and rear so that they opened from the center up, like a jackknife. In honor of the novel bodywork, the car had been rechristened the Flip-Top. Better still, Miles had managed to get his hands on one of the Ford 390s, which were in such short supply that they seemed to be made of unobtainium rather than aluminum. Miles took the car to the Bahamas, ready to cut a few new notches in his holster.

Despite the big motor, the Flip-Top weighed a mere eighteen hundred pounds, and it promised to do to the Corvette Grand Sport what the 289 Cobra had done to the Sting Ray. Sure enough, Miles made mincemeat out of the competition at Nassau. Racing strictly for bragging rights, he put the Flip-Top on the pole of the Tourist Trophy, outqualifying not only a pair of Grand Sports but also two mid-engine Ferrari 250 LMs. At the start, he blasted off into the lead. "Ken left that bloody Grand Sport standing—and pissed Roger [Penske] off," Charlie Agapiou remembered with great satisfaction.[10] As Miles crossed the start-finish line to end the first lap, there wasn't another car in sight. He was having so much fun that he forgot to turn on the diff cooler, and he ended up frying the rear end. But it didn't matter. Shelby saw which way the wind was blowing, and he placed an order with AC for one hundred 427 Cobras.

The year-end races in Nassau were a pivotal event in Shelby American history for another reason. Plenty of Ford executives were there, ostensibly for work but mostly because a week in the Bahamas was a palatable alternative to Dearborn during the frigid depths of December. They were delighted to see the Flip-Top Cobra stick it to GM's Grand Sports. But they were dazed and confused—and more than a little bit dismayed—by the pitiful performance of the Ford GT40s, which were slow before breaking early. The Le Mans prototype program was the most expensive and highest-profile element of Ford's growing motorsports empire, and the lack of results to date was taken as a personal affront by the company's CEO, Henry Ford II.

After crashing the original 427 Cobra, aka The Turd, at Sebring, Miles had the car reworked with a beefed-up frame and lightweight bodywork. Now known as the Flip-Top, the Cobra ran away and hid from the Corvette Grand Sports at Nassau at the end of 1964. Miles was so far in front that no other cars were in the picture—literally—until a fried differential ended his day. *Revs Institute / Eric della Faille Photograph Collection*

The Deuce, as he was known, was the eldest grandson of company founder Henry Ford and one of the most formidable figures in corporate America. He'd greenlit the Ford GT program the previous year out of a sense of personal grievance after a distasteful incident involving Enzo Ferrari. Il Commendatore had let it be known through emissaries that he might be willing to sell his company. Ford was in the midst of expanding its Total Performance portfolio, and acquiring Ferrari seemed like an easy way to jump-start the program. Don Frey was dispatched to Maranello, where torturous face-to-face negotiations with Enzo ensued. A deal was hammered out after a week of contentious horse trading: Ford would buy Ferrari for $10 million, and two companies would be created—Ford-Ferrari to sell road cars and Ferrari-Ford to go racing. But on the evening of May 20, 1963, as Frey and Enzo went over the proposed contract in Ferrari's office, they reached an impasse.

"Dottore Ingegnere," Ferrari said, politely referring to Frey as an engineer, "if I wish to enter cars at Indianapolis and you do not wish me to enter cars at Indianapolis, do we go or do we not go?"[11]

"You do not go," Frey said flatly.

To which Ferrari responded with an operatic speech worthy of a Puccini opera. "My rights, my integrity, my very being as a manufacturer, as an entrepreneur, as the leader of the Ferrari works, cannot work under the enormous machine, the suffocating bureaucracy of the Ford Motor Company."[12] Or maybe he just said, in Italian, "No deal," which was more or less how Frey remembered it.

Frey returned to Dearborn (with an ironic parting gift from Ferrari—an autographed copy of Enzo's memoir). When he got there, Frey was summoned to a meeting in Henry Ford II's private dining room. The Deuce hadn't been especially eager to buy the Italian carmarker; that had been Iacocca's fantasy. But Ford was every bit as autocratic as Ferrari, and his temper flared when he realized that Enzo had left him standing at the altar like the hapless loser in a rom-com. "You go to Le Mans," he told Frey, "and beat his ass."[13]

Ford engineer Roy Lunn was charged with doing just that. He conceptualized a sleek prototype with a mid-mounted Ford engine standing a mere 40 inches high, hence the name GT40. (The car was also known simply as the Ford GT.) But no builder in the States had the technical acumen to bring his plans to life, so an alliance was formed with Englishman Eric Broadley, the founder of Lola Cars. A few months earlier, Broadley had built a car known as the Lola GT, which was a sleek prototype with a mid-engine Ford V-8 (installed with the help, coincidentally, of none other than Phil Remington). A wholly owned subsidiary called Ford Advanced Vehicles was established to design, build, and race the new car. John Wyer, Shelby's one-time team manager at Aston Martin, was hired to oversee the operation, and Lunn traveled to the UK with three Ford engineers to work with Broadley.

The Ford GT debuted at the Nürburgring in 1964. It failed to finish. Three cars raced at Le Mans the next month. They all failed to finish. Three cars raced at Reims the month after that. Again, no finishers. The races in Nassau produced two more DNFs. Earlier in the year, management of all of Ford's racing programs had been given Leo Beebe, a buttoned-down marketing executive who'd never actually seen a race before getting the job. After the embarrassment of Nassau, he led a testy postmortem with the team. "I don't know anything about racing," he said, beginning with what had become his standard homily, "but there is one thing that has become increasingly apparent to me in the past few months—you don't either."[14] Ford executives decided that Wyer was the wrong man for the job. But who was going to replace him?

Shelby desperately wanted the GT40 program. Besides being the jewel in Ford's motorsports crown, it promised the biggest payout. But Shelby knew he had competition in the form of John Holman of Holman & Moody, the Ford-contracted stock-car leviathan in Charlotte. Shortly before a meeting with the Ford brass in Dearborn, Shelby sternly told a roomful of Shelby American managers, "No drinking."

Huh?

"Did you see who's out there?" Shelby snapped.[15] "John Holman. You know what he's here for? He wants our business. The Mustang and everything else—he wants a piece of it. You guys say something wrong, and we'll be going home on a bus. So no drinking until after this is over."

In the end, Shelby's road-racing experience and success with the Cobras won over Ford executives, and they decided to put their in-house snake charmer in charge of the Le Mans program. The formal announcement was made at the annual pre-Christmas dinner Ford traditionally held for its race teams around the world. Dignitaries would show up from Canada, England, Germany, Australia, wherever. Imagine a banquet bringing together the first families of the Cosa Nostra. The boss of all bosses stands ups in front of the hushed audience and declares that so-and-so is being given such-and-such a territory to administer and plunder. Here, Shelby was anointed as the Chosen One. Wyer and Holman weren't happy about it. But as long as Shelby didn't screw things up, the job was his.

Two GT40s were disgorged from a TWA air freighter at LAX on a dreary day in late December, still covered with grime from Nassau. The job of cleaning them was given to two freshly designated crew chiefs—Ohlsen, who'd been pulled off the 427 Cobra project, and Frank Lance. Lance was one of growing number of new hires who'd been brought in to handle Shelby American's broadening workload. At the top of the org chart was "Big" Jim McLean, a former executive at Philco and General Dynamics, who was installed as executive vice president. Newcomers to the shop floor included Colin Riley, who'd done consecutive stints at Indy with Jim Clark and Dan Gurney; renowned custom car painter Dennis Ercek, who'd been working on funny cars; and Ron Butler, a

New Zealander who'd raced sports cars in Hawaii with Al Dowd and who would become one of Shelby's most treasured employees.

"Dowd called me and said, 'We need mechanics,'" Butler recalled.[16] "He picked me up at the airport and took me straight to the shop. The first thing I see is the biggest bloody tire I've ever seen before, and then there was Miles working on a Tiger there in the doorway. Jack Hoare had an engine on the dyno. He was throttling it to seven thousand, and the bloody windows were rattling. Then he introduced me to Granny— John Collins. He showed me the bloody heliarc. I'd never seen one before; all I knew was gas welding. I went to the office with tears in my eyes. 'I'm sorry,' I told Dowd. 'I can't do this.' And he said, 'I'll put you with Granny. You'll pick it up.'"

Lance was a native Texan who'd worked at Carroll Shelby Sport Car in Dallas and then on Jim Hall's Chaparrals in Midland. He'd left John Mecom's operation in Houston because he'd heard that Shelby American was paying overtime. He accumulated plenty of it during the next ten weeks as he and Ohlsen struggled to get the GT40s ready for Daytona. First, the cars were retrofitted with Cobra race motors. Then they were painted the new team color, a darker blue called Guardsman Blue. The exotic dry sump was replaced with a simpler—and more reliable—wet-sump oiling system. Lance swapped out the straight-cut gears in the fragile Colotti transaxle with spiral bevel ring-and-pinion gears for better durability. When Miles and Bob Bondurant first tested the cars at Willow Springs, they were still running wire wheels instead of Halibrand mags. This would soon change—along with just about everything else as the cars went through a seemingly endless loop of testing during the day and development at night. "We can react to a suggestion—we can do something—*right now*," Miles explained.[17] And they did. Brake ducts were rerouted, oil and gearbox coolers relocated, body panels lightened, British fasteners replaced. It wasn't merely that Shelby American had taken possession of the GT40s. The team also wanted to remake the cars in its image.

Shelby himself remained one step removed from the action. It was his genius as a leader to hire the right people and then let them do what they did best while avoiding the temptation to micromanage. But he kept tabs on the project in his own way. When he saw Ralph Falconer rummaging around the engine bay of a GT40, he asked him, "How's that run, boy?"[18]

"It runs good, Mr. Shelby," Falconer told him.

"Have you driven it yet?"

"No."

"Well, go drive it!"

At the time, the marina that gave Marina del Rey its name was still under construction, but the streets for the development had already been built. "Somehow, Shelby had gotten permission to go on the property so we could rip around there for a while and see how everything drove," Falconer said.[19] "I drove the GT40 up Lincoln Boulevard to Venice Boulevard and into the marina. Can you imagine giving a twenty-four-year-old kid the license to drive a GT40? I shifted the gears up and down a few times and drove back. It was wild."

To race the two GT40s in addition to the Cobra Daytona Coupes, two more fresh bodies were brought in as the team prepared for Daytona. One was a baby-faced twenty-year-old with a reputation as a Weber carburetor whisperer. A skeptical Remington marched him over to one of the GT40s and said, "Start tunin'."[20] His name was Gordon Chance, and he massaged those Webers so expertly that he became known as "Ricky Nelson, the Teenage Tuner." Out-of-work race car driver Carroll Smith, meanwhile, had contacted Shelby after what he'd decided would be his final season running Formula 3 cars in Europe. "What you need is a good team manager, and I is one," Smith wrote.[21] Shelby agreed, and the deal was done.

Smith's team shirt identified him at "Smitty," but he was often called "Scat," which was short for "Scattershit." Smith left tools and papers everywhere, driving the crew batty. But he maintained meticulous records of driver feedback cross-referenced with mechanical adjustments. This gave him unique insight into how to improve a car's performance. Before Smith, changes to race cars were made by crew chiefs, who were essentially the senior mechanics on a team. Smith more or less invented the role of the modern race engineer, who serves as a technical liaison between driver and crew, and his input was essential to the team's success.

Shelby American needed two transporters to get all its cars to Daytona—two GT40s and no fewer than four Daytona Coupes, which were mounting a full-court press to win the GT World Championship that had eluded them the previous year. After Le Mans in 1964, Carrozzeria Gransport had built four more cars, so Shelby American went into the new season with six Daytona Coupes, and all of them would see action before the year was over.

Lots of cars meant lots of mechanics. About fifteen of them were hanging out in a room in a shabby Florida motel when Chance walked in, unobtrusively placed a small package in a bedside drawer, and walked out. A few seconds later, the drawer exploded into hundreds of pieces, plastering the wall with splintered wood—an M-80 assault. In the unlikely event that the motel owner didn't hear the detonation, he surely saw the smoke seeping out of the room. Irate, he threatened to have everybody arrested. Shelby was summoned and told it would cost sixty dollars to replace the nightstand. "Just put it on my bill," he said.[22] "The boys have to have some fun." Shelby had his detractors. But, generally speaking, his mechanics weren't among them.

Reigning F1 World Champion John Surtees qualified fastest in a works-in-all-but-name Ferrari 330 P2 prototype, but Bondurant blasted past him at the start in the GT40 he'd tested so often at Riverside and Willow Springs before suffering a major brain cramp. "I hadn't listened very well at the drivers' meeting, and I thought we were supposed to do two laps of speed around the oval," Bondurant said.[23] "I was flat-out through Turn Four when I realized that the course markers had been put out across the oval signaling that we would make the turn into the infield. I thought, 'Oh shit, I'm never going to stop!' And I didn't. It was one of my most embarrassing moments."

Gurney and Jerry Grant dominated the first half of the race in a lightweight Ford-powered Lotus 19—the first-ever race entry for All American Racers, which was a joint project between Gurney and Shelby—until holing a piston. Bondurant and Richie Ginther then led until their starter motor failed on their last pit stop. Miles and easygoing Texan Lloyd Ruby, who'd been pacing themselves to save their brakes, inherited the win, with Bondurant and Ginther third. The Daytona Coupe shared by Jo Schlesser and Hal Keck was second, and a second coupe was fourth. This was not only the GT40's first win. It was the first time the car had ever finished a race! Back in Dearborn, the Ford brass was convinced that Shelby walked on water.

Shelby holds court in a roomful of racing royalty before the 12 Hours of Sebring in 1965. Seated, (from left) are Miles, Dowd, Johnson, Bob Bondurant, Phil Hill, Carroll Smith, Ford PR rep George Merwin (obscured), Shelby, Jim Adams, and Bruce McLaren. Standing on either side of the doorway in dark shirts are Ray Geddes (left) and Cramer (right). Torrential rain threw all of the pre-race instructions out the window. *Ford Motor Company*

Four weeks later, the team was at Sebring, expecting more of the same. Instead, it ran into two nasty surprises. The first was Jim Hall's Chaparral 2, which was lighter and more powerful than the GT40. Developed with under-the-table support from GM, this was the most technologically sophisticated car in the world. Technically, it shouldn't have even been in the race, but organizer Alec Ulmann gave it a special dispensation to compete, and it was in another class, figuratively and literally, from the Fords. The second surprise was the weather, which was Africa hot and even more humid than usual. Sweltering inside his Daytona Coupe, Lew Spencer was suffering from heat prostration after thirty minutes. "I said to myself, 'If I could just lay my head down on my shoulder and have a little nap, I would be fine,'" he said.[24] "That's when I realized something was wrong, and I pulled into the pits."

Spencer was unconscious by the time Bill Eaton yanked him out of the car. A physician deposited him in a Lincoln Continental with wet towels on his head and the air conditioning blasting. While he was out, there was a downpour of biblical proportions. The rain was so torrential that blinded drivers steered inadvertently into parking areas. In another coupe, Bob Johnson was up to his waist in water, running slower than the MGs, until mechanics punched holes in the belly pan to drain the cockpit. Ed Leslie drove for several laps holding the circuit breakers in his hand to prevent them from shorting out. When the car finally flooded, he had to push it back to the pits. Mounted tires floated like beach balls down pit lane while Butler did the breaststroke between them. The Chaparral stopped in the pits and sat there for ten minutes without losing the lead until the rain dissipated. Red Pierce was electrocuted when he climbed in the Shelby American truck and ended up in the hospital. When Spencer came to, totally disoriented, he was astonished to see Phil Hill desperately trying to push-start his waterlogged coupe.

"I decided to go help him out," Spencer said.[25] "It was probably a stupid thing to do, running out onto the track, but I was still groggy. I realized that we could be disqualified if I helped him, but what did we have to lose? He obviously wasn't going to get it started by himself. By the time I got there, he was just thrashed, completed exhausted. I told him to get in the car, and I pushed until it started. If any of the flagmen saw me, they must not have realized that it was illegal."

Hill, Spencer, and Bill Adams soldiered on to finish way down in twenty-first. A Chaparral won handily, with the Miles/Bruce McLaren GT40 a distant second. Well, technically, they were first in class because the Chaparral wasn't eligible for World Sportscar Championship points, but nobody on the team was crowing about it. Schlesser and Bondurant salvaged some of Shelby American's pride by driving their Daytona Coupe to a GT class win. The team was ready to tackle the European season. But first, they had to stop at LAX—and not to catch a flight.

For the past few months, space had been so limited in Venice that the operation looked like a teenager who'd outgrown his hand-me-down wardrobe. Now that Shelby was gearing up to produce as many as five hundred GT350s a year, it was obvious that a bigger—*much* bigger—

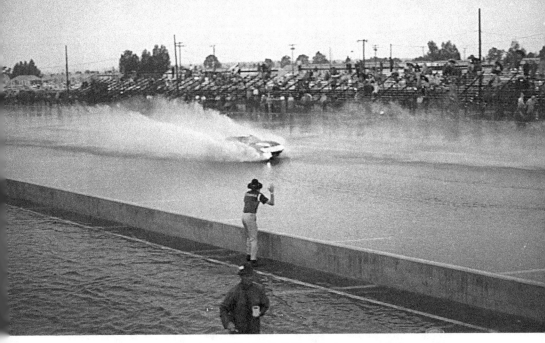

Is this a car race or a boat race? The biblical Florida downpour that marred Sebring in 1965 has ended, but the floodwaters haven't yet receded. Shelby leans over the pit wall to offer encouragement to the Miles/McLaren GT40. The car slogged to a first-in-class finish, but it was beaten badly in the overall standings by Jim Hall's Chaparral. Still, Daytona Coupes finished one-two-three in the GT class. *Ford Motor Company*

plant was needed. Peyton Cramer led the effort to find suitable shop space. A deal to lease a piece of Northrop property in Hawthorne was closed, but Northrop got cold feet and backed out at the last minute, so Shelby American scrambled for an alternative. A pair of cavernous hangars on the southern edge of Los Angeles International Airport where North American Aviation had built F-86 and F-100 fighter jets emerged as a possibility. Shelby was dubious. "What are we going to do with all this space?" he asked Bruce Junor.[26]

Junor, who'd come from the aerospace industry, pointedly ignored the question. "This is perfect," he said. "We don't have any columns— none, zero. The building is free span, three hundred feet long and two hundred feet wide." Shelby was persuaded, even if he wasn't convinced. Grumbling about the cost, he signed a lease for 6501 West Imperial Highway in El Segundo.

The 12.5-acre site came with ninety-six thousand square feet of covered space. Junor and Balch reconnoitered the buildings and laid out rough plans. The western hangar had a partition separating the race shop from the show-car services Shelby American provided to Ford. The paint shop, with a couple of spray booths, was also there along with a dyno room at the back of the building. The eastern hanger housed a genuine assembly line for the GT350, a dedicated space to put together 427 Cobras, the parts department, and the warehouse. Along the north wall was a mezz-anine with a long row of offices offering a panoramic view of the airport. Shelby's was at the end, with a private stairwell so that he could come and go in his Lincoln Continental without being seen. Below, part of the hangar was partitioned off for his airplane, initially a Cessna 206, later an executive DC-3. Outside, a concrete blast wall separated the facility from the runway and provided a safe space for parking and shakedowns.

The move to LAX was chaotic—a symptom, no doubt, of the prob-lems encountered by a small artisanal company transitioning awkwardly into a more formalized corporate entity. Even though it had been com-ing for months, most of the employees were caught by surprise. Moving trucks and car haulers were in short supply, so about fifteen unsold 289 Cobras had to be driven across town to the airport. The assignment was given to John Morton, fellow racer Earl Jones, and three young production-side mechanics with no racing experience. You didn't have to be clairvoyant to see the future. Morton—who refrained from street racing—said the other Cobras sped down Lincoln Boulevard at 140 mph, and the racket they made bombing through the tunnel under Sepulveda Boulevard was loud enough to drown out the sound of the jetliners passing overhead. When they reached LAX—without getting ticketed, amazingly—a van ferried them back to Venice so they could do it all over again.

Unfinished GT350s also had to be driven over surface streets to the new facility. This was a problem for several R-Models because the stock gas tanks had already been removed but the new race-spec ones hadn't yet been installed. "I finally came up with the idea of using the windshield washer fluid containers," said Dick Lins, another former GM Styling engineer who worked under Cantwell.[27] "They were little sacks, actually, not even bottles. We would fill them with gas and hook a temporary rubber tube to the inlet of the fuel pump, and we could drive them just long enough to go from Venice to LAX."

The move from the cramped facilities in Venice to a pair of gargantuan hangars at LAX greatly expanded Shelby American's horizons as well as enlarging its footprint. Here, mechanics work on comp Cobras and GT40s while R-Model GT350s are being built behind them. The west hangar also housed the paint shop, engine dyno, and show-car operations. Meanwhile, street GT350s rolled down a legitimate assembly line in the east hangar. *Dave Friedman*

The northeast corner of the production hangar was reserved for the Cobra II, as the 427 was often called. The first 427 chassis, CSX3001, had been sent to Ford and restyled into an ungainly alternative to the Sting Ray. CSX3002 was delivered to Shelby American in October 1964 and largely ignored until Shelby ordered an old acquaintance, Andre Gessner, to put the car together. Gessner, who today uses the surname Capella, was an expert machinist who'd built several road-racing specials from the ground up. "There was nobody to tell me what to do," he said.[28] "In fact, every time I said, 'How should I do this?' it was always, 'You're the expert. Do it however you want.' And that's what I did. I built it the way I thought it should be built."

Gessner designed and fabricated 375 individual parts, from the bracket to mount the clutch master cylinder to the wiring loom. In many cases, he cut out paper templates that 427 project engineer Jim Benavides later converted into blueprints for future production. Although Gessner could draw on other mechanics for help with specific tasks, he basically built the first five or six cars in Venice by himself. When the company moved to LAX, he accepted a job as foreman in return for a dollar-an-hour raise and use of a company GT350. Working with a crew of four, he was able to assemble a 427 in about a day-and-a-half.

This wasn't nearly fast enough for homologation purposes. But the bottleneck was on the AC end, not in LA. Only twenty-three cars had been shipped to Shelby American by the end of January, and the pace slowed after that. On April 29, when FIA inspectors showed up, they found only fifty-one 427s on site—barely half the number required for homologation for the GT category. Shelby had made a good-faith effort to meet the letter of the law, and he fully intended to put the car into production. But the FIA was still feeling the heat for its refusal to homologate the Ferrari 275 GTB the previous month—a decision that would be reversed during the summer—and it wasn't willing to incur Enzo's renewed wrath by giving Shelby the benefit of the doubt. So the homologation application for the 427 was denied.

As far as Shelby was concerned, the news was as welcome as a stiff breeze in an outhouse. Since it hadn't been homologated, the 427 Cobra would be classified as a prototype in international motorsports, where it would be hopelessly outclassed. The car would be eligible to compete in SCCA races in A Production, where it was virtually guaranteed to clean up. But the market for $9,995 cars for club racing was thin, and before too long, everybody who wanted one had one. Shelby immediately ordered AC to stop building 427s as race cars and instead to dumb them down with less sophisticated components to sell as street machines. Meanwhile, unsold cars piled up in long rows outside the hangars at LAX. The sight would have looked reasonably impressive were it not for the fact that the 427s were parked on jack stands because the supply of Halibrand wheels had dried up. Around this time, McLean sent out a company memo announcing that the cars would be known from this point forward not as Cobra IIs but 427 Cobras. "White elephant" might have been more appropriate.

The GT350 program, on the other hand, was humming. Junor had overcome a host of technical and regulatory hurdles to excavate a

Nobody was going to confuse it with Ford's gargantuan River Rouge complex, but the east hangar at LAX housed a legitimate assembly line that cranked out dozens of cars a day. Here, Shelby American crews transform humdrum notchbacks into fire-breathing GT350s as Mustangs roll over the pit designed by Bruce Junor. At this station, mechanics are installing exhaust manifolds and headers along with oil pans and valve covers bearing "Cobra" legends.
Chuck Cantwell / Greg Kolasa Collection

150-foot-long pit in the concrete floor of the eastern hanger to serve as the foundation of a real assembly line. No longer did mechanics on creepers work underneath cars balanced on ramps. Instead, when the cars were brought inside, they were positioned on wheeled diamond-plate carts and rolled the length of the pit while mechanics above and below the Mustang installed GT350-specific components. Compressed air, oil pumps and tools were positioned at stations along the way.

Peter Crane worked in the pit. As an apprentice mechanic in England, he'd applied for a job by mail. When he didn't hear back, he decided to come to the States anyway. In Detroit, he bought a battleship-class Pontiac Bonneville convertible and followed Route 66 straight to Shelby American. He was hired then and there, right around the time that a letter arrived at his parents' home in England stating that no jobs were available. Co-workers would later take him to Lions Drag Strip in Wilmington, which set him on a path that would lead him to a Top Fuel ride and membership in the British Drag Racing Hall of Fame.

"Working in the pit was quite fraught to begin with because the line was moving at the speed the people were building on top of you, and there was an awful lot to do down below," Crane recalled.[29] "I had to do the front anti-roll bar, Pitman and steering arms, hang the exhaust headers, put the Konis on. We had had a lot of problems with the cast-aluminum sumps because they were so porous. The night before, we'd fill the pans with a kerosene-and-oil mixture and see if it would soak through. If it didn't, the pans would go on. If they did, they were binned."

The production run for the 1965 model year lasted only eight months, with nearly half of it constrained by the cramped conditions in Venice, where no more than two dozen cars were built. The pace increased exponentially after the move to LAX, where the young guys on the assembly line worked to the backbeat of "Wooly Bully," "My Girl," and "Mrs. Brown, You've Got a Lovely Daughter." The total build was 526 street cars and thirty-six race cars. Priced at $5,950, the R-Model—a turn-key race car you could trailer directly to the track—was a steal. The street GT350 didn't generate as much enthusiasm. With a sticker price of $4,547, it was nearly twice as expensive as a base-model Mustang and slightly more than an entry-level Corvette, and while the car offered spectacular bang for the buck, it also came up short in certain areas.

"The '65 GT350 was a hot-rodder's idea of a sports car—a rough-riding bronco that was as exciting to drive as a Maserati 300S, and about as marketable a proposition," *Car and Driver* wrote from a vantage point in 1967.[30] "The traction bars clanked, the side exhausts were deafening, the clutch was better than an advanced Charles Atlas program, and when the ratcheting-type limited-slip differential unlocked it sounded like the rear axle had cracked in half. It rode like a Conestoga wagon and steered like a 1936 chain-drive, solid-tire coal truck . . . and we loved it. It was a man's car in a world of increasingly effeminate ladies' carriages. You drove it brutally and it reacted brutally. Every minute at speed was like the chariot-racing scene in *Ben Hur.*"

The GT350 fared far better as a race car. The first customer car was pre-ordered by Tom Yeager four months before it was actually delivered in April 1965. Altogether, thirty-four R-Models were built, along with the two prototypes used as factory race cars. Although Miles had raced the car in its first outing, the win at Green Valley in February, he was too busy—and, frankly, too important—to spare the time to compete in lowly SCCA club races. So Shelby strolled into the offices of *Sports Car Graphic* and had a talk with John Christy's right-hand man, technical editor Jerry Titus. "I got this Mustang," Shelby said, "Don'tcha think it'd be fun if we raced it?"[31]

Short, feisty, and fearless, Titus would become a principal player in the Shelby American drama. He came to racing via a circuitous route. A classically trained musician who played trumpet in the jazz band of Jack Teagarden, he also did a stint as a mechanic with famed East Coast race car builder Bill Frick. Having to deal with the media for the publicity-shy Frick led to a gig *in* the media, and Titus eventually graduated to *Sports Car Graphic.* Along the way, he raced everything from go-karts to the wayward Cheetah, winning SCCA titles in Porsches and Elvas. Titus was thirty-six when Shelby tapped him to race the GT350, but that didn't prevent him from keeping up with guys like Gurney and Parnelli Jones. "Jerry was on the ragged edge an awful lot, and he crashed a lot, but he was amazingly easy on a car," Spencer said. "Jerry did a hell of a job for us all those years."[32]

Shelby decided to chase after a B Production championship, but with most of his resources earmarked for Europe, he tried to do it on the cheap, with Titus's GT350 supported by a lone sports car dealership mechanic. "Well, that lasted until the car started needing maintenance," Cantwell said.[33] "And then we had a debacle at Riverside where everything broke." Shelby agreed to bring the program in-house, where it was staffed by Cantwell, Spencer, and three mechanics—Schwarz, Mike Sangster, and Bernie Kretzschmar.

Kretzschmar had been working in a speed shop when he drove his cherry '32 Ford roadster over to the shop in Venice a few months earlier see what all the fuss was about. "It was crazy," he remembered. "I mean, they were testing cars on the city streets and running the dyno wide-open with a tract of homes two blocks away. I don't know how they got away with all that. I said to myself, 'While I'm here, I'm going to fill out an application.' And they ended up calling me and asking me two questions: Do you have your own tools, and can you weld? I said, yes and yes."[34]

With the crew in place and Titus behind the wheel, the GT350 pretty much ran the table in B Production on the West Coast. At a national at Willow Springs, when it looked like there wouldn't be enough cars competing for Titus to get full points, a second GT350 was entered for Cantwell. Jim Adams, in a Sunbeam Tiger slickly modified by Doane Spencer, took the lead at the start. Going up the hill on the first lap, Adams short-braked Cantwell, who left the track to avoid him. Cantwell waited for Titus to pass him (since the whole object of the exercise was maximizing points for his teammate). The two GT350s then ran in tandem—until they reached Turn One, where Titus spun. His tires blew out on the sharp rocks that make the runoff areas so treacherous at Willow Springs, and he spent the rest of the race as a spectator. By this time, Cantwell was ten seconds behind Adams. "I had to run pretty hard to chase him down," Cantwell said.[35] "Just when I caught him, he raised his arm and pulled off the track." Cantwell finished his career as a GT350 racer with a perfect record—one race, one win.

Near the end of the year, with the Southern Pacific B Production title in the bag, Titus drove Vacek Polak's Porsche-powered Elva in the big *LA Times* Grand Prix. Miles was supposed to race a privately owned GT40 campaigned with Essex Wire sponsorship. When this ride fell through, he decided to do the preliminary production car race in a GT350. The car had already been stickered up with Essex Wire graphics. The crew peeled off the "ES" and "WIRE," leaving "SEX" in big black letters on the door. "Miles had a cow when he saw it," Kretzschmar remembered.[36] The crew grudgingly replaced "SEX" with "Hi-Performance Motors," and Miles cantered to an untroubled victory in his second and last race in a GT350.

Shelby American's new GT350 laid waste to SCCA competition after it was introduced in 1965. Racing on a criminally dangerous circuit laid out in the parking lot of Candlestick Park in San Francisco, Jerry Titus cruised to a win in B Production, with Leslie second in a second team car. Titus would earn the national championship by winning the American Road Race of Champions at Daytona at the year's end. *Revs Institute / Duke Q. Manor Photograph Collection*

The SCCA's year-end championship, known as the American Road Race of Champions, was held that year at Daytona. There, the Shelby American guys were wrong-footed by a little-known, pudgy-faced Brown University engineering grad. This was Mark Donohue. In years to come, Donohue would put Penske Racing on the map. But at the time, he saw the ARRC as an opportunity to make his mark on the big-time racing world, and he'd painted his impeccably prepared customer GT350 blue with white stripes just to annoy Shelby. Benefiting from a hot engine and oversized tires, Donohue qualified on the pole and was leading handily until his right-rear tire shredded after rubbing against the fender. With Donohue out, Titus came home first, ahead of Johnson in another GT350. Meanwhile, in the same race, Keck was at the head of a trio of 427s that finished one-two-three in A Production.

Two national championships for two brand-new cars was an impressive achievement, and Shelby was pleased. But at the same time, he was acutely aware that world domination in amateur SCCA racing in the

States wasn't going to placate his overlords in Dearborn if the multi-million-dollar GT40 program went south, which it was in the process of doing. Although the season had opened on a high note with the win at Daytona, Sebring had been a disappointment, and the shift to Europe spotlighted flaws in the cars and the team that ran them. Shelby American wasn't in the same league as Scuderia Ferrari at Monza or the Nürburgring, and the lone GT40 in the Targa Florio broke. Even if the Fords made it to the finish at Le Mans—a long shot, based on recent experience—they didn't seem to have the pace to outrun the Ferraris.

But the Blue Oval boys had an ace up their sleeve, namely, a 427-cubic-inch engine. A big-block motor had been wedged into a GT40 by Kar-Kraft, an engineering firm in Dearborn that served as Ford's unofficial skunkworks. (Although it was owned independently, Kar-Kraft's one and only client was Ford Motor Company, and Ford engineers routinely moonlighted there on motorsports projects.) Six weeks before Le Mans, Miles flew to Michigan to test the mongrel at the Michigan Proving Grounds in Romeo, about ninety minutes north of Detroit. It didn't take him long to push the car past 210 mph while cutting a lap at 201.5 mph, amazing himself as well as the Ford engineers.

"What does everyone think?" Lunn asked after the session was over.[37]

"That's the car I want to drive at Le Mans this year," Miles said immediately.

Chance, aka Ricky Nelson, the Teenage Tuner, was sent to Dearborn to help Kar-Kraft activate a crash program to prepare two big-block cars. The new models were designated as Mark IIs. Shelby American took both of them to Le Mans—crew chiefed by Chance and Walter "Davy Crockett" Howell—along with a trio of standard GT40s. A sixth car was entered by Wyer and Ford Advanced Vehicles. The massive Ford fleet also included five Cobra Daytona Coupes looking to defend their GT title. During the run-up to Le Mans, two engines were dyn-oed daily at LAX. The cars, on the other hand, got very little test time. The first Mark II had barely been run, while the second hadn't turned a wheel, before being shipped to France, and the lack of development showed. The cars were so unstable at high speed that Remington and his crew spent most of their time during practice snipping out strips of aluminum and affixing them to the cars in strategic locations—under the nose as air dams, on the front fenders as canards, on the rear deck as tailfins, and on the tail as rear spoilers. Although the appendages looked agricultural, they did the job.

The Fords were fast. Really fast. Stop-the-presses fast. During a Friday night practice session, Shelby ordered Hill to "let it out a little."[38] Free to run hard, Hill snagged the pole in the Mark II he was sharing with Amon, posting a lap time 5.1 seconds faster than Surtees's Ferrari. That ended the snide comments Chance had been hearing about "Ricky and the cast-iron monsters." Bondurant was third quickest in one of the 289s, Bruce McLaren fourth in the second Mark II, and Bucknum fifth in another GT40. Besides monopolizing the pointy end of the grid, the team also looked suave and debonair in the quilted, white Shelby American jackets Brock had designed for the occasion. But Ford officials weren't content to leave well enough alone.

It was almost midnight by the time the crew got the cars back to the Peugeot garage they were using in downtown Le Mans. There, they found three wood crates. Inside each one was a Ford engine—a small-block V-8 stroked to 325 cubic inches, delivered at the eleventh hour to give the team an edge it didn't need. "We stayed up all night swapping out engines," Lance said.[39] "Bill Eaton was my helper. He was a great guy and a great fabricator, but he wasn't a mechanic. So I just about changed the engine out by myself and had to get it to the track by ten o'clock the next morning. Oh, man, I was dead tired." Another mechanic told Amon about the hellish overnight scene in the garage: "I've been to everything from county fairs to public hangings, and I've never seen anything like this before."[40]

The race began as though Ford had scripted it. Amon led at the start in the blue and white Mark II, laying down rubber as McLaren tucked in behind him in the sister car. "I remember leading onto the Mulsanne straight, and Bruce slipstreamed past me, and I can remember looking in the mirror as we came over the hump, and the closest car—which was Surtees in the Ferrari—was six hundred meters behind us," Amon said. "We were so much quicker than anybody else. We were just cruising around, basically."[41]

McLaren and Amon were seventy seconds clear of the Ferraris after the first hour. In the VIP section overlooking the pits, Ford executives were giddy. The command the Deuce had issued to Frey two years earlier was being fulfilled: Ferrari's ass was being whipped in front of God, country, and four hundred thousand spectators. But as anybody who's been around this sport for very long knows, the race isn't always to the swift. As the hands of the giant Dutray clock hanging over the pits swung around the dial, GT40s and Daytona Coupes kept pitting with problems. Gearbox. Head gasket. Head gasket. Head gasket. Clutch. Repeat as necessary. Ten of the eleven Fords failed to finish. Only the wounded coupe entered by AC Cars took the checkered flag, crawling home forty-four laps behind the race-winning Ferrari 250 LM.

The failure of the small blocks didn't come as a complete surprise. "The 289 was not great for head gaskets to begin with because of the bolt pattern, and the cylinder head was thin there," Ryan Falconer said.[42] The problem was usually solved by sending engines to Kelly's Block Welding Service in El Segundo to have the upper coolant transfer passages welded up. But in this particular case, the overheating issues were traced to defective head bolts, which stretched when they got hot, allowing water to seep past the head gasket. Remington diagnosed the problem early in the race, but there was nothing even he could do about it. Ironically, the 427s in the Mark IIs ran like locomotives, but the new heavy-duty T-44 transmissions Kar-Kraft had developed to handle the additional torque came up short due to insufficient testing. Remington figured this was something he could address, so over and over, when the cars pitted, he dove underneath to remove safety wire and work on hot trannies with his bare hands. But it was a lost cause, and the Mark IIs joined the GT40s and Daytona Coupes in the dead-car park.

Miles called it "the greatest defeat ever suffered by a team in the history of motor racing."[43] Even allowing for a hyperbole discount, the results were appalling. But there was a silver lining in the defeat—the certainty that the Fords had the pace to win. All they lacked was durability. After the race, Shelby playfully shoved his black Stetson on the head of Walter Hayes, Ford of Britain's powerful public relations czar, and told him, "We're gonna make the [427] right." Beebe convened a team meeting back at the Hotel de Paris.[44] "Gentlemen, this is a victory meeting," he told the bedraggled and disbelieving crew.[45] "We start this instant to plan our victory next year."

McLaren leads Chris Amon as the new big-block GT40 Mark IIs dominate early at Le Mans. But the fun didn't last long. Both Mark IIs broke. So did all but one of the other GT40s and Daytona Coupes in the eleven-car Ford armada. Miles called it "the greatest defeat ever suffered by a team in the history of motor racing." Ferrari won for the sixth straight year. *Revs Institute / Eric della Faille Photograph Collection*

The mood in Dearborn was less upbeat. "When a single would have won the ball game for us, or even a walk, we got over-exuberant and went for another home run," read an in-house postmortem.[46] "We struck out. We did not win, we did not finish, we fell flat on our face. We lost the ball game. We got what we deserved. We failed to attain our objective at Le Mans because we took our eye off the ball." Two years after the GT40 had been approved, the Le Mans program seemed to be back where it started. Ford did what major corporations often do when they confront a thorny issue: it created a committee to study the problem. But the Le Mans Committee was more than mere window dressing. Its members included Beebe, Hayes, Frey, executive vice president Charles "Cast-Iron Charlie" Patterson, Engine & Foundry chieftain Bill Innes, public relations maven Ted Mecke, and comptroller Sev Vass, plus technocrats of every description. They weren't making recommendations to upper management. They *were* upper management. They had the authority to take action. And that's just what they did.

During the summer, the Le Mans Committee made three critical decisions. First, the GT40s wouldn't race again that season. Instead, the rest of the year would be devoted to testing in preparation for 1966. Second, the team would double down on the 427. This meant the Mark II was now the weapon of choice while 289-powered cars would be left to the privateers. Third, no longer would all of Ford's eggs be left in the Shelby American basket. This meant Holman & Moody was being given a piece of the Le Mans program. Shelby wasn't pleased. As far as he was concerned, Holman was a rival to be trounced rather than a teammate to be embraced. "Someday," Shelby told Smith, "you're going to get beat, and it better be by Ferrari."[47] And not, Smith understood, by Holman & Moody.

But the 1965 European season wasn't a complete write-off for Shelby American, thanks to the Cobra Daytona Coupe. Inevitably, perhaps, Brock's former Folly had been overshadowed by the newer, shinier, faster GT40s. Ford was determined to win Le Mans overall, so it was devoting the vast majority of its considerable road-racing resources to the Anglo-American prototypes. No money was budgeted to send the Daytona Coupes to Europe in 1965. But scoring class wins at Daytona and Sebring at the start of the season suddenly gave the team a gigantic lead in the GT class standings. Then, after the FIA declined to homologate the 275 GTB, Ferrari announced it wasn't planning to contest the championship, leaving only privateers with year-old 250 GTOs as the main competition. The title was Shelby American's to win—if the money could be found to send the coupes to Europe.

Former Shelby American marketing manager Fred Gamble had watched over the coupes' performance the previous year from his lofty perch as director of Goodyear's international racing program, and he was eager to see the cars return to action. He'd also been impressed by the professionalism of the team run by an enterprising Brit named Alan Mann. The previous year, Mann had successfully campaigned Ford Falcons in the Monte Carlo Rally and Ford Mustangs in the Tour de France. Gamble approached Hayes with a proposition: "The Cobra Coupe can get the job done, but Ford has said, 'No more money.' If you can con Ford in Detroit out of three Cobra Coupes, I'm sure you and Alan Mann can win the championships."[48]

Even though Hayes was based in the UK, he had enough clout to make things happen in Dearborn. Once again, Ray Geddes came to the rescue. This time, his financial legerdemain involved agreeing to buy old rally parts from Mann in return for Mann's commitment to race a pair of coupes on the continent. Mann's team had limited circuit-racing history, so Charlie Agapiou was sent overseas to make sure the British mechanics didn't screw up the cars. One car would be raced by Mann's own drivers, Jack Sears and Sir John Whitmore. The others, chosen by Shelby, were Bondurant and Allen Grant, whose deal required him to wrench on the GT40s as time permitted while he was in Europe.

Mann's brief was to win the world championship, full stop. He knew going in that the coupes were in a class of their own. Basically, if they finished, they were virtually guaranteed to win. But what should have been a cakewalk turned out to be season-long study in aggravation. Not because of the competition on the track but because of the tension within the team. Mann sensibly wanted to adopt a conservative approach, going only as fast as necessary to win. Bondurant, on the other hand, was angling to climb the motorsports pyramid and make it all the way to Formula 1. For him, it wasn't enough just to win a team championship. He wanted to win with style, beating not only the Ferraris but also his teammates.

Mann met Bondurant at Heathrow Airport. "Before you pick up your bags, I have to alert you to one thing," Mann said.[49]

"What's that?" Bondurant asked.

"Sir John Whitmore is my Number One driver, and Jack Sears is Number Two, and if you choose to stay, you're Number Three."

"No, I have a contract right here in my briefcase from Shelby saying that I'm the Number One driver."

"You don't understand. You're in England now. Things have changed."

Bondurant immediately called Shelby, who was sympathetic but noncommittal. "Well, he's running the team. I have to go by that," Shelby said. "Just smoke 'em off anyway."

The Monza 1,000 Kilometers in April established the template for the races to come. Bondurant qualified on the GT pole, a whopping

6.2 seconds faster than Whitmore. Almost as soon as the race started, Mann held out the "SLOW" sign, and with good reason. The coupes already had amassed an insurmountable lead, and the cars were bouncing so badly on the banking that the paint on the drivers' helmets wore off from banging against the roof. "The banking was poured in probably twenty-foot sections of concrete, and some of them settled and some of them didn't," said Grant, who was sharing a car with Bondurant.[50] "When you hit a bad section, the back end would shoot out about five feet, so you'd have to correct, back off, and get on it again."

Bondurant would go by the pits in third gear to show Mann that he was complying with team orders, then speed up when he was out of sight. Near the end of the race, Mann directed Bondurant to slow down even further so Sears could catch up to finish in formation. But Bondurant was afraid that Sears would snatch the win away from him, so he maintained his lead. That night, at dinner, Sears told Bondurant, "You're a terrible sport. You didn't wait for me."[51]

To which Bondurant replied, "I waited for you all race."

Game on.

Bondurant was generally the fastest of the team drivers, but that was due, at least in part, to the fact that Sears and Whitmore were good soldiers who obeyed Mann's orders to race at less than ten-tenths. Bondurant also benefitted from engines that Hoare tuned especially for him at Shelby American. (The shipping crates were marked so Agapiou would install the hot motors in the "right" car.) By the time the team reached Reims in midsummer, the title chase was all but over. Ford of France wanted native son Jo Schlesser in a Cobra when the coupe clinched the championship. Schlesser graciously gave his ride to Grant, who therefore drove the final race of his career not in a Daytona Coupe but in a Ferrari 250 GTO—two rivals with almost nothing in common besides four wheels and an engine. "It's like comparing a sewing machine to a Briggs & Stratton motor," Grant said.[52]

Mann declared that the Sears/Whitmore car would win the twelve-hour night race. Bondurant grudgingly maintained station through the darkness. When Schlesser passed Whitmore during his stint, Mann flagged him into the pits, where he told the Frenchman to get with the program or get out of the car. Schlesser went with Option A (though his wife threw a bottle at Mann in protest). Come Sunday morning, to Bondurant's delight, Sears slowed and trundled into the pits with a broken motor. By this time, the Ferrari competition was long gone, and Bondurant was in position to clinch the championship. Nevertheless, Mann was adamant that the second car be repaired. Not for championship points but because he'd bet forty bottles of champagne with a local merchant that both coupes would finish the race.

When Agapiou removed the oil pan, he realized that one of the wrist pins had broken. "Get a connecting rod cap from the spare engine in the truck," he yelled.[53] Then he and Alan Mann Racing mechanic Roy Butfoy performed emergency surgery in the hot pit. "We jammed the piston up to the top [of the cylinder], took the connecting rod out completely, and put a secondary cap around the crankshaft so that the two caps bolted together and the engine would hold oil pressure. We put the oil pan back on. Off he went, and he was only about a second off his pace. It was unbelievable."

Whitmore's car sounded more like a gravel truck than a race car, but the engine continued to run on seven cylinders. The two blue-and-white coupes took the checkered flag side by side. It was July 4th, Independence Day, a fitting occasion for the Cobra Daytona Coupes to win the first championship for an American manufacturer in international competition. Mann called Shelby that night, rousing him out of bed at three o'clock in the morning, "He didn't mind a bit," Mann recalled.[54]

It was, for Shelby, a watershed moment. He'd won Le Mans as a driver in 1959, and he'd scored a class win there as a constructor the previous year. In years to come, he would win Le Mans overall not once but twice. But it was the title clinched at Reims that he was proudest of when he looked back on his career because it represented the culmination of the improbable dream that had begun with the first Cobra being assembled in Dean Moon's humble shop in Santa Fe Springs three-and-a-half years earlier.

"The most satisfying thing I ever did was winning the world championship," he said.[55] "I was just subcontracting the work from Ford on the GT40. I owned all the Cobras. Shelby American—that was mine. It was gratifying to win that championship. But I still had a chapped ass over the old man pulling that bullshit deal in 1964. We should have won it both years."[56]

Driving the definitive version of the definitive American sports racer, Bondurant and Jo Schlesser steer their Daytona Coupe through French Champagne country to a class win at Reims, clinching the GT manufacturers' title for Shelby American—the first claimed by an American team in international competition. Although Shelby won Le Mans as a driver and would win it twice as an entrant, he called this his greatest achievement in racing. *Revs Institute / Eric della Faille Photograph Collection*

The coupes would race only one more time, in the Coppa Città di Enna. In mid-August, while the crew at LAX watched smoke rising from storefronts torched during the Watts Riot ten miles to the east, the Alan Mann team unloaded two cars in the paddock outside a lake in Sicily. Although Sears was supposed to win, Bondurant hounded him mercilessly—so mercilessly that the nose of his car was sandblasted by gravel and his windshield was cracked. Bondurant used the damage as an excuse to pass Sears and win the race. Mann was furious. By all accounts a brilliant and admirable team owner, Mann understood Bondurant's unwillingness to obey orders, but he didn't excuse it. "Once again Bob behaved as if we were running the Bob Bondurant Racing Team," he said.[57] "Bob's refusal to act as a team driver was unshakable to the end."

The Daytona Coupes never raced again. For Brock, the retirement of the cars came as a bittersweet moment. Yes, the machines he'd created had done exactly what he'd designed them to do. But he'd dreamed of more than that—of winning Le Mans outright. At the tail end of 1964, he found an ally in Miles. By that point, the GT40 program had been given to Shelby, but drivers hadn't been selected, and with Ford calling the shots, it seemed likely that Miles would end up in the Daytona Coupe. So he, Agapiou, and John Collins lightened and upgraded the car in preparation for testing it with a road-racing version of the 255-cubic-inch engine that Ford had developed for the Indy 500. (This was the motor used in the original version of the GT40.) Remington was in England at the time. When he got back and saw the changes that had been made in his absence, he went ballistic. "Ken doesn't run this shop. I do," he told Collins and Agapiou. "Put the car back to the way it was before."[58]

There were a couple of factors behind Remington's decision. The most obvious was that he wanted to focus the team's resources on the GT40s, which had more upside potential, not to mention the full financial and technical support of Ford Motor Company. But there was also longstanding tension between Remington and Miles, not personally but on a philosophical level. Although Miles was a car builder, he wasn't a craftsman. Fast-and-dirty solutions were fine with him as long as they worked. Remington was renowned for his on-the-spot fixes, but he was also an artist. Given time, he drew sketches so clear and accurate that, it was said, only a complete nitwit could fail to follow them properly. (According to legend, these sketches came with a legend: "Draftsman: Remington. Designer: Remington. Engineer: Remington. Approved: Remington.") Remington had his blind spots, to be sure, but he also recognized Miles's limitations.

The GT40 seemed to be the car of the future. But Shelby was hedging his bets. Months earlier, he'd commissioned construction of new-and-improved version of the Daytona Coupe that Brock had designed around a 427. The idea was to use the new chassis and suspension that Negstad had developed with AC Cars for the big-block Cobra. Brock planned to sheathe it in a long, sleek body that built on the lessons he'd learned with the Daytona Coupe. Because the car was designed to be raced in 1965, he named it the Type 65. In years to come, it came to be known as the Super Coupe.

Brock had wanted Carrozzeria Gransport, the Modenese coachbuilder responsible for the Daytona Coupes, to handle the project.

Instead, to save money, Cramer hired a British firm, Harold Radford and Company, to build the prototype. Radford was already doing the interiors of the GT40s, and the company specialized in bodywork for upper-crust customers. But it had never built a race car, and months passed without any progress reports. Finally, Remington visited the shop while he was in England, and what he saw prompted him to tell Brock and Shelby that they'd better fly over and take a look for themselves—pronto.

"We went downstairs into a tiny room with a dirt floor and a single white bulb hanging down," Brock recalled.[59] "The car was so grotesque; I just couldn't believe it. It reminded me of a thalidomide baby. I thought, 'My God, I've made an incredible mistake.' But then I began really looking at it and the plans tacked up on the wall. I said, 'Do you have a tape measure?' They didn't even have a tape measure. They had to run around to find one. When I finally measured the distance from one side of the open door to the other side of the open door, it was eight inches too wide. *Eight inches too wide.*"

A half-inch off would have been understandable. A full inch might have been acceptable. But eight inches? And that wasn't the only problem. Besides failing to follow Brock's blueprints, the Radford "craftsmen" had built the car out of thick steel plate and iron pipe. Brock was heartbroken, and Shelby was pissed. Radford, desperate to retain the GT40 business, agreed to redo the car for free. A new chassis was delivered by AC Cars, and the second effort was better than the first, but the proportions were still off, especially the rear deck, which looked like it had been squashed by a giant hand. "It was like a caricature of what it was supposed to be," Brock said.[60] By the time the car was shipped to Shelby American, its moment had passed, and the team was committed to the Mark II. Rendered redundant before it ever turned a wheel, the Type 65 sat forlornly in the shop, mocked as the Super Slug.

The Daytona Coupe enjoyed one final—and unlikely—moment in the spotlight. In November, Shelby got a call from his old friend Tony Webner of Goodyear. The tire company had rented the Bonneville Salt Flats so that Craig Breedlove and Walt Arfons could make land-speed record attempts. But they were running behind schedule, and Goodyear would forfeit its rights to the salt if no record runs were being made.

Webner asked Shelby if he could provide a Cobra on short notice to run at Bonneville.

"The only thing in the shop that's even running is the old proto-type, and it's pretty tired," Shelby said.[61] "We haven't gotten around to rebuilding it since Le Mans last June. We just use it for auto shows. It's the oldest car we have, and I can't guarantee that'll hold up for even an hour. Besides, it's set up for racing, not record breaking."

Webner was in no position to bargain, so he gratefully accepted Shelby's offer to put a new Cobra race motor in CSX2287. Because Shelby American personnel were busy with other projects, Tom Greatorex, who had been the mechanic on the Cobras run very successfully by Johnson, stepped in to prep the car. When he got to Bonneville, Greatorex took the car out for a run on the salt and accelerated up to about 180 mph with no drama.

As soon as Breedlove saw the coupe, he told Greatorex to remove the mirrors, rear spoiler and any other appendages that would produce drag—standard Bonneville practice. Before Breedlove could drive the car, he had to be taught how to use an H-pattern gearbox(!). His first trial run was a hair-raising affair. "This car is the most evil thing I've ever driven!"[62] he said after maxing out at a mere 168 mph. "It was like driving on ice." Next up was Bobby Tatroe, the driver of Arfons's Winged Express LSR car. Tatroe was a sprint car ace by trade, so he was accustomed to big power and armloads of oversteer. But he spun after the first mile and sheepishly admitted that he couldn't keep the car straight above 5000 rpm. Greatorex was baffled. Here were these two hero drivers who couldn't get the thing past 168 mph, and yet he'd gone 180 mph driving like the little old lady from Pasadena. He climbed back into the cockpit, and as soon as he got up to speed, he identified the culprit—the missing rear spoiler.

The instant Greatorex pop-riveted the aluminum strip back on the rear deck, the Daytona Coupe felt solidly planted, and Breedlove had no problem mashing the pedal to the metal. The next morning, he went 187 mph and set a G Class national record, then five more in the afternoon. The next day, he and Tatroe ran the car for twelve hours and 1,931 miles on a twelve-mile loop marked out on the salt, collecting an additional seventeen FIA and USAC speed records.

A quarter-mile stretch of the loop was on dirt rather than salt, and as it got rutted, it beat the car up. By the time Greatorex towed it back to LAX, it was junk—tired engine, blown clutch, sagging suspension, broken windscreen, headlights hanging out, and generally looking like it was ready for the crusher. "The salt had eaten into everything," Butler remembered.[63] "It was dripping between the aluminum panels and out the magnesium brakes. They offered it to me for $3,000. The car is probably worth $20 million now. But I looked at it and said, 'Shit, I wouldn't give you two bob for that thing.'"

The immensity of the salt flats at Bonneville sometimes seems to swallow up the machines that race there. But at the end of 1965, a Cobra Daytona Coupe prepped by mechanic Tom Greatorex managed to stand out. Drivers Craig Breedlove and Bobby Tatroe set twenty-three speed records—maxing out at 187 miles per hour—in a series of straight-line passes and during a twelve-hour endurance run over a twelve-mile loop. The Daytona Coupes never raced again. *Dave Friedman*

CHAPTER FIVE

WORLD DOMINATION

1966

Shelby American was going through ch-ch-ch-ch-changes as 1966 dawned. Most of them were all about the ka-ching. A sign of the times was the unlikely deal general manager Peyton Cramer had negotiated to sell one thousand special versions of the GT350 to Hertz Rent-a-Car. Hertz Rent-a-Car! The largest rental-car company in the world was planning to make a major buy of thinly disguised race cars from a Lilliputian manufacturer that had built fewer cars in three years of production than GM knocked out every day. The Hertz connection said a lot not only about Shelby American's growth but also about the maturity of the GT350.

The original version of the car suffered from the headache endemic to boutique production, namely narrow customer appeal coupled with high unit costs. Ford wanted to broaden the car's sales potential. This inevitably sent the GT350 down the path of so many other sports cars, which almost always grow flabbier with age, to the eternal frustration of enthusiasts. Still, from Ford's perspective, jettisoning some of the more expensive and uncompromising high-performance components would make the car both cheaper and more pleasant to drive—an apparent win-win. At the same time, Ford understood that it was critical to retain the GT350's cachet, so it continued to trumpet the association with Carroll Shelby's influential brand image. Under the headline "It's been a long time since bib overalls," Ford commissioned an ad featuring a photo of the tall Texan, dressed in a suit, tie, and cowboy boots, leaning insouciantly against a 1966 GT350, with a 427 Cobra in the background. After enumerating many of the go-fast features of the car, the copywriter concluded, "You don't have to go zero to sixty in 5.7 seconds, but it's nice to know you can."

It's been a long time since bib overalls.

Street cars often sell on the basis of their subjective image as much as their objective merits. To stir up interest in the 1966 GT350, the marketing mavens put Shelby—dressed elegantly in a suit and tie—front and center with the memorable "It's been a long time since bib overalls" ad campaign. "The Shelby G.T. 350 starts with a Mustang Fastback," the copy read, "and there the similarity ends." *Ford Motor Company*

That farm boy outfit and the big black hat cropped up everywhere from Le Mans to Riverside. On tortuous racing circuits around the world, Carroll Shelby learned what a car should be...power when you need it, handling when you need it. And he proceeded to build America's first true sports car...the 289 Cobra. Laurels are not for resting on. Now, here are the new ones...the sensational 427 Cobra and the road hungry G.T. 350 from Shelby-American.

The Shelby G.T. 350 starts with a Mustang Fastback and there the similarity ends. The high performance Ford 289 has been reworked with an aluminum high rise manifold, four barrel carburetion and tuned exhaust headers. The result? 306 horse. Completely new front suspension geometry, torque controlled rear axle, the close-ratio Borg Warner gear box (high performance automatic optional) front discs and sintered metallic rear linings deliver superlative handling characteristics. Then add the rear quarter panel windows, functional hood and rear brake air scoops, tach, competition seat belts and optional fold-down rear seats. You don't have to go from zero to sixty in 5.7 seconds, but it's nice to know you can.

The Cobra is the perfect sports car. Those are strong words but they can be proven. The 7-litre Ford 427 is fitted out with two four-barrel carbs and delivers 425 horsepower. That's right, 425. The result is an acceleration curve that's as close to vertical as you can get. For instance, Ken Miles did zero to a hundred to zero in 13.8 seconds with street tires. The all-new computer-designed frame with independent coil sprung suspension is one of the most sophisticated designs on the road today. Anti-dive and anti-squat characteristics are excellent. And as far as braking is concerned...well, those massive Girling discs will really haul her down from top speeds. If you need roll up windows for perfection, then forget it.

SHELBY
G.T. 350
COBRA

A host of changes were incorporated in the 1966 models. Some of them were purely cosmetic. Candy Apple Red, Ivy Green, Raven Black, and Sapphire Blue were added to a palette that had previously consisted of any color as long as it was Wimbledon White. Consumers wanted to see a more visible distinction between the GT350 and the significantly less expensive Mustang GT, so Dick Lins proposed a plexiglass rear quarter panel to replace the louvered insert. The functional rear brake ducts that Peter Brock had mocked up the previous year were resurrected, and Chuck Cantwell came up with a relatively easy way to pop-rivet them to the rear fenders. Mustang-style fold-down rear seats were offered as an option. (Virtually every buyer went for them.) So was an automatic transmission, which also proved to be very popular.

Cutting production costs was a major theme when the 1966 model was being spec'd. Adopting the Mustang GT's instrument panel and faux-wood steering wheel was a no-brainer. But the big money was saved in areas that most customers wouldn't see. No longer would new bolt holes be laboriously drilled to relocate the front control arms, and the high-line Koni shock absorbers were replaced with middle-of-the-road Gabriels, saving $8.63 per corner. The GT350 team also junked the so-called override traction bars at the rear because fitting them into the car was such a time-consuming operation. Instead, Traction Master developed an "underride" system that could be installed without cutting a hole through the body structure. The switch had no impact on performance. Not so for the decision to remove the Detroit Locker from the list of standard equipment. The gripe about the differential was that the signature *thunk* it made when it locked and unlocked sounded like a bowling ball rolling around in the trunk. The Locker would still be offered, but only as an option.

A handful of additional mods were made on the cars earmarked for the Hertz Rent-a-Racer program. The most obvious was the color: The vast majority of GT350Hs were black with striking gold stripes and rocker panel decals. The most important—and most troublesome, as it happened—change was the addition of power brakes. Hertz cars also were fitted with radios. This was more complicated than it sounded because, as Lins had discovered, static from the ignition interfered with the signal in cars with fiberglass hoods. He even tried lining the underside of the hood with tinfoil and grounding the chassis to that, but no joy. And the hoods posed other, more serious problems. "They were ill designed at first and were so wide that they required six or eight men to force them in place so the holding screws and bolts could be put in," production foreman Bob Wyatt said.[1] "I used to think to myself, 'My God! I hope these bolts don't ever come unsprung in a group of people or while driving down the road. It will kill someone!'"

The fit and finish of the fiberglass pieces provided by vendors were a perennial source of frustration. "I took care of all the supplies for the paint shop, and one of the biggest items that I bought was Bondo," said Dennis Eshelman, who was only seventeen when he was hired by lead painter, Dennis Ercek.[2] "The fiberglass pieces came out of the mold pretty rough back then. So there was a lot of Bondo used on those plastic parts in those cars."

Initially, GT350s were offered through a limited network of roughly ninety high-performance Ford dealers. Although the cars encouraged foot traffic through the showrooms, they didn't translate into much income. "We are programmed at about two hundred [cars] per month, but sales thus far have averaged about one hundred," Leo Beebe wrote to Don Frey.[3] "We are offering the car to dealers throughout the California area, on a test basis, to see if we can reach program volume. Failing this, we'll have to reshape the Shelby program because he cannot subsist with present overhead and limited volume."

Don Coleman of Ford's GT and Sports Car Department was dispatched to Southern California to help buttress Shelby's bottom line. "There was an opportunity to develop some more revenue with a fairly extensive Shelby American parts program," Coleman said.[4] He began working with Tim Foraker. With an MBA and a degree in mechanical engineering, both from Stanford, Foraker was the perfect guy to revamp Shelby's aftermarket parts program. Ironically, he'd been rejected the first time he applied for a job, when the company was still in Venice. He'd walked into the Carter Street facility, where a man was sitting at the front desk with his back to the door and his feet up on a credenza, talking on the phone. When the call finally ended, the man turned around and glared at Foraker. "Well, what do you want?"[5]

"I've been following Shelby," Foraker said mildly, "and I'm kind of interested in exploring if there are any job opportunities here."

"Have you ever raced cars?"

"No."

"Have you ever sold cars?"

"No."

"Have you ever been a mechanic on cars?"

"No."

Without saying a word to Foraker, he turned around, threw his feet back up on the credenza and picked up the phone.

Miffed, Foraker sent a letter to Shelby outlining his qualifications—and didn't hear anything. Months later, Cramer hired him as the parts and accessories manager. When he started, Shelby American already had a small trinkets-and-trash operation, selling tchotchkes to the public. There was also an extensive in-house parts program, supplying the components necessary to build Cobras and GT350s. As Foraker established a formal inventory-control system, he realized there was money to be made selling components used on Shelby American products to retail customers. The problem was that Ford owned the rights to the Cobra name, and Shelby was contractually obligated to sell Cobra-branded parts through Ford dealers. That's when Foraker had an epiphany.

"I went to management, and I said, 'We could rebrand the Cobra parts as Shelby parts, and put together a catalog to sell them,'" he said.[6] Pure gold. Eventually, Foraker had about a dozen people working for him in the warehouse and purchasing department. By the time he left, parts and accessories were generating $300,000 in profits on annual sales of $1 million of products ranging from intake manifolds, valve covers, oil pans, and air cleaners to fender badges, anti-sway bars, drag-race cylinder heads, and ZF-5DS-25 transaxles.

Meanwhile, GT350 production was booming, at least by Shelby American standards. After building 526 cars the previous year, the company cranked out 1,377 GT350s and 1,001 GT350Hs during the 1966 model year. Production peaked in April at 429 units, and the record was thirty-two a day. Naturally, this had entailed a rapid expansion of manpower. During the Venice years, there had never been more than fifty or so employees. Now, about that many were devoted to nothing but Mustangs, and Wyatt held shop meetings from 2 to 4 p.m. every Friday.

When cars came into the shop, four men were responsible for installing the new intake manifold, carburetor and valve covers, then tuning the carb and reinstalling the air cleaner. Next, the Mustangs were mounted on green carts and rolled over the pit, where Lonnie Brannan and Paul Kunysz headed up two twelve-man crews. At any given time, there were about five cars on the line, advancing through various stations. At the end of the line, cars proceeded to the paint shop in the west hangar, where the hoods were installed. After that came a test drive in an area staked out between the hangars and the concrete blast wall. Nobody was going to confuse it with Ford's monstruous River Rouge Complex, but it was an assembly line all the same.

The character of Shelby American changed as it morphed from a scrappy, scruffy start-up into a multi-million-dollar company with many of the trappings of corporate America. To keep track of everybody, security badges were issued—and fines were levied if they were lost. Once upon a time, the shop in Venice had been a casual hang for enthusiasts from all over California. Now, visitors had to pass through a guard booth off Imperial Highway just to enter the property, and a special credential was needed to get into the race shop. A lot of the guys who predated the move to LAX either quit or got fired—Peter Bryant, Bruce Junor, Frank Lance, Dick Lins, John Ohlsen, Ted Sutton, the Falcolner brothers. John Morton got the axe and never found out why. Peter Brock left to chase his own fortunes and ended up butting heads with Shelby over a contract to run the Toyota racing program. Allen Grant moved on when Shelby told him he was selling the Lola T70, which Grant had been promised a ride in, to a customer because "I need the money."[7] Jere Kirkpatrick quit, then came back to work on the GT350 production line. "I was welding in traction bars, and then they put me over on doing front-end alignments and lowering the A-arm," he said.[8] "It was a boring, brain-dead job. I finally got tired of the bullshit at the airport. It wasn't the same anymore. I was working for Ford Motor Company and doing exactly the same thing every fucking day."[9]

As Shelby American grew, so did the PR department. This created an opportunity for twenty-year-old Diana Trampe, a recent college graduate who was distraught after flubbing a secretarial skills test at Hughes Aircraft. Sobbing beside her father's truck, she looked across Imperial

Highway and saw an orderly collection of white cars—Mustangs ready to be converted into GT350s. For some reason, she thought they were Studebakers, and to cheer herself up, she decided to take a tour of the Studebaker factory. She drove up to the guard booth and was directed to a portable building. Before she could ask about taking a tour, the woman who greeted her said, "Are you the girl for the PR job?"[10] Trampe may have been young, but she wasn't stupid. "Yes!" she said immediately, even though she didn't know what "PR" meant.

During her job interview with PR director Don Rabbitt, Trampe finessed her lack of secretarial skills. (She'd just earned a degree in political science.) Rabbit told her that she had to talk to somebody named Carroll Shelby. She was ushered into another area, where she met a lanky, middle-aged man with curly brown hair and a Texas accent. After a few minutes of nervous conversation about her college experience, she asked him, "Is Miss Carol coming soon?" Shelby muffled a laugh and told her, "Miss Carol is allowing me to do the interview." Then he called down the hall to Rabbitt, "She's fine!"

As a PR assistant—and, later, director of public relations—Trampe ghostwrote magazine articles for Shelby, initiated an in-house newsletter called the *Cobra Crier*, and was responsible for providing cars and factory tours to celebrities ranging from Jerry Lewis, James Garner, and Tony Curtis to Twiggy, Gus Grissom, and Scott Carpenter. (Years later, after leaving Shelby American, she married Ray Geddes.) She also fielded complaints from air-traffic controllers at LAX whenever a Shelby American employee got busted for antics like racing at the airport. She would march down to the shop floor, put her hands on her hips and sternly declare, "You have to *stop* testing on an active taxiway. They want to shut us down!"[11] And almost as soon as she'd climbed the stairs back to her office, she could hear tires squealing. "It was like the Wild West," she said.[12]

Mark Waco was a repeat offender. Before moving over to the race shop, he worked on GT350 production, installing scoops and valve covers. "Fortunately, I was at the end of the line, so I got to drive the cars off," he said.[13] "We found ways to drive them onto the taxiway. Today, you'd be dead in five minutes doing that. But back then, the pilots would just wave at you and give you the A-OK sign."

Of course, Waco was only nineteen at the time, so he deserved something of a free pass. But the anything-goes mentality evidently applied equally well to veteran engine man Jim O'Leary. After working for hours to cure a miss in a 427 Cobra, he ran the car around a makeshift test track behind the hangars—though not on an active taxiway—to make sure the engine was okay. The wheels were spinning so luridly that the speedometer showed 100 miles per hour even though the car was going only 50 mph. But he thought to himself, "If Ken Miles can do it, I can do it." So he kept his foot in the throttle—and spun the car just as Shelby and some Ford execs were walking out. "And I thought, 'Wow, this is my last day!'" O'Leary said. "But they never said a word."[14]

But the worst offenders were the pro drivers. Case in point: Bernie Kretzschmar remembers looking out the window of the west hangar one day and seeing Jim McLean showing off row after row of neatly parked GT350s to Dan Gurney and Jerry Grant. Gurney jumped in one and started turning tire-roasting 360s—with Grant right behind him, enveloping the cars in a cloud of smoke. Then Gurney peeled off past a row of brand-new cars, did an arcing U-turn at 80-plus mph and screamed in between two other rows of Mustangs. And where was Grant while Gurney was turning the parking lot into a temporary racetrack? Playing bumper tag with Gurney! "And I'm thinking, 'Man, if they wreck in between all those cars. . .'" Kretzschmar recalled.[15] They didn't wreck, of course. Gurney and Grant parked the GT350s, and everybody went back to work—until Jerry Schwarz hollered, "Hey, one of the cars is on fire!"

Black smoke was swirling up from the car Gurney had been driving. The crew ran outside and checked under the hood. Nothing. Then they checked under the car and found the problem. Gurney had been standing on the brakes so hard that the rubber boot around the pistons in the calipers had caught fire. "Just another day at Shelby American," Kretzschmar said.[16]

Over in the west hangar, the race shop was busier than ever. Ford was determined to do whatever it took to avenge the beatdowns that Ferrari had administered to the GT40s the previous year. After Le Mans,

Henry Ford II had summoned Don Frey to his office. "You got your ass whipped?" the Deuce said.[17]

"Yes, sir," Frey said.

"You win that race."

"Yes, sir. How much money do I have?"

Ford stared at him. "Who said anything about money?"

While digging deep into the FoMoCo treasure chest, Ford kept its eyes laser-focused on the prize: Le Mans. The two US races at Daytona and Sebring would serve as trial runs. After a seemingly endless series of tests conducted by Ford and Shelby American, the big-block car had been updated to Mark IIA spec. The Daytona Coupe was history, but as a reward for delivering the GT World Championship the previous year, Alan Mann had been brought into the Le Mans program as a junior partner. Holman & Moody was getting a much bigger piece of the pie in 1966. But Shelby American was still first among equals, and it would remain the tip of the spear unless it failed to deliver the head of Enzo Ferrari on a platter.

During the summer of 1965, to pay for this reorganization, $1.845 million of Ford's $6.8 million racing budget for 1966 was funneled into the Le Mans effort. By January 1966, Leo Beebe was already warning Frey about "a possible $1.5 million overrun," and even this number was just a starting point, not a final figure.[18] (Total expenses for 1966 turned out to be $5 million.) "Mr. Ford wants to win Le Mans so bad he can taste it," Executive Vice President Charlie Patterson told Beebe over lunch.[19] "You tell us what needs to be done with those powertrains. If necessary, we'll gold-plate every one of them!"

Ford's largesse extended to Shelby American, which had a cost-plus contract that guaranteed Shelby an agreed-upon profit over and above his expenses, no matter how outlandish. "We all made lots of money, and where else could I call up Homer Perry, our liaison with Ford, and say, 'Homer, I need another million dollars?'" Al Dowd said, exaggerating only slightly.[20] "And where else could I have heard him answer back, 'Okay, Al, it's just a stroke of the pen.' The money was always there for whatever we needed, and we never had to wait for it to arrive." Perry had his own take on the nonexistent budget. "You don't understand," he told Carroll Smith. "If you win Le Mans, it doesn't matter how much money you spent—you're a hero. If you lose Le Mans, it doesn't matter how much you spent—because you're fired."[21]

Racing is a uniquely fickle endeavor, and money alone can't guarantee victory. But in this particular case, it paid for a testing regimen unlike any ever seen before in the sport. "Making this car go twenty-four hours has been like trying to win the war in Vietnam!" Beebe wrote to Frey.[22] "We simply have not had a vehicle—powertrain or otherwise—capable of that distance. So we've been testing and developing as rapidly as possible in an attempt to run twenty-four hours flat-out. We tried in August at Daytona, again in October, and again in December. This last time, we made it on a cumulative basis, but with interruptions for engine and brake repairs that would have put the car out of the race."

In February, Ford was back at Daytona again, but this time, it wasn't just a test. Shelby American unloaded three cars and about three dozen people—two drivers and four mechanics per car plus additional personnel ranging from Shelby and Phil Remington to O'Leary and fellow engine man Steele Therkleson to truck driver Bob Parker and four German timekeepers. Holman & Moody had two additional cars, so new that the team had been forced to work 24/7 to prep them for Daytona. Mann attended the race as a spectator; he would make his debut as a team principal at Sebring.

By this time, the 427 was rated at 463 horsepower at 6300 rpm. So power wasn't an issue. But weight was an ongoing concern despite an aluminum head, aluminum water pump, aluminum front cover, aluminum hub on the vibration dampener, a lightened flywheel, and a magnesium oil pan housing a dry sump. "No one knew how to make brakes last on a three thousand-pound race car. After the brakes warmed up—in two or three laps—I had to push so hard on the pedal that I couldn't concentrate on driving the car," wrote Mark Donohue, who was sharing a Holman & Moody car with Walt Hansgen.[23] "Nothing worked. No matter what, in a few laps, they would all go to hell." Fortunately, Remington had already come up with one of his patented fixes—spring-loading the brake pads for quick changes.

For the first time ever, Daytona was being run as a twenty-four-hour enduro. Ken Miles had a vexing steering issue during practice, but as soon as the steering rack was replaced, he shattered the lap record and qualified on the pole. Jo Bonnier, co-driving with Phil Hill—who'd defected from Ford—was a tick behind in the new Chaparral 2D, with its distinctive periscope air intake. Enzo Ferrari, for his own inscrutable reasons, had chosen not to send any factory cars to Daytona, but hard chargers Pedro Rodriguez and Mario Andretti started third in a quasi-works North American Racing Team 365 P2. It seemed to be shaping up to be a tough, grueling race. It wasn't. The Chaparral led the first lap before Miles swept past on the banking and motored into the distance, as placid as a soccer mom driving a minivan in the carpool lane. Hansgen led briefly during a pit stop exchange and Gurney set the fastest lap, but nobody was in the same zip code at the finish as Miles and co-driver, Lloyd Ruby, who was so relaxed that he napped in between stints. Gurney and Jerry Grant were second, eight laps back, with Hansgen and Donohue third, and another Mark IIA fifth.

Despite the uncomplicated win, the guys at Shelby American remembered—oh, how they remembered—what had happened twelve months earlier, when Miles and Ruby won at Daytona and the team then spent

Lloyd Ruby flat-out on the banking at Daytona as he and Miles breeze to a crushing victory in the twenty-four-hour enduro. Shelby American Mark IIAs finished first, second, and fifth, not only humbling Ferrari but also putting Holman & Moody in its place in the Ford motorsports hierarchy. The frustrations of 1964 and 1965 seemed like ancient history as the Ford prototypes swept through an undefeated season in 1966. *Ford Motor Company*

the rest of the year getting clobbered by Ferrari. Also, the next race, at Sebring, promised to be much more challenging, and not just because the circuit was much harder on machinery. Ferrari had deigned to send a team car to Florida—the all-new 330 P3, manned by Mike Parkes and Bob Bondurant, who hoped that consorting with his one-time enemy would launch him into Formula 1 orbit. Jim Hall was bringing not one but two Chaparrals in preparation for making a full-blown assault on the World Sportscar Championship. (Unlike GM, Ford had no interest in any of the European races except Le Mans.) Holman & Moody again had a pair of Mark IIAs, but this time the team had a lot more experience under its belt than it'd had at Daytona. Also, Mann was making his prototype debut. But instead of running Mark IIAs, he'd commissioned a pair of lightweight GT40 chassis and covered them with thin aluminum bodies so he could use a 289 and still have roughly the same power-to-weight ratio as the 427s.

Shelby entered a pretty blue Mark IIA for Gurney and Grant along with a somewhat ungainly looking open-top car with an aluminum chassis. Chris Amon had been racing the roadster in Group 7, the precursor to Can-Am, but in that class, it wasn't powerful enough to be competitive. In fact, it was such a dog that the crew referred to it not as the X-1, its official name, but as Big Ed, short for Edsel. Notwithstanding its checkered past, Shelby reasoned that the open-top car had a future in endurance racing because it was 250 pounds lighter than a Mark IIA. Remington assigned a team led by Bill Eaton to prep it.

"There were no drawings, and we were way, way behind," Eaton recalled.[24] "At about three o'clock on the day before they were getting ready to leave, I still hadn't gotten around to the roll bar. When Phil found out, he really laid into me. Then he rolled up his sleeves and said, 'You weld, and I'll hammer.' We were gas-welding aluminum, which is pretty painful. I had to pre-flux the rods and clean everything off after each one. He was working the power hammer, and he made the parts so fast, I could hardly keep up with him. The whole shop stopped to watch us."

The mix of cars near the front of the starting grid at Sebring suggested that the race was going to be a dogfight. The V-12 Ferrari was second, Graham Hill and Jackie Stewart an impressive third in the

Mann lightweight, Hansgen and Donohue fourth in the lead Holman & Moody Mark IIA, Miles and Ruby next in the scarlet X-1, then Jim Hall in a Chaparral. But Gurney was in a class of his own. He qualified on the pole with a two-second gap. At the start of the race, he flooded the engine and got away last, then proceeded to zigzag through the field like a car in a video game. He took the lead after ninety minutes while setting a lap record. Miles tried to chase him down until Shelby jumped up on the pit wall and furiously waved a wheel knock-off hammer at him. Miles gave Shelby the finger the next time by, but he finally slowed down.

Later, in the pits, Charlie Agapiou—who usually was the crew chief on Miles's car but was working for Gurney at Sebring—asked Miles what was going on. "You're going to be a lap down pretty soon," he said.[25]

Miles shrugged. "Dan's overrevving that thing," he said. "He's pulling me too easily."

Bumpy and twisty, Sebring was always a long, hard slog. This particular edition of the race was marred by two fatal accidents. Canadian Bob McLean died when his GT40 hit a utility pole, flipped, landed upside-down, and burned like a Viking funeral pyre. Later, four fans were killed when a car spun into an area that was supposed to have been closed to spectators. But the race droned on. Both Alan Mann cars and the Chaparrals were gone by nightfall, and the Ferrari expired shortly thereafter. The Holman & Moody cars were still running at the finish, but they'd made so many stops to change brake rotors that they might as well have been competing in a different race. Miles, who had brake problems of his own, was lapped shortly before the finish. Gurney motored on serenely, only to go missing with three minutes left in the race.

"Where's Gurney?" everybody asked frantically in the pits. "Where's Gurney?"

Gurney was parked on the apron of the last turn before the pits, where a rod bolt in his 427 had failed while he was within sight of the finish. As Miles came around to unlap himself, he was astonished to see Gurney pushing the car down the pit straight. Gurney was greeted with a huge ovation as he shoved his Mark IIA across the finish line—and was promptly disqualified. (Drivers were allowed to push their cars only *off* the track.) The only person more disappointed than Gurney was Mike Donovan, who'd been preparing to accept the trophy for the winning crew chief. An elated Miles took the checkered flag. "I was in the shower when I found out I had to go to victory lane," Ruby said.[26] "What a shock that was, 'cause Gurney and them guys was supposed to win that race, and they should have. We were really lucky in that one."

Hansgen and Donohue officially finished second, twelve laps down to Miles and Ruby. But the people at Ford knew the score. The Mark IIA had shown itself to be clearly superior to the Ferrari, and Shelby American had demonstrated that it was the top dog in the Ford lineup. For the first time ever, an American manufacturer would go to Le Mans as the odds-on favorite, and a team of Southern California hot-rodders would be its standard bearer.

Sebring proved to be an affair to remember for another reason. The day before Miles won the 12 Hour, Sebring had hosted the inaugural race of the Trans-American Sedan Championship, which later became one of Shelby American's favorite hunting grounds. Trans-Am was an attempt to attract manufacturers to SCCA with a pro series for production-based four-seat sedans. Shortly after the series was announced, Cantwell and Lew Spencer met with Ford reps and decided to dip their toe in the water. The fastback GT350 wasn't eligible; ironically, the changes SCCA had demanded to make the car legal for B Production as a two-seater rendered it ineligible for Trans-Am. The team would have to start with a fresh Mustang and go from there. "Shelby gave us five thousand dollars to do the first Trans-Am car, and that included going out and buying the car," Cantwell recalled.[27]

At the time, no notchbacks were available from the assembly plant in San Jose. Cantwell searched around until he found a light-blue metallic Hi-Po 289 at a Ford dealership in Newhall, a far-northern suburb of LA. After Schwarz picked it up from the showroom, it was retrofitted with a suite of GT350 equipment—aluminum oil pan, 715 CFM Holley, lowered front suspension, traction bars at the rear, gauge cluster, et cetera. Cantwell had a Ford graphic artist doctor the homologation

The Shelby American team takes a curtain call after an untroubled win at
Daytona. Miles and Ruby should have been oil and water—an acerbic, demanding
Brit and a laid-back, accommodating Texan—yet they made a perfect team.
That's them to the left, Smith in the cowboy hat behind the car, and mechanics
Bill Eaton, Mike Donovan, Max Kelly, and Charlie Agapiou on the right.
Ford Motor Company

photograph to show American Racing wheels instead of the stock
steelies. The car was approved for SCCA's A Sedan class, which also
made it eligible for Trans-Am.

Shelby had no interest in racing the Mustang himself because Trans-
Am was shaping up as the low minors of pro racing. But there seemed to
be a commercial opportunity to provide turn-key cars for customers who
dreamed of earning a little bit of cash from what was, for most of them,
just an expensive hobby. Twenty hardtop Mustangs would eventually
be delivered from San Jose. Cantwell and his team turned sixteen of

them into Trans-Am cars, while the others were completed as European rally cars. Trans-Am drew an oddball mix of cars during the inaugural season, but Mustangs were among the most successful.

With all the emphasis on the Le Mans program, Shelby chose not to race the GT350 in 1966, instead letting privateers have the field to themselves. (Shelby American offered contingency money—$150 for first place and $75 for second—and low-key aeronautical engineer Walt Hane would win the national B Production championship.) But before shutting down the factory program, Shelby decided to indulge himself by competing in what he described as a "low-pressure event" at Green Valley Raceway in Dallas.[28] "Howja like to drive the Mustang in my hometown?" he asked Jerry Titus. "They have a little regional race down there, and I'd like to hep 'em out."[29]

It was all hands on deck during the run-up to Le Mans in 1966, as Shelby American was responsible for building two new Mark IIAs from scratch and completely overhauling a third, which hadn't raced since winning at Daytona. Here in the west hangar at LAX, one of the cars destined for France is examined by, (from left) mechanic Ron Butler, Ford engineer Chuck Mountain, Smith, and Remington. *Ford Motor Company*

Titus didn't have anything else on his dance card, so he eagerly accepted the offer. He and Schwarz towed the original prototype on an open trailer to Texas. When they arrived, they discovered that a Ford dealer in Galveston had hired the ultra-aggressive Pedro Rodriguez to drive a customer GT350. "There went our relaxed weekend down the tubes," Titus said. Although Titus qualified fastest in B Production, Rodriguez slipped past at the start, and despite "driving like a mad idiot"—Titus's words—Titus could never elbow his way past the notoriously difficult-to-overtake Mexican.[30] The result supported Cantwell's claim that he was giving customers the same components that the Shelby American team was using. Still, Shelby was annoyed about the rare defeat. "We send you guys all the way down there with a factory car, and you got your ass beat," he groused to Schwarz.[31]

The only other 1966 GT350s specifically designed for racing were the Drag Unit cars. Besides being equipped with a bunch of drag strip–friendly components such as torque control arms and a driveshaft safety loop, these cars were delivered with a cast-iron scattershield, a heavy-duty clutch, and a pressure plate in the trunk. (The idea was, since the motor had to be removed prior to installation of these items, engine work would be done at that time.) The program had been spearheaded by Shelby sales rep and drag racer Don McCain the previous year, when he set a B/Sports record of 12.93 seconds and 107.10 mph in the quarter mile. A total of eight Drag Unit cars were sold in 1965 and 1966.

Another special-order model in 1966 was a GT350 pumped up with a Paxton supercharger. Joe Granatelli of Paxton Products had pitched Shelby on the blower when the car debuted. Given a car to play with, Granatelli supercharged a GT350, then walked away from Shelby's 289 Cobra in an impromptu street race near LAX. The Paxton unit looked impressive inside the engine bay, and it reportedly increased the power rating from 306 horsepower to over 390. But the magazine reviews were tepid, and as a $670 option, so were sales. Eleven supercharged cars were sold in 1966 and twenty-eight in 1967, and a few dozen Paxton superchargers were sold separately through Foraker's growing parts department.

The GT350Hs being built for Hertz were a much bigger deal, not to mention far more important to Shelby American's profit-and-loss statement. Back in 1958, Hertz had created the Hertz Sports Car Club, replete with a driving test that had to be passed before you were issued a membership card. In previous years, it had featured cars like the E-type Jaguar, and the Corvette Sting Ray had been slated for inclusion in 1966 until Cramer instead sold the company on a lightly modified GT350. Hertz promoted what it marketed as the Rent-a-Racer program with magazine ads showing a black-and-gold GT350H barreling into a corner. "There are only 1000 of these for rent in the entire world," the headline read. "Hertz has them all." Depending on the location and time of year, rates ranged from thirteen to seventeen dollars a day, or fifty-four to seventy dollars a week, and thirteen to seventeen cents a mile. The only restriction was that renters had to be twenty-five or older.

By rental-car standards, performance was otherworldly. In a nuts-and-bolts report in *Sports Car Graphic*, a GT350H equipped with a T-handle, three-speed automatic was timed at 0-to-60 mph in 7.9 seconds and 0-to-100 in 21.1. In a more irreverent review, *Car and Driver* enthused, "The taut suspension, well controlled geometry, and big tires suffice to keep it on the road at insane speeds, and when it starts to slide, you can wrestle the slide in the direction of your choice."[32] In its ads, Hertz crowed, "Why a rent-a-car with all this performance? We could have gotten a fleet of high-powered pseudo-sports-cars. But we figured you'd want to try a champion. Not just another imitation."

The major mechanical difference between the GT350H and the standard car was power brakes, which was one of Hertz's non-negotiable requests. At the time, Ford didn't offer power brakes for the Mustang, so Shelby American had to come up with a system of its own. Once again, Remington came to the rescue. Not with a fix this time. But because he knew so many vendors in so many backwaters of the automotive ecosystem, he located a supplier in Minnesota that sold two-stage master cylinders—imagine a piston within a piston—for industrial applications such as forklifts. The beauty of the unit was that it could be mounted to the firewall (with a bracket designed by Cantwell) without modifying the brake pedal assembly or the brakes themselves. The downside was that it produced a strange hard-then-soft-then-hard-again brake feel. And that wasn't the only sticking point.

The other issue was that the GT350's brake system had been optimized for road racing, not rental-car duty. "We had racing pads on the front and ceramic metal brakes on the rear drums," Cantwell said, "and those guys didn't start doing their job until they got about three laps on a racetrack."[33] As a result, there were reports of renters rear-ending other rental cars before even getting out of the parking lot. Eventually, the aftermarket master cylinder was junked, and Hertz reverted to the original GT350 brake system with softer pads at the front and rear shoes from a Ford station wagon. Oh, and a label was affixed to the dashboard of each rental car: "This vehicle is equipped with competition brakes. Heavier than normal brake pedal pressure may be required." Who knows what renters made of that warning?

Although Hertz promoted the GT350H through the Rent-a-Racer program, the company prohibited renters from actually racing the cars. Yet Shelby lore is rife with tales about scofflaws who bolted in roll bars, ran the cars in SCCA events, and removed the bars before innocently returning the cars to the Hertz lot. The vast majority of these stories are undoubtedly bogus. But Jim Gessner, aka Vettefinder Jim, insists that he helped some California racers change the wheels and tires of their Hertz rentals before running them in SCCA autocrosses and then erasing the evidence of any crimes at a quarter car wash. Tom Greatorex, who was the mechanic at Bonneville when Craig Breedlove and Bobby Tatroe set speed records with the Cobra Daytona Coupe, figures in another favorite account. During a twelve-hour enduro at Marlboro, Tom Yeager's Mustang wasn't running properly. Greatorex cured the problem by pulling a carburetor from an unattended GT350H he found parked in the paddock. The kicker is that the car had been rented from Hertz by none other than John Bishop, the SCCA honcho who'd helped Shelby conceptualize the GT350 in the first place.

Although he wasn't on a racetrack, Kretzschmar had a high-speed misadventure with a GT350H he rented during a vacation in Alabama. He got the car up to 125 mph—"blowing sparks out the back," he says—on a rural interstate before seeing flashing red lights in his rear-view mirror.[34] He killed his lights and slid to a stop beneath an underpass, but his efforts to elude the police didn't work, and he spent the night in jail. Dowd also had several unpleasant experiences with rental Shelbys. On various occasions, he smelled exhaust fumes in the cockpit and heard valve clatter so deafening that he couldn't listen to the radio.

There was also a car so badly aligned that he had to keep both hands on the steering wheel at all times. Unlike a stock Mustang, a GT350H was a high-strung beast that needed to be looked after on a regular basis. After Dowd wrote a scathing letter to Hertz, the company did a better job of staying on top of maintenance. Although several clutches were roasted on the hills of San Francisco, GT350Hs generally fared no better or worse than the rest of the cars in the Hertz fleet. It's not clear if this reflects how well Hertz customers treated the Shelby cars or how badly they treated *all* rental cars.

As 1966 GT350 production was winding down, unwanted 427 Cobras continued to stack up at LAX. The 427 was a better car than the 289 by virtually every measure. It was bigger, faster, more powerful, more refined, rode better, cornered harder, and, to most eyes, looked more bitchin'. Today, it's rightfully considered to be the poster car that best embodies the intoxicating testosterone-fueled vitality of the Cobra. As *Motor Trend* wrote in its first review of the car, "Periodically, some psychiatrist grabs himself a headline by proclaiming that the reason men like sports cars is because the car compensates for a sense of sexual inadequacy. We've never bought that theory but if there is anything to it, the cure is simple. Rx: one 427 Cobra."[35]

Miles demonstrated the truly awesome performance of the car by taking on the unofficial record for going from a dead stop to 100 mph and back to zero, which had been set years earlier by Aston Martin at 27.4 seconds. Despite using rock-hard Goodyear Blue Dot street tires on the slippery concrete surface behind the hangar at LAX, Miles managed the feat in either 13.2 seconds (according to *Sports Car Graphic*) or 13.8 seconds (so said *Car and Driver*). Both times were quicker than marks posted a half-century later in *Road & Track* tests of a Ferrari 575M Maranello, a Dodge Viper SRT-10, and a Lamborghini Murciélago. The 13.2-second 0-to-100-to-0 time became an essential element of the 427 Cobra legend.

The big-block Cobra just might be the most imitated car in history, which says something about its enduring appeal. But what gets lost in all the hosannas back in the day and the astronomical prices paid for the cars

More Miles, this time showing off the prodigious power of the 427-cubic-inch V-8 as well as his cat-like car-control skills. Here at Sebring in 1966, Miles and Ruby would score the open-top X-1's first—and last—win as they lucked into Victory Lane after Gurney's Mark IIA, leading by more than a lap, failed on the last corner. Gurney pushed the car over the finish line—and was promptly disqualified. *Ford Motor Company*

by contemporary collectors is the indisputable fact that, when the 427 was being built, it was a sales catastrophe. By the start of 1966, only sixteen of the fifty-two race car chassis that had been shipped by AC Cars had been raced. The rest were sitting on jack stands outside the hangars at LAX, unsold and apparently unsellable. When East Field Services Rep Charles Beidler visited Shelby American, the sight of all those unpainted Cobras inspired a eureka moment: Why not dumb down the race car ever so slightly and sell it as a street machine that could be billed as the fastest production car ever built? And so the 427 S/C was born.

Exactly what S/C stands for is a matter of some dispute. "Semi-competition" is the most likely possibility, but votes also have been cast for "street competition." Could be both, might be neither. The point is, the S/C is a magnificent kludge, a classic case of turning lemons into lemonade. The only major changes were subbing out the full-on race motor for a street-car engine and sticking a muffler on the exhaust. Beidler himself was responsible for selling the first S/C. Naturally, it overheated on the way home from the dealership. Future cars were fitted with electric cooling fans for the radiator.

Efforts were made to make the S/C more palatable to non-racing customers. Header expert Robert Krauss was hired to work with Miles on exhaust development. He fabricated various prototypes of conventional tailpipes, but none of them panned out. "You know," he told Miles, "the only way we're going to get the ground clearance you want and the tuned length of the headers is to go through the body."[36] Side pipes, in other words. After yet another prototype got torn up, Miles reluctantly agreed, and Krauss created the system now found on all S/Cs. "Performance-wise, it worked perfect," he said. "Clearance-wise, it worked perfect." The only problem was proximity to the shins of the cars' occupants, which is why virtually every S/C owner wears a side-pipe burn scar as a proud emblem of membership in a very exclusive club.

Shelby American eventually found buyers for all twenty-nine of the S/Cs. But AC Cars was still delivering street versions of the 427 Cobra. These were de-contented much more ruthlessly than the S/Cs. "The race cars got all the good stuff," said Andre Gessner, who ran the 427 production unit.[37] "The street cars didn't get the side pipes and roll bars and stuff like that. Shelby was a good businessman, but let's face it, he was cheap as hell. He told me, 'Get 'em built, and get 'em out of here. Don't do any more work than you have to.' It got down to: Don't spend any more money on them than you have to. And we didn't."

Despite the downgrades, the 427 Cobra was still the baddest street car on the planet. Even with a cast-iron head and a compression ratio backed down to 10.4:1, the engine made 425 horsepower at 6000 rpm and a stump-pulling 480 lb-ft of torque at 3500 rpm. This was a car that ran low 12s at nearly 120 mph straight out of the box. But priced at $6,995, it was nearly two grand more than a big-block Sting Ray, which offered far more in the way of creature comforts. So sales were, well, what's worse than pathetic?

Under the circumstances, the temptation to cut corners was impossible to resist. One of the dirty little secrets of the Cobra world is that nearly a third of the cars sold as 427s were actually equipped with 428-cubic-inch Police Interceptor V-8s designed to motivate Thunderbirds and Galaxies. Instead of getting a lightly detuned race motor with twin Holley four-barrels, buyers of these impostors received a mass-production street-car engine with a single Autolite carb. At the time, it was said that the change was made because 427s weren't available. But in retrospect, it's clear that it was all about the Benjamins. While Shelby American paid $730 for 427s, 428s could be had for a mere $320. Shelby wasn't happy about the switch. "I'm not putting the station wagon motor in my cars," he insisted.[38] "I'm just not going to do it." But considering what an albatross the big-block Cobra had become, the math was very persuasive.

On a spec sheet, the numbers didn't look too bad, and even now, the faux 427s have their advocates. Although the stock 428 was rated at 333 horsepower, Shelby claimed the modded version in the Cobra made 390 horsepower, which was nothing to sneer at. But on the street, much less the track, the Police Interceptor couldn't keep up with the 427. "The 428 wasn't worth a damn," Gessner said.[39] "Hell, a Mustang would beat a Cobra with the 428 in it. It just didn't have any power. I changed the cams on all seventy motors we put in there to try to give them some horsepower. But even then, the car would stall on you when you went around a corner because it didn't have a center-pivot carb, like the Holley."

All 427s were shaken down at a track before leaving Shelby American. Gessner did a lot of this testing himself. But on one occasion, Miles joined him at Willow Springs. While flying a company airplane, Miles dinged the wing during a tricky crosswind landing at the track. "He was lucky he didn't crash and hurt anything really bad," Gessner said.[40] The plane wasn't flyable, so they arranged a convoy to move the damaged bird five miles down a two-lane highway to an air park in nearby Rosamond. "I drove the truck and the trailer in front, waving people off the road, and he followed me with the airplane, using the motor and propeller to power it," Gessner said. "It was just another one of those crazy things."

Ron Butler vividly recalls another ill-fated 427 test session when Miles *wasn't* there. Butler had been pursuing a career as a race car driver when Dowd called to offer him a job as a mechanic at Shelby American, and he didn't want to bail on his dream. "Well, if I come," Butler asked, "can I get a ride in one of the Cobras?"[41]

"I can't guarantee it," Dowd said. "But you'll never get a ride over there. If you come here, you've got a chance of getting one." Is it any wonder they called him Greasy Slick?

After moving to LA, Butler continued to pester Dowd, but he never got anywhere. Finally, Butler spoke directly to Shelby. "How's my ride coming along?" Butler asked.

Shelby put his arm around Butler. "You know what?" Shelby drawled amiably. "We need people like you here in the shop."

Miles, at least, let Butler test cars unofficially. And when the team was conducting endurance tests of the 427 prototype, Miles sent Butler to Riverside to log laps. Butler had gotten down to within a half second of Miles's time. Looking for a few extra tenths, he misjudged his entry speed into Turn Seven and went over the hill with all four wheels off the ground. The brakes locked up when he landed, and he nosed into a dirt embankment, pushing the right front wheel back into the chassis. "The oil tank blew the cap off the top and bloody oil squirted out all over the car," Butler said.[42] "When the dust settled, the whole car was covered in oily dust, and I was hanging onto a bloody steering wheel with bent spokes."

Butler trailered the wounded car back to the shop and used a Porto-Power to try to push the fender back out. At about 10 p.m., while working underneath the car, he spotted a pair of cowboy boots. It was Shelby. "Where are you working next week, boy?" he asked.

To Butler's immense relief, Shelby didn't fire him. Shelby couldn't afford to lose any seasoned race mechanics, not now, with Le Mans looming on the horizon. But there was more to it than that. As a former race car driver, Shelby had a special appreciation—and respect—for what race mechanics did and how tirelessly they worked, so he was generally willing to cut them a lot of slack. Kretzschmar remembers driving into the LAX parking lot in his Model A hot rod after an extra-long liquid lunch at a topless bar that had just opened on Imperial Boulevard. Shelby walked over, and Kretzschmar figured he was about to get reamed out. He was right. But Shelby couldn't have cared less about the topless bar. "Bernie," he said, "you got Firestone tires"—pronounced "tars"—"on this car. Get 'em off there."[43]

It was time to head to France, not for the race but to practice at Le Mans. The 24 Hour was traditionally run during the summer solstice in mid-June, when there were only six hours of absolute darkness. Because

162

the circuit was stitched together out of public roads—France's admirable Route Nationale system—there was no opportunity for teams to shake down their cars on the track prior to the race. So Automobile Club de l'Ouest typically closed the roads for a single Le Mans Test Day roughly two months before the race. This year, Ford brought five cars and all three of its factory teams to the test.

The test marked the first official appearance of the J-Car, which was designed to be the sharpest arrow in Ford's quiver. From the beginning, the biggest knock on the GT40 was its excessive weight. Thanks largely to the cast-iron lump in the engine bay, the car was a porker. So almost from day one, Roy Lunn had been searching for ways to put it on a diet. The previous year, Ford engineer Chuck Mountain had discovered a honeycomb-aluminum material that was being used to make fighter aircraft instrument panels. Super light yet extremely strong, it seemed to be perfect for racing. Kar-Kraft engineer Ed Hull fashioned a monocoque out of sections of honeycomb-aluminum bonded together with industrial-grade adhesives cured in ultra-high-heat ovens. Designers at Ford Styling designed unconventional bodywork featuring a nose that looked like lobster claws and a high, flat rear deck that inspired the nickname The Breadvan. Officially, it was called the J-Car because it had been built to meet Appendix J of the FIA regulations.

Light rain fell steadily when the circuit was opened. While most of the drivers ran a few slow laps before returning to the safety of the pits, Hansgen continued to pound around the track with water spraying off the tires of his Mark IIA. After several years as the resident ace in Briggs Cunningham's team, Hansgen was now Holman & Moody's lead driver. He'd finished third at Daytona and second at Sebring. Now, he was determined to put his stamp on the session. Twice, he was called into the pits and told to slow down. Instead, he went faster, clicking off a lap at 3:59, then a 3:48.5, then a 3:46.8. "I don't know what he was doing, but he was going like hell," Amon said.[44] And then, disaster.

Hansgen bombed past the pits. As he bent the car under the Dunlop Bridge, the tail twitched violently. Veteran driver that he was, Hansgen calmly collected the slide and steered the car up the escape road to the left. Under normal circumstances, that would have been the right play. But what Hansgen didn't realize was that a giant pile of dirt had been deposited in the escape road in preparation for a construction project. He hurtled into it at better than 100 mph. The car flipped end over end and the chassis folded in half, trapping him inside, injured horribly. It took twenty minutes to cut him out of the car, and he died five days later without ever regaining consciousness.

The tests resumed, and as the track dried, lap times tumbled. Fords ended the day one-two-three-four-nine. The J-Car, surprisingly, was fastest of all. But last year's calamity at Le Mans had taught Ford all it needed to know about the recklessness of tackling a twenty-four-hour endurance race with an experimental car. Stewart and Sir John Whitmore had been reasonably quick in Alan Mann's 289-powered lightweights, but both of them preferred the Mark IIs, so Ford made a command decision to shelve the small-block. "To get the power you needed to be competitive, you had to run 8000, 8500 rpm, and the engines got tired after a while at a twenty-four-hour race," Ford engine engineer Hank Lennox explained. "But the 427 could loaf [because] they didn't have to work real, real hard. Unless somebody over-revved it or had a horrible, horrible shift or something, those engines weren't going to break. They had a ton of power, but you never really used all of it because you didn't need it."

The big-block Mark IIA had already scored decisive victories in the first two races of the season, and there was no reason to think it wouldn't keep its streak alive at Le Mans. The ACO, sensing which way the wind was blowing, invited Henry Ford II to serve as the race's honorary starter. The Deuce had no intention of being made to look like a fool at Le Mans. He made a copy of his acceptance letter to the ACO. On the bottom, in longhand, he wrote "You better win."[45] It was signed "HFII." He sent this copy to Leo Beebe. When Beebe had been given control over Ford's motorsports portfolio, his brief had been to win the Indy 500, Daytona 500, and Le Mans—a tough trifecta. Against all odds, Ford had won Indy and Daytona. But Beebe knew that if the Mark IIAs didn't come through at Le Mans, he would be remembered for this signal failure, not his many successes. To him, the Deuce's note wasn't a friendly exhortation from an old comrade in arms. It was an order from his commander-in-chief, and if Beebe's best-laid plans went awry at Le Mans, he would be expected to fall on his sword. Beebe kept

The glorious program cover for the 12 Hours of Sebring in 1967 shows the previous year's winner—the red open-top X-1 driven by Miles and Ruby—alongside the blue Gurney/Grant Mark II that coulda, woulda, shoulda won the race. *John Gabrial Collection*

the note in his wallet for the rest of his life. He also reproduced it on the back of a 1966 Le Mans race poster and gave a copy to every member of the team.

Ford's strategy for Le Mans was to win by brute force. Not since D-Day had an expeditionary force this large landed in France. Including the Deuce's delegation of beautiful people, there were eight race-ready cars (and a spare), seven backup engines, twenty-one tons of parts, an eight-thousand-pound set-up plate and a Coca-Cola machine, or what Henry Manney described in *Road & Track* as "more materiel than Hannibal took over the Alps."[46] Holman & Moody contributed a forty-foot-long trailer equipped with a lathe, mill, hydraulic press, sheet-metal bender, bead roller, surface grinder, belt and disc sanders, generator, air compressor, gas and electric welding rigs, bathrooms, showers, and, on the roof, canopies and cots for sleeping. The Shelby American contingent consisted of fifteen mechanics and two parts men plus Shelby, Remington, Dowd, and Smith. John Holman figured his ace in the hole was the Wood Brothers racing team, renowned in NASCAR for their lightning pit stops. Glen Wood, who was dubious about the European adventure, arrived at Charlotte Airport with huge suitcases overloaded with cases of potted meats and Vienna sausages. "We ate every can he had," stock car racer Dick Hutcherson said.[47]

American racers had been popular in France at least since the liberation of Paris in 1944. French fans had cheered the Cadillac special known as Le Monstre, the Hemi-powered Cunninghams, the all-American Corvettes, and the early GT40s. American drivers, too, were crowd favorites—the handsome Hill, the boyish Gurney, the bespectacled Masten Gregory, and, yes, the colorful Texan, Carroll Shelby. The Ford brass didn't want the Shelby guys, with their reputation as hell-raisers, coming off as ugly Americans. "Our crews should look like racing crews and behave like gentlemen," Beebe wrote longhand on an inter-office memo.[48] Shaves and haircuts were strongly suggested before flying to Europe.

Ford was also sensitive to complaints about the enormity of its Le Mans expedition. As British PR maven Walter Hayes put it: "I am naturally not anxious for a 'poor little us [meaning Ferrari] against the rich giants' story to grow too large, because it merely magnifies the 'Ford pours millions into Le Mans' stories that we can do without anyway. Pyrrhic victories are also of doubtful value."[49] But twenty-one tons of parts is still twenty-one tons of parts, no matter how you try to spin it. "Operation Overkill," John Wyer called it.[50] Or as former GT40 driver Dick Attwood said, "That was really using a sledgehammer to break a nut, wasn't it?"[51]

Nobody roots for Goliath. The ACO did what it could to hamstring the Fords. During practice, Holman & Moody driver Dick Thompson—the racing dentist—neglected to mention a minor accident to race officials. The ACO reacted to this petty infraction by disqualifying the car. Beebe was incensed when he heard the news. But he'd lettered in baseball at the University of Michigan, so he knew how to play hardball. He told the ACO that he'd withdraw the entire Ford team if the car was disqualified. The ACO saved faced by DQing only Thompson, and little-known Australian driver Brian Muir was hired at the last minute to replace him.

Fords dominated practice. After the first session, Bruce McLaren sat in his car with a frown on his face. Smith was puzzled. He knew that Miles had tested this particular chassis at Riverside before it was flown to France. In fact, he'd liked it so much that he told Smith he wished he were driving it at Le Mans. "What the hell is wrong?" Smith asked McLaren.[52]

"The car is so [naughty word deleted] good, I just don't want anybody else to know about it." McLaren said. "They'll take it away from me."

Mark IIA claimed five of the first six starting positions, with the Shelby American entries one-two-four. Gurney and Grant were on the pole in a red car with white stripes (and a roof blister to accommodate Gurney's helmet). Miles and Denny Hulme, a little-known but promising F1 driver from New Zealand, were second in a baby blue Mark IIA with bright red eyebrows that Agapiou had painted around the headlights so he could identify the car from a distance. McLaren and Amon, both Kiwis, qualified fourth in a black car with silver stripes, New Zealand's sporting colors. The Ferraris and Chaparrals, not to mention the Holman & Moody entries, couldn't keep up. As was traditional at Le Mans, the cars were parked diagonally in the pits in their starting order while the drivers lined up on the other side of the track. When Henry Ford II waved the tricolor, the drivers sprinted across the front straight, jumped into their cars and hauled ass onto the track, usually without bothering to latch their seat belts.

The race that unfolded was one of the most controversial, most contentious, and most confounding in the annals of motorsports. Historical mysteries are usually the product of not having enough information to properly understand and contextualize what happened. In the case of Le Mans 1966, there's *too much* information—too much conflicting information, that is. Virtually every eyewitness to the events in question left some sort of testimony about the race, but it's impossible to reconcile the various accounts. There was widespread confusion as the race was going on, and there's still widespread confusion to this day.

Miles had trouble closing his door at the start, and he pitted after the first lap so Agapiou could secure it properly. To make up for lost time, he set a lap record of 3:31.9. After an hour, the Fords were one-two-three, with Gurney at the front after clocking a 3:30.6, which translated into an average speed of 142.979 mph. (Yes, Le Mans was crazy fast.) Rain fell on and off, generally leaving the track greasy rather than truly wet. Amon and McLaren had to pit repeatedly because their Firestone intermediate tires kept throwing treads. None of the other Fords were having trouble because they were using Goodyears. The dilemma for McLaren was that Firestone was a major sponsor of his fledgling race team, which was gearing up for both Formula 1 and Can-Am. But he obviously wasn't going to win the race unless he made a change. So he made the politically inexpedient decision to ask Firestone officials to release him from his contractual obligations, which they did. Goodyears were then bolted onto the black-and-silver car, now several laps behind the leaders. As Amon was about to leave the pits, McLaren leaned into the cockpit and shouted, "Let's drive this thing flat-out. If it finishes, it finishes. If it doesn't, it doesn't. We've got nothing to lose."[53]

The Chaparrals didn't last long, and only one of the Ferraris had the pace to hang—barely—with the Mark IIAs. By half distance, the Ferrari was toast and McLaren and Amon had made up the time they lost with the Firestone intermediates, so the Shelby American trio was running one-two-three. But shortly before dawn Sunday, Grant pitted with the water temp gauge pegged, and after a brief stint on life support, the car he was sharing with Gurney expired. Hutcherson was third, but ten laps down, in the last remaining Holman & Moody car. This left the Mark IIAs of McLaren/Amon and Miles/Hulme poised to fight for the lead—except that fighting was exactly what Ford didn't want them to do.

Spare a little sympathy for Leo Beebe. Shelby owned the team running the cars at the front of the field, but Beebe was the man on the spot. He had the Deuce's you-better-win notecard burning a hole in his pocket, with his boss literally watching over his shoulder. He remembered 1964, when all three GT40s broke, and last year's fiasco, when all *six* cars had puked. This year, five of the eight Mark IIAs were already out of commission, and there were still seven hours to go. Making sure that one of the surviving cars made it to the finish in front was all he cared about. "As far as I was concerned, it didn't make any difference to me who won," Beebe said. "I wanted Ford to win."[54] To prevent the remaining drivers from overstressing the cars, he ordered them to shift gears at 5000 rpm instead of 6200 and slow down to lap times of four minutes flat, a pace that a ham-fisted club racer could have managed without scaring himself. "It took me something like ten laps of concentrated effort to slow down to this speed," Amon admitted.[55]

At this point, the 1966 edition of Le Mans ceased to be a race in any conventional sense. Lap charts show that the lead changed hands on several occasions between the Miles/Hulme and McLaren/Amon cars over the last eight hours, but not because the drivers were dicing furiously on the track. No, the ebb and flow was simply a function of the timing and the type of the pit stops—fuel only; fuel and brake pads; or fuel, pads, and brake rotors. Lap after lap, hour after hour, the big Mark IIAs pounded around the track while Shelby and the Ford brain trust debated how to play the endgame.

But Beebe wasn't the only one making calculations. Miles and McLaren also understood the score. (Hulme and Amon were junior partners who were content to follow the lead of their older mates.) They realized that Ford wasn't going to let them off the leash so they could have a knock-down, drag-out grudge match. The trick would be to position themselves in the right place at the right time for the finish. Miles was operating under the assumption that possession was nine-tenths of the law. It appears that he flouted team orders and turned a few quick laps to make sure that he was in front when, presumably, the positions were frozen. At least, that's what McLaren and Amon claimed. And Beebe agreed with then. Miles had been ordered to slow down in several previous races, and here at Le Mans, Beebe described his behavior as "spirited" and "devilish."[56]

McLaren came up with a more creative solution. In a letter he later wrote to his father—"not printable, of course"—he claimed that he approached Ford officials with a cheeky proposition.[57] "Why don't you bring the cars over the line together? It would be much better public relations."[58] Really? Amon, who was a friend of McLaren, didn't know anything about this conversation. And the pitch itself was bizarre. The whole point of staging a race is to identify a winner. What major motor race—or horse race or pennant race or presidential race—has ever ended in a tie? And why would the ACO agree to reduce its crown jewel into a promotional extravaganza for a carmaker it despised?

Still, from Ford's perspective, McLaren's suggestion was inspired. "We had three cars running up at the front as the race was drawing to its conclusion," explained Jacque Passino, whose opinion was second in importance only to Beebe's.[59] "Ken Miles was in one, and Dick Hutcherson and Bruce McLaren were in the others. All of those guys were real racers. Miles would race his grandmother to the breakfast table, and the other two weren't much better. We figured that in order to ensure a Ford win and keep those three guys from racing each other to the end, we would have a dead-heat finish. We didn't want to risk those guys crashing each other or breaking the cars. In hindsight, we probably should have done it differently, but we were trying to control our destiny and ensure a Ford win, and we did just that."

Unbelievably, the ACO signed off on the dead-heat scenario. Miles was ordered to back off and let McLaren catch up. "So ends my contribution to this bloody motor race," Miles snapped as he flung down his sunglasses.[60] In the pits, nobody was sure what was happening, but they could tell something was up from the intense discussions between the Ford executives wearing suits and worried expressions. As Miles buckled up his seat belts before beginning his final stint, Smith leaned into the cockpit and said, "I don't know what they told you, but you won't be fired for winning Le Mans."[61]

Less than an hour before the race was scheduled to end, while Miles and McLaren were on the track, a Ford functionary hustled into the Ford pits and breathlessly informed Beebe that the ACO had decided that a dead-heat finish wouldn't be allowed after all. If two cars crossed the finish line together, then the one that had covered the greatest distance would be declared the winner. Since McLaren had qualified two spots behind Miles, he would have driven about twenty-five feet farther. What to do now? This was long before cars were equipped with in-car radios, so there was no way to explain the situation to Miles and McLaren short of having them make unscheduled pit stops. And, of course, once the drivers realized that it was every man for himself, the shit *really* might have hit the fan. Doing nothing, Beebe knew, was the safest strategy, so nothing is precisely what he did.

The three big Mark IIAs maneuvered into a loose formation and trundled along the slick track with the two Shelby American entries side by side and Hutcherson's bronze car bringing up the rear. McLaren was slightly ahead when the checkered flag dropped. Even so, Miles thought he and Hulme were the co-winners of the race until French officials blocked their car to prevent them from approaching the victory rostrum. "I think I've been fucked," Miles told Agapiou out the side of his mouth.[62] Looking back on the scene, Agapiou said, "They treated us like bloody dogshit. Ken was *so*, so disappointed. He took off, and I didn't think he was coming back."[63]

Amon was as confused as anybody when the race ended. He'd sensed the tension in the pits and knew that something was up. But McLaren hadn't confided in him during the race, and nobody from Ford or Shelby

The denouement at Le Mans in 1966 was so confusing that not even the drivers knew what had happened. Miles, thinking he'd co-won the race, drives down the narrow dirt path to the victory rostrum, with Hulme on the roof, while the car shared by Amon and McLaren trails behind them. A few seconds later, officials barred Miles and Hulme from proceeding, and victory garlands were handed to Amon and McLaren. *Revs Institute / Max LeGrand Photograph Collection*

American bothered to tell him anything about what was going on. He didn't realize that he'd won the race until he and McLaren reached the rostrum. Holding their victory garlands, Amon and McLaren wore smiles that looked tentative, if not sheepish—not the expression you'd expect on the faces of drivers who'd scored the biggest win of their careers. The only person who looked positively elated was Henry Ford II, who was oblivious to the machinations that had just decided the finish. All he knew was that it was payback time, and revenge was sweet indeed.

Miles eventually was cajoled into joining Amon, McLaren, and Henry Ford II for the celebration, and he quaffed a flute of champagne through gritted teeth. After the race, Ford was excoriated by critics who felt that faceless bureaucrats had botched what should have been—and was—a glorious moment in American motorsports. Conspiracy theories abound to explain what went wrong. The most elaborate was promoted by factory engineer Bob Negstad, who insisted that a Ford official petitioned the ACO to dock Miles a lap to make sure he didn't win the race. Like most conspiracy theories, this one requires a gigantic leap of faith.

To begin with, it would have required the acquiescence—and inexplicable silence—of a large number of people with conflicting interests and no love for Ford. And why, exactly would Ford have done this? Because Miles was an Englishman, as if it was somehow better for the race to be won by two guys from New Zealand? Others believe that Ford was afraid that, by winning the triple crown of endurance racing—Daytona, Sebring, and Le Mans—Miles would have been showered with the publicity that Ford wanted to monopolize for the company. This overlooks the inconvenient fact that there was no triple crown at the time because Daytona was relatively new to the schedule and both it and Sebring were far less prestigious than the classic European races at Spa, Monza, and the Nürburgring. Anyway, winning Le Mans didn't come with enough glory then or now to make a driver famous. Gregory, the Kansas City Flash, had won the race the previous year, and most Americans would have had a hard time recognizing his name, much less picking him out of a police lineup.

Most conspiracy theories are based on the assumption that Beebe was a villain who held a grudge against Miles. There's no denying that Miles didn't suffer fools gladly and made enemies easily. But there was

Ford win ad
from 1966
Le Mans
spotlights
the victorious
McLaren/Amon
Mark II while
omitting the
controversy
about the finish.
*John Gabrial
Collection*

no bad blood between them. "I loved Ken Miles dearly," Beebe said.[64] "It was purely pragmatic. Ken wanted to play a little, and we felt he was endangering our chances of winning—including his own. So we pulled him in and slowed him down. We had to." Beebe never second-guessed or deflected responsibility for his decision. "To have Ken win would have been more expedient and more popular," he admitted. "But the extent to which McLaren and Amon had played exactly according to our rules militated against Miles."

Another popular take holds that McLaren goosed the throttle at the last instant to steal a victory that belonged to Miles. Alternatively, some people contend that Miles purposely backed off to signal his contempt for Ford's clumsy effort to stage-manage the finish. The evidence for both arguments are photos of the sodden conclusion of the race, which clearly show McLaren a few feet ahead of Miles when the flag was thrown. But Miles said later that the actual finish line, marked by an electronic timing wire, was ten yards before the spot where the flag was waved. "At the start-finish line, I believe we were side by side," he said. "Certainly, having been ordered by Ford to do this, we made a serious effort to do it."[65]

Shelby was conspicuous by his absence after the race. He later said he felt remorse for his failure to stand up for Miles when Beebe and company were deciding how to choreograph the finish. "I've regretted it ever since," he said, "but I went along with what they wanted."[66] This mea culpa, however heartfelt, struck some cynics as too little, too late. As Brock Yates wrote caustically in *Car and Driver*, "Shelby was later to say wistfully, 'I would have given fifty thousand dollars to have Ken win.' All it would have taken was a pit signal."[67]

Not true, really. And truly unfair. Shelby wasn't calling the shots at Le Mans, any more than Miles or McLaren were. What Shelby may have regretted more than anything was that he, too, had become a cog in the Ford corporate machine. A month after the race, Miles sat for a radio interview and talked about his obligations as a Ford factory driver. "They're running the cars. It's their money. They're paying the piper, they can call the tune," he said. "I'll do what they tell me to. I don't necessarily like it, but I'll do it."[68]

The muddled and unsatisfying finish left a bad taste in the mouths of both the winners and the losers. "You think about the decision now, and it seems kind of dumb, but we've all done a lot of dumb things in our lives before," Passino admitted later.[69] "It's one of those things that happens, but we were trying to control our destiny, and looking back, maybe we should have done it differently." But how? Whatever Ford did or didn't do, the result was going to be two enormously unhappy drivers. The only question was which two drivers were they going to be?

Two days after the race, Ford invited the media to an elaborate, champagne-soaked victory banquet at Le Chanteclair, the elegant French restaurant in midtown Manhattan run by retired Grand Prix driver René Dreyfus. A gigantic enlargement of the photo finish had been mounted on the wall behind the head table, where the drivers were seated. Nobody wanted to be there; all they wanted to do was go home. As Beebe delivered a tedious speech awkwardly trying to put a positive

The controversial finish at Le Mans in 1966, with McLaren in the dark car next to Miles in the light one and Dick Hutcherson bringing up the rear. McLaren and co-driver Amon were awarded the win not because they were ahead at the finish but because they started the race about twenty-five feet behind Miles and Denny Hulme. Therefore, officials ruled, Amon and McLaren had covered more ground than Hulme and Miles. *Ford Motor Company*

spin on the results, the blown-up photo fell off the wall and engulfed the drivers. "It was a funny night," Ford PR man Paul Preuss said later.[70] "I was so tired that my memory is still kind of a blur. All I know is that it did not go according to Hoyle. And when this crazy picture fell down over the head table, it was the straw that broke the camel's back."

Most people figured that Ford would cancel the Le Mans program after the one-two-three finish. Henry Ford II had underwritten the project with a single goal in mind—to beat Ferrari. Mission accomplished. At LAX, there was a schedule taped to the office outside the race shop listing the dates of upcoming races and test sessions. After Le Mans, one wag had scrawled, "See you at the employment office." But the Deuce had other plans. Jazzed by winning Le Mans, he stunned his underlings—and just everybody else—by declaring ebulliently, "We'll be back next year."[71]

By winning Daytona, Sebring, and Le Mans, Ford had already amassed enough points to clinch the World Sportscar Championship, so it was decided to spend the remainder of the season developing the cars in preparation for 1967. Two months after the disappointment at Le Mans, Miles was testing an experimental semi-automatic gearbox in the J-Car at Riverside. It felt like an oven, with an unforgiving sun beating down and heat waves eddying up from the pavement. Miles's son, Peter, was there, practicing parallel parking in a borrowed rental car. "I heard my dad driving around the track," he said.[72] "On that last lap, it seemed like he was working the car really hard, and it sounded like he was doing power slides. Then it got quiet. I happened to look down at Turn Nine and saw a fireball flying through the air."

Several Shelby American crew members were there by the time Peter arrived at the crash. The car was still burning. "Can't we get him out of the car?" the teenager asked.

"He's not in the car," Smith told him.

Miles lay crumpled on the ground about twelve feet from the smoldering remains of the J-Car. His helmet was next to him. Witnesses said that car had been going about 100 mph in the brake zone for Turn Nine when the wheels locked. The car pirouetted around, left the track broadside, vaulted over an embankment, and cartwheeled several times. Miles was ejected on the third rotation. He died at the scene of massive head trauma.

The cause of the accident was never determined, though there was no lack of speculation. The brakes or the transmission might have locked up. Some observers thought the honeycomb-aluminum structure literally came apart. Others suspected that aerodynamic instability was the cause or that an upright broke. Nobody thought Miles was to blame. He was the third driver to die in a Ford prototype in five months. His loss was the low point in the history of Shelby American and gruesome proof that the costs in racing aren't calculated in dollars and cents alone.

While the team focused on the mission to win Le Mans, the inaugural Trans-Am season was unfolding without any direct involvement from Shelby American other than building and selling cars for customers. This wasn't yet the celebrated series that would feature epic battles between Boss 302 Mustangs, Chevrolet Camaros, AMC Javelins, and Dodge

Challengers, along with fenders being banged by Donohue, Gurney, Parnelli Jones, and George Follmer. The races of 1966 were modestly attended enduros lasting from four to twelve hours, and the entry lists included Saab 96s, Volvo 122s, and Renault Gordinis. Privately owned Mustangs won three of the first six races of the year, but a Dodge Dart had won twice and a Plymouth Barracuda once. Going into the final race at Riverside in September, the manufacturers' championship was a toss-up between Ford and Chrysler. At the last second, Ford asked Shelby to race a factory Trans-Am Mustang to secure the title.

The problem was, there *was* no factory Trans-Am Mustang. Shelby had been so determined to minimize his investment in the program that, after Cantwell built and tested the prototype, Shelby told him to sell it. Now, with Ford's backing, Shelby told Cantwell to prep an unsold customer race car for Riverside. Titus was the obvious choice to drive the car. He justified his selection by qualifying on the pole after only three laps of practice, shattering the lap record for sedans by a full second.

The four-hour race was scheduled to start Le Mans style on the back straight. To ensure that the engine would catch cleanly, mechanic Ron Sampson stabbed the gas pedal a few times to prime the carburetor. But when he shut down the electric fuel pumps, they sucked the fuel out of the engine. When the race started and Titus turned the ignition key, the engine cranked but refused to light. By the time Titus got going, he was dead last. No problem. After eight laps, he was already in the lead and disappearing fast. But with a bit more than an hour to go, while passing a backmarker in the Esses, he drifted wide and ran over one of the half-buried tires that Riverside used in lieu of guardrails. When Titus tried to straddle it, the tire ripped off the oil filter. "I drove it two miles back to the pits with absolutely no oil pressure, figuring that'd finish it," Titus said.[73]

Trailing white smoke, Titus braked to a stop and climbed out of the car, sure it was Game Over. While Titus sparked a cigarette, Sampson—working without gloves—yanked off what was left of the old oil filter and fitted a new one. Schwarz dumped in four quarts of oil, just guessing at how much the engine really needed. Titus climbed back in the car and hustled back onto the track. By lap ninety-five, he'd retaken the lead, and he held it for the next forty laps. Lew Spencer called it "the cheapest championship Ford ever bought."[74] Better still, the victory at Riverside persuaded Ford to hire Shelby American to run a full-on Trans-Am Mustang program in 1967. The Trans-Am series would become a major part of Shelby's racing portfolio for the next three years.

But if the fall of 1966 opened up a new vista for Shelby American, it also marked the end of an era. While 427 Cobras continued to dominate SCCA A Production racing, winning on Sunday didn't translate into sales on Monday. Shelby made a few half-hearted attempts to gin up interest in the street cars. About thirty cars were shipped with less voluptuous rear fenders, but these so-called narrow-hipped 427s didn't set the marketplace on fire, and AC quickly reverted to the original bodywork. Four Cobras were equipped at LAX with automatic transmissions, but they, too, failed to move the needle.

Still, the 427 could have soldiered on indefinitely, selling in dribs and drabs, if the bulk of the Federal Motor Vehicle Safety Standards hadn't been scheduled to go into effect on January 1, 1968. Among other requirements, the new regulations demanded that cars be equipped with shoulder belts, collapsible steering columns and other features that would allow occupants to survive a 30-mph head-on collision. "I was

Ford wasn't interested in the inaugural Trans-Am series in 1966—until it looked like Mopar might claim the manufacturers' title. At the last minute, Shelby was commissioned to run a Mustang at Riverside. Chuck Cantwell pulled a customer Trans-Am car off the line, and Titus was tabbed to drive it. Despite a kerfuffle at the start and a mishap during the race, he romped home first and made Ford a champion. *Ford Motor Company*

the guy who had to go in and tell Carroll we couldn't build the Cobra anymore," Fred Goodell said.[75] "It was one of the hardest things I've ever had to do in my life. Because he loved that car."

Goodell was a top Ford technocrat who'd joined Shelby American as chief engineer in October 1966, mostly to ride herd on the Mustang programs. Although he didn't come from the high-performance car milieu, he understood what the Cobra stood for. One of his first acts after moving to LAX was to put the kibosh on selling 427 Cobras with 428-cubic-inch Police Interceptor engines. When the finance guys complained, he told them, "Hell, why don't you guys use 352s—they're even cheaper yet!"[76]

By 1966, Shelby American was selling accessories through a hefty catalog. What's weird about this ad is that it mentions the Mark II winning Le Mans in 1966 yet shows a GT40 that failed to win at Daytona in 1965. *John Gabrial Collection*

179

Goodell investigated the possibility of updating the 427 to meet the new standards, but it didn't take long for him to realize that the car was simply too antiquated to be modernized successfully. "It would not pass anything," he said. "It wouldn't pass front-end crash, head swing or rollover; the door locks were no good. . . . There wasn't anything on the car we could fix—it was just too far gone. That's why we decided to go with a completely new car."[77]

The all-new car, code-named Cobra III, turned out to be an unfortunate one-and-done flop that barely merits a footnote in the Shelby American saga. The last 427 Cobra, CSX3360, was billed by AC Cars on December 14, 1966. Hardly anybody noticed. Believe it or not, unsold 427s were still languishing on new-car lots as late as August 1968, almost two years after being shipped to LA. Total production of the 427 was 343 units, this on top of the 655 leaf-spring 289s that had been built previously.

As of January 1, 1967, Shelby American was out of the Cobra business. Before the year was over, the company would be out of business altogether.

CHAPTER SIX

VICTORY AND DEFEAT

1967

Racing is the ultimate just-in-time proposition. The annals of motorsports are rife with tales of race cars that were literally being buttoned up as they were being loaded on the trailer for their first event. Shelby American embodied this ethos with almost perfect fidelity. Time and time again, race car debuts were prefaced by insane thrashes. "The overtime was crazy," Bernie Kretzschmar said.[1] "We'd go into the evening six days a week, some nights going home at midnight. For the big races, it was seven days a week." The pace was even more frenetic at the racetrack, where Phil Remington famously, and repeatedly, improvised instant solutions under preposterous time pressure. And Remington wasn't the only one adept at cut-and-paste engineering. As Ken Miles once put it, "We don't have to go through elaborate procedures of putting through formal design changes. If we decide we don't like something, we take a hacksaw and cut it off."[2]

But building production cars by the thousands requires not only a different strategy but also a different mindset. Designs have to be set in stone months before the assembly line gears up. Budgets have to be finalized, parts ordered, paint colors selected. Hard deadlines are established, and if they aren't met, the large and complex machine grinds to an expensive halt. American cars typically started reaching showrooms during September of the prior model year, so Job One—production of the first sellable car—was usually slated for no later than August. There's a long tradition of pulling all-nighters to finish a race car at the last second. But that's not a feasible business model for big-time carmakers with millions of dollars on the line.

Ford had generally been content to let Shelby operate as the sovereign monarch of his plucky little empire in Los Angeles. But with production of Shelby Mustangs expected to rise above three thousand units during the 1967 model year, Ford wanted more control over the mavericks at LAX. Ford exec John Kerr was brought in as general manager after Peyton Cramer left to buy Dana Chevrolet, which had its own well-known high-performance department. Another Ford import was chief engineer Fred Goodell, who knew nothing about racing and very little about sports cars when he joined Shelby American. But he understood how the industry worked. "I never met anyone who knew more about automobiles—inside and out—than Fred Goodell," designer John Chun said. [3] Shelby also recognized that Goodell could bring a more rigorous brand of discipline to the production-car business. "You know, Freddie," he told Goodell, "I think we got too many fuckin' racers around here. See what you can do to straighten it all out."[4]

The new Shelby Mustang promised to be especially challenging because Ford was introducing an all-new version of its original pony car for the 1967 model year. On the other hand, this gave the crew at Shelby American a chance to address a gripe they'd been hearing for years—that other than hard-core car guys, nobody could tell a GT350 from a spiffed-up Mustang. "So in 1967," Chuck Cantwell said, "there was a definite emphasis on appearance and in doing as many things as possible to make the cars look better."[5]

Ford stylist Charlie McHose, an Art Center grad, arrived from Dearborn in May 1966. His first assignment was to design a paint scheme for Shelby's DC-3. But after that, he was flat out on the GT350. He quickly hired not one but two clay modelers and set up shop in a studio on the mezzanine of the east hangar, above the 427 Cobra assembly area. Two bodies, one steel and the other fiberglass, were forklifted up to the second floor, then turned on their sides and manhandled through several offices before being deposited in the studio. By July, McHose wrote in a memo to Ray Geddes, he and the clay modelers were camped out in their lair seven days a week, twelve to sixteen hours a day. The next month, he felt compelled to explain in another memo to his boss in Dearborn why they hadn't worked the previous Sunday: "We had worked sixteen days straight, so it was suggested by Mr. Shelby that we take a day off."[6]

At Shelby's direction, McHose lengthened the hood, which gave the car a sleeker and much racier look than the stock Mustang. McHose was also inspired by the Mark IIs being fettled next door in the west hangar to add boy racer touches like a giant scoop in the quarter panel window—although it looked like a brake scoop, it actually extracted air from the cockpit—and an elegant ducktail spoiler. Other graceful touches include a stylishly integrated scoop in the fiberglass hood, Mercury Cougar taillights and a steering wheel made of actual wood. Visually, the car was a bull's-eye.

Because the new Mustang was being built on a larger platform, it could now accommodate a big-block engine. The possibilities weren't lost on Cantwell. Long before Shelby American got its hands on one of the next-gen Mustangs, he ordered Jerry Schwarz to lead the complicated "front-end reconstruction" necessary to squeeze a side-oiler 427 into an unsold R-Model GT350.[7] Cantwell tested it at Willow Springs, where, he said, "It was better than I expected."[8] The car was then shipped to Michigan, where, Cantwell was told, it turned a faster lap on Ford's handling track than any car other than a Mark II driven by Dan Gurney. Unfortunately, though the surgery was a success, the patient died, which is to say that the retail price of a Mustang, even a Shelby-ized Mustang, couldn't justify the cost of a race motor.

Still, everybody was sold on the concept of a big-block option. So instead of a 427, the car would get the Police Interceptor 428-cubic-inch engine. Like the rest of the car, it was a good-looking piece, topped with a Cobra-branded cast-aluminum air cleaner top and valve covers. Fitted with hydraulic lifters and twin 600 CFM Holleys on top of an aluminum intake manifold, it made 355 horsepower and 420 lb-ft of torque. The new model was named the GT500, not because "500" actually stood for anything but to denote that it was the GT350's bigger brother. Well, that and because size matters, and Ford wanted to make sure buyers understood that the engine packed more cubic inches than GM's 427 and Chrysler's 426 Hemi.

Despite all the planning, the build was the production cycle from hell. When the fiberglass hoods, scoops, deck lids, and nosepieces started arriving at LAX, Jack Khoury and his production team discovered to their horror that they fit worse than wooden dentures. The problem wasn't the vendors. It was that the body McHose used for the styling buck had been bent during earlier inertia-reel seat-belt tests. Originally, the team thought the damage was limited to the rear but, no, it turned out that the entire unibody had been tweaked. "That's why every 1967 Shelby Mustang had the left side of the hood sticking up a half-inch," McHose said.[9] "All those hoods were cockeyed when they were built." Hoods weren't the only problem. "When they built the cars, they had to really loosen everything up and readjust the whole front-end assembly," Cantwell said.[10] "It was murder trying to get cars off the line."

Eventually, better-fitting parts were produced, and the pace—and quality—of production improved. But the headaches caused by the fit issues had profound long-term effects on the Mustang operation. Ford already had questions about Shelby American's ability to handle the program, especially since the production numbers were expected to climb even higher during the 1968 model year. The lease at LAX was due to expire in the fall of 1967, so a new facility would again have to be found and outfitted. It was clear that the fiberglass vendors in Southern California weren't equipped to fill large-scale orders. Kerr opened a dialogue with executives at A. O. Smith Corporation in Ionia, Michigan, which had for many years supplied fiberglass bodies to Chevrolet for the Corvette. The company had recently lost the Corvette contract, and it was eager to find a new customer. It wasn't long before the folks at Ford started wondering if it might be cheaper and easier to build the cars closer to home.

But that was a discussion for another day. To reduce costs in Southern California, numerous performance items that had been standard in 1966 were axed in 1967—traction bars, Pitman and idler arms, tubular steel exhausts, cast-aluminum oil pans, three-inch racing seat belts. Even the plexiglass quarter window disappeared. Because it was closer to stock than previous iterations, the new GT350 was $433 less than the old one, and the big-block 1967 GT500 was cheaper than a small-block 1966 GT350. The cars also looked racy, but they were more show than go. While this offended purists, the softer ride and more luxurious appointments greatly extended the reach of the Shelby Mustangs. "It is a substantially better and more practical machine, without compromise in the performance area," Jerry Titus wrote about the GT350 in *Sport Car Graphic*.[11] In the same review, he called the GT500 "surprisingly good," which was something less than a rave. *Road & Track* also damned the car with faint praise. After questioning the optimistic quarter-mile times quoted by the factory, the reviewer wrote, "As for handling, the GT500 is something less than we've come to expect from Shelby's cars but still very good in comparison to the typical American sedan."[12]

The new-for-1967 GT350 was probably Shelby American's most successful compromise between show and go. The model year also brought the debut of the even more popular GT500, packing a 428-cubic-inch V-8, which, despite the extra cubic inch, was far less impressive than a full-tilt 427 race motor. In this ad, Ford touted the cars' FPM, or fun per mile. "For more FPM," the copywriter suggested, "see your Shelby dealer PDQ." *Ford Motor Company*

want
more

F.P.M.?*

try a Shelby GT

*That's Fun-Per-Mile—yours aplenty in these two great new GT cars from Shelby American.

There's more F.P.M. when you have reserve performance. The GT 350 carries a 306 horsepower 289 cubic inch V-8. The GT 500 is powered by the 428 cubic inch V-8, descended from the 1966 LeMans winning Ford GT.

The F.P.M. is higher when steering is competition-quick, suspension is firm. Driving's *fun* with the safety of an integral roll bar, shoulder harnesses, disc front and drum rear brakes, wide-path 4-ply nylon tires.

Driving's fun with the Shelby brand of comfort and style. For more F.P.M., see your Shelby dealer P.D.Q.

SHELBY G.T. 350 and 500 **The Road Cars** *Powered by* Ford

Shelby American, Inc., 6501 W. Imperial Highway, Los Angeles 90009

Sales were brisk, by specialty-car standards. Total production was 3,225 for the year, with the more expensive GT500 accounting for nearly two-thirds of the sales. But these numbers had been achieved by transforming what had once been an authentic sports car into a grand touring machine. "No more wham-bam, thank-you-ma'am," *Car and Driver* wrote, somewhat disapprovingly.[13] The magazine sounded a note of skepticism when Shelby, creator of the legendary Cobra, declared in a paroxysm of PR speak: "This is the first car I'm really proud of."[14] Which prompted *Car and Driver* to write sarcastically: "Right. We've come a long way since bib overalls too, Shel."

In retrospect, this assessment seems unreasonably harsh. Yes, the GT500 came perilously close to poseur territory. But the GT350 offered a neatly calibrated combination of looks, practicality, and performance— the sports car as daily driver. Nevertheless, among the self-appointed keepers of the flame, there was a palpable sense that, with the new cars, Shelby had sold out.

The GT500 was the first product to come out of Shelby American with no racing aspirations whatsoever. And as the 1967 models were being developed, the company hadn't planned to race a Mustang either. Ford was getting into Trans-Am in a big way, but the company wanted Shelby to focus on the Le Mans program, and the stock-car champions within the racing department were able to steer the business to NASCAR mainstay Bud Moore. Tough, crafty, and crusty, Moore had earned four Purple Hearts while fighting on D-Day and in the Battle of the Bulge before becoming one of the most creative and successful team owners on the stock-car scene. He would be representing Ford Motor Company with a fleet of Cougars, Mercury's upscale version of the Mustang. The cars and their high-profile drivers, Gurney and Parnelli Jones, were introduced at a swanky press event in Carmel in November 1966.

Shelby American, it seemed, had been left out in the cold. But once again, Geddes came to the rescue, finagling a deal to get the SoCal gang back in the game. Naturally, it helped that the team had secured the championship for Ford the year before with Titus's win at Riverside. Even so, Don Frey had to intercede personally shortly before Christmas to get three notchback Mustangs shipped from San Jose to LAX so they could be prepped for the opening race at Daytona, only five weeks away. Ultimately, Shelby American would build twenty-five Trans-Am-eligible Mustangs in 1967. Four of them were campaigned as factory cars; the rest were sold to privateers. "We were the backdoor team, not the official team," said Lew Spencer who managed the operation.[15] "We didn't have any of the trick stuff, and we did everything on our own."

Shelby hired Titus to drive his lead car. He was an unconventional choice. Titus was still working at *Sports Car Graphic*, and he'd be racing against no-quarter-given pros including Jones, Gurney, Mark Donohue, and David Pearson. Titus maintained a poker face when Shelby offered to pay him $1,000 per race, plus expenses and 50 percent of the prize money. The package was like winning the lottery. The instant Titus stepped out of Shelby's office and closed the door behind him, he yelped with bottled-up joy. The Trans-Am gig enabled him to quit his job as an editor and purse racing full time, and his gritty performances in 1967 proved that Shelby had made the right call. To race the second car, Shelby negotiated a deal with Grady Davis, the vice president of Gulf Oil, who put Dick Thompson—The Flying Dentist—behind the wheel. Both machines were supported by the crew in the west hangar at LAX, with engines provided by John Dunn, who later went into business with another ex-Shelby employee, Ryan Falconer.

The cars were finished in time to be shaken down at Willow Springs, where Cantwell—who was serving as the team engineer—was a tick faster than Titus. But the timeline was so tight that the Mustangs arrived at Daytona still painted Wimbledon White and carrying virtually no graphics other than race numbers. Because Bud Moore Engineering was the "official" team, Ford tried (not very successfully) to camouflage its association with Shelby American, so Titus's car was entered by Dallas attorney David Witts. He and Shelby owned a vast tract of arid wasteland near the desolate Southwest Texas ghost town of Terlingua, which was said to be home to seven Texans, nine goats, and two burros. The two of them often flew down there on Shelby's DC-3 with like-minded merrymakers for weekend bacchanals of drinking and off-road motorcycling. Later that year, it was the site of the first World Championship Chili Cook-off. As an inside joke, they named their Trans-Am operation the Terlingua Racing Team.

The 1967 season opened at Daytona, not just for Trans-Am but also for the World Sportscar Championship. With two Trans-Am cars and three Ford GTs on hand, plenty of Shelby American crewmen were in town, and they had access to plenty of rental cars. Racers have long had a love-hate relationship with rental-car companies. That is to say, racers love rental cars while rental-car companies hate racers. There are endless stories about rental-car street races gone awry and drivers who are personae non gratae at various rental-car agencies. The most famous tale of all involves Augie Pabst driving a Ford Falcon rented from Hertz into the swimming pool at the Mark Thomas Inn in Monterey to win a $100 bet with Roger Penske. (Pabst stripped down to his skivvies beforehand, and his teammate, Walt Hansgen, had to dive in afterward to retrieve his suitcase from the trunk.)

At Daytona, a dozen Shelby American mechanics piled into a rented Ford LTD station wagon driven on the beach by Charlie Agapiou. When he finally got the wagon up to speed, he cranked the wheel and threw the transmission into park to spin the car. This went over so well that he did it several more times. Only the weight of a dozen occupants, laughing uproariously, kept the station wagon upright. "The next morning, the car wouldn't move from the parking lot," Kretzschmar said.[16] "We had to get another one. The transmission had been turned to junk."

In the Trans-Am race, Gurney and Jones locked out the front row in their red Cougars, with Titus third on the grid and Donohue next to him in a Sunoco-blue Penske Camaro. Jones and Donohue banged doors early on, a scenario that would be repeated on countless occasions over the next four years. Titus powered into the lead, but he tangled with a pokey Porsche in the infield and tweaked the right rear fender enough to cause the tire to rub. At 160 miles per hour, while the car was fully loaded on the banking, the tire disintegrated. Although the car started to spin, Titus made an amazing save, and he hammered sideways around the banking like a drift king with the bare wheel sparking against the pavement. Kretzschmar hustled back to the garage to grab the cutting torches and was thrilled to get a lift back to the pits from a passing golf cart, whose driver just happened to be track owner Bill France. After the damage was repaired, Titus roared back onto the track. Second verse same as the first. After another tire failure and another 160-mph near-spin on the banking, the crew used the torch to cut a larger fender opening. Titus finished fourth, a lap down. Thompson was leading shortly before half distance when a wrist pin broke and a rod ventilated the engine block. "I should have won that damn race," he said.[17]

The day after the Trans-Am race, Daytona was also the site of the twenty-four-hour enduro marking the start of Ford's campaign to defend its Le Mans title. Alan Mann had been rendered redundant as Ford decided to give Shelby and John Holman equal shares of the prototype program. The cars had been rechristened Mark IIBs after punishing off-season development that didn't produce any radical changes but made everything incrementally better. Ford waltzed into the new season fat, dumb, and happy, expecting an effortless replay of the previous year's undefeated season. Enzo Ferrari had a different scenario in mind.

The J-Car was the lightweight, all-American, honeycomb-aluminum prototype that had been built by Kar-Kraft to replace the GT40. Driven here by McLaren, it turned the quickest lap during the Le Mans Test Day in 1966. But several drivers were spooked by the handling, and the car looked strange, hence its nickname—the Breadvan. The J-Car's stock fell even further after Miles was killed testing it at Riverside two months after Le Mans. *Ford Motor Company*

After suffering through an uncharacteristically down year in 1966, Ferrari had commissioned a new prototype built around a lovely twin-cam 4.0-liter V-12 making 450 horsepower. The car was down about 40 horses to the Mark IIB, but it was nearly one thousand pounds lighter, and it cornered like a dream. Gurney squeaked out a pole lap by bolting on a set of super-sticky gumball tires, but the Ferraris were right there with him, and so was Jim Hall's new Chaparral 2F, with its gigantic driver-adjustable rear wing. Ford brought six Mark IIBs—three each for Shelby American and Holman & Moody. None of them were fast enough to keep up. Even worse, all of them were victimized by roasted transmissions, which kept getting swapped out until the team ran out of spares. "We got so good at changing transmissions that we were doing it in less than twenty-five minutes," Bill Eaton said.[18] The smart-asses later claimed that the little red wagon used to carry trannies between the pits and paddock logged more miles than the race cars. Only the Bruce McLaren/Lucien Bianchi car finished, slowed by a blown head gasket and using a gearbox that had been salvaged from a J-Car sitting on a transporter.

Phil Hill crashed while his Chaparral was way in front, allowing Ferraris to finish one-two-three en route to executing the picture-perfect finish that Ford had flubbed at Le Mans the previous June. Chris Amon, who'd decamped from Ford to join Ferrari, added insult to injury when describing his race-winning P4. "It's beautiful," he said. "By comparison, the Ford Mark II is a truck."[19] Ouch! Ford later traced the gearbox failures to improperly heat-treated output shafts—provided by a vendor—that snapped under load.

But fragile gearboxes were the least of Ford's concerns. The bigger issue was that the Mark IIBs had been outpaced in a straight-up fight, and after six months of solid development, the teams had run out of ideas to make the cars significantly faster. Which was an existential problem. Ford had always gone to Le Mans confident that it would win if its cars made it to the finish. Now, the company was looking at the very real possibility of having to rely on reliability as the key to victory, and that didn't look like a good bet after the debacle at Daytona. As happened so many times when Shelby American needed a quick fix, Remington was the man with a plan. The week after the race, he, Eaton, and painter/

body man Dennis Ercek hopped on a plane at LAX and embarked on one of the most remarkable makeovers in racing history.

Although the J-Car was the obvious alternative to the Mark IIB, it came with a lot of baggage. Ford management wasn't entirely sold on the car, which had never been conclusively faster than the Mark II, and at Shelby American, a lot of guys blamed it for Miles's fatal accident. But unlike Shelby, who thought the J-Car was a colossal waste of time and money, Remington's only complaint about the car was that the boxy bodywork was "really draggy."[20] So at the Kar-Kraft facility in Brighton, Michigan, where the J-Cars had been built, he, Eaton, and Ercek performed cosmetic surgery.

"We took the old body off and saved the center section, which had the doors and the windshield," Remington said.[21] "We had about three guys from Ford Styling helping us. We built the thing up with plaster and eyeballed it until it looked right." Eaton confirmed Remington's recollections. "We did the work entirely by eye—no drawings, nothing" he said.[22] "The nose was created with welding rods and tubes. We knew the tail was about a foot or a foot and a half too long, so Phil built it in such a way that it could be unzipped and shortened in the wind tunnel."

While leaving the center section unchanged, Remington and his team dramatically reshaped the rest of the car. The blunt front end got a sleek new nose while the flat bread van tail was replaced with a rear deck that sloped gracefully down from the cockpit. After a week of day-and-night labor, the mockup was hauled into the Ford wind tunnel and tested. At 120 mph, it generated one hundred pounds less drag than the J-Car, confirming empirically what the Shelby American guys knew by intuition. "Phil Remington designed the car inside his mental wind tunnel," said Mario Andretti, who would win his first major endurance race in Remington's creation.[23]

A female mold was made off the mockup, and a fiberglass body was laid up at Ford Styling. This was bolted back on the J-Car chassis, and it was shipped to Ford's proving grounds in Arizona for a head-to-head comparison with a Mark IIB. After adding an unobtrusive rear spoiler to generate some downforce, the modified J-Car topped out at 215.62 mph, four mph faster than the Mark II. The car was then shipped to Shelby American. "We took a splash off of that and made our own bodies,"

Remington recalled.[24] "We changed the inlets to get the air a little bit better to the carburetors, and we put two little spoilers at the edge of the radiator exits to keep the air from washing off to the side. Those were about the only modifications we made."

The updated J-Car was designated the Mark IV. Ford decided to use the upcoming 12 Hours of Sebring as a gong show between old and new cars. Shelby American sent its Mark IV, now painted bright yellow, for Andretti and McLaren. Holman & Moody had a lone Mark IIB to be driven by A. J. Foyt and Lloyd Ruby.

After the debacle at Daytona, there were no rental cars for the mechanics, so they were reduced to hitching a ride back to their hotel

A week after the Mark IIBs got shellacked at Daytona in 1967, Remington flew to Kar-Kraft and redesigned the J-Car's bodywork by using what Mario Andretti called "his mental wind tunnel." The car was then tested in Ford's actual wind tunnel. Here, Remington looks over his handiwork with (from left) Ford's Homer Perry and Mountain, the engineer who'd come up with the original idea for building a monocoque out of honeycomb-aluminum. *Ford Motor Company*

with Foyt. Driving a rented Ford Galaxie, he pulled up at a stoplight behind a Corvette convertible. When the light turned green, the Corvette stayed put. Foyt lightly tapped his horn. The driver in front gave him the finger and refused to move. Not a wise decision. Foyt leaped out of the car, ran over to the Corvette, and grabbed the driver by the scruff of the neck. But before Foyt could do any damage, the driver mashed the throttle, forcing Foyt to let go and ripping his Rolex off his wrist. After picking up the watch, Foyt sprinted back to the Galaxie, threw it into gear and bombed through red lights as he chased the 'Vette. The Corvette veered down a side street, hoping to escape, only to find it was a cul de sac. Foyt pitched his car sideways and screeched broadside to a halt, blocking the road. The guy in the Corvette jumped out of the car with a beer bottle, which he proceeded to break and brandish at Foyt. Ignoring the jagged glass, Foyt marched over and bopped the guy in the nose—hard. He went down in a heap, bleedingly profusely. Lights winked on in the houses nearby, and police cruisers rolled up with sirens blaring. "They took all of us to jail," mechanic Ron Butler recalled.[25] "Shelby had to bail us out."

This turned out to be the highlight of Foyt's weekend. In the Mark IVs' first outing, McLaren claimed the pole, 5.6 seconds faster than the Mark IIB. Come race day, the high-wing Chaparral of Phil Hill and Mike Spence ran the Mark IV tough for seven hours, but after it broke, Andretti and McLaren cakewalked home, miles ahead of Foyt and Ruby. The Mark IV won its first race out of the box and, in so doing, demoted the Mark IIB to also-ran status. Ford ordered Kar-Kraft to immediately start building four more Mark IVs. Because that was the car, Ford realized, that could beat Ferrari and win Le Mans.

Sebring also marked the second race on the Trans-Am schedule. Since Daytona, the Shelby American Mustang had been painted pale yellow. Nobody's sure who picked the color, but it's generally accepted that Shelby's boon companion, Bill Neale, deserved credit for the name: Gawd-Awful Yellow.

A Dallas advertising executive by trade, Neale was also a terrific graphic and fine artist with a special knack for painting images that captured the essence of the motorsports experience. He and Shelby shared East Texas roots, stints as military aviators during World War II and an affinity for spinning yarns with a sly sense of humor. According to legend, Shelby—who was a serial divorcé—once asked Neale to fly to California on short notice to serve as his best man. "Shelby, I've got a card game," Neale drawled. "I'll be best man at your next wedding." Neale designed the ornate shield that served as the Terlingua Racing Team logo—a jackrabbit holding up its right foot. The three feathers below the rabbit, he explained to Shelby, represented the three Indian tribes whose three languages, or *tres lingues*, gave the town its name, while "1860" referred to the year of the first race in the region, between mercury-ore wagons pulled by six-mule teams.

"Neale," Shelby said, "that's a hell of a story. Where did you find it?"

"Shelby," Neale said, "I didn't read it in a book. I made it up!"

Titus grabbed the pole in his Gawd-Awful Yellow Mustang, but he expected the fiercely combative Jones, who'd qualified next to him, to try a Hail Mary pass to get by on the first lap. Before the race, Titus confided to Cantwell, "I think I know where I can get Parnelli."[26]

Sure enough, halfway through the first lap, Titus went deeper than usual in the brake zone for the hairpin before throwing out the anchor, and Jones flew off the track trying to out-brake him. Titus was three hundred yards clear down the backstretch, and nobody came close to him thereafter. Donohue was the only driver on the lead lap, and Thompson finished third. The plot for the rest of the season was established: If Titus didn't run into trouble, he was unbeatable.

Green Valley was a racetrack where he found trouble—lots of it. The headaches began when Titus rolled his Mustang during qualifying. The roof was caved in almost down to the steering wheel, and the rest of the car was boogered up so badly that an insurance adjuster would have totaled it on the spot. Shelby found a local Ford dealer who was willing to provide access to a body shop and a new Mustang to use as a parts car. "We took off the fender, the door, and the windshield, and we porta-powered the roof up and dropped the windshield in," Kretzschmar said.[27] "We painted it at about four o'clock in the morning, lined up the front end, went back to the hotel, slept for two hours, and went to the track. We would do anything for Jerry."

The four-hour race was held during a fiendishly hot Texas broiler. Gurney later said it took him two weeks to recover from the race, and he's the guy who won it! After winning the qualifying race to make the feature, Titus started last and quickly rocketed to the front. But the crew hadn't had time to install the quarter window panel, which he usually turned sideways to funnel air into the cockpit. Without any ventilation, Titus was getting roasted like a Thanksgiving turkey. He stopped twice so Schwarz could dump buckets of water on him, and mechanic Ron Sampson used an air chisel to punch a hole in the roof, but Titus was beyond help.

A faux classified ad showing the mangled car appeared in *Sports Car Graphic*. "Very low mileage. Driven only on weekends by conservative magazine editor. Absolutely no highway miles. Color is beautiful tequila yellow with mesquite black trim."[28] Cantwell later took the repaired car directly to Willow Springs. After one very slow lap, he told Schwarz, "Take it back [to LAX] and take anything that you might use again off it and junk the rest."[29]

The Mustangs were pretty fragile even when they weren't being wadded up into a ball. The Trans-Am cars of 1967 were much closer to street cars than they would be even a year later. At Sebring, Thompson had bent a tie rod cutting some corners, prompting Shelby to tell him, "This is a cheap, little car, and you aren't supposed to do things like that."[30] Even when he played nice with apexes, Thompson said the tie rods would stretch over the course of a race, radically changing the front-end alignment.

Shelby American's secret weapon was that it had years of familiarity with its Mustangs, which were based on the first GT350s of 1965, whereas Moore and Penske faced much steeper learning curves with their Cougars and Camaros. At Lime Rock, Titus dominated the first two-thirds of the race before throwing a fan belt. Two weeks later, at Mid-Ohio, he was again untouchable, winning despite spinning on the last lap and being pushed back onto the track—probably illegally. And that wasn't the only stroke of luck. "When we tore the engine down at technical inspection, there wasn't a drop of oil left in it," mechanic Bobby Boxx said.[31] "If that race would have gone one more lap, we wouldn't have finished."

Shelby got the glory, but Titus, the team's lead driver, and Chuck Cantwell (left), the project engineer, did the heavy lifting during the 1967 Trans-Am season. Here, they celebrate after winning the four-hour enduro at Sebring. Titus won three more races in 1967, but it was Bucknum's second-place finish at Kent at the end of the year that clinched the manufacturers' title for Ford. *Chuck Cantwell Collection*

Titus had started the season with a modest reputation. But race after race, he proved that he was the equal of drivers with much more impressive pedigrees. At the same time, he also benefitted from three fast ones that Cantwell and Don Coleman of Ford's GT and Sports Car Department had pulled when they filed the homologation papers for the Mustang. First, they specified traction bars for the rear axle, which made the Shelby American cars more stable under braking and hard acceleration than the Cougars built on the same platform. Coleman also made sure the Mustang had a one-inch-wider tire than its FoMoCo stablemate. And third, Coleman explained, "The Chevrolet engine was much better for road racing. We were competitive engine-wise only because we were able to homologate two four-barrel carburetors in the 289."[32]

But Penske and Moore hadn't just fallen off the turnip truck, and they deployed their own bag of tricks as they played catch-up. Penske chased after the unfair advantage with gray-area practices such as acid-dipping bodies (to save weight) and icing down the fuel (to load more gas in the tank). And Moore came from the world of NASCAR where, it was said, if you ain't cheatin', you ain't tryin'. His Cougars were often ballasted before being weighed after races with tires filled with water and lead hidden inside door panels—and even inside the drivers' helmets! By mid-season, competition in the series had heated up to the point that David E. Davis wrote in *Car and Driver*, "The most In races in the country are the Trans-American sedan races, but the Sports Car Club of America is so Out they don't know it."[33]

The team returned to LAX for the summer break in the Trans-Am schedule. Production of the 1967 GT350s and GT500s was winding down, but Goodell was busy with a bunch of special projects that

The 1967 Trans-Am season was defined by one car/driver/paint job combination, and this is it—Titus in Mustang notchback painted Gawd-Awful Yellow. To half-heartedly hide Shelby American's involvement in the program, the car was entered by the Terlingua Racing Team. The Mustang was the cream of the crop in 1967, and when Titus didn't run into trouble—including three hellacious wrecks during the season—he was the man to beat. *Ford Motor Company*

seemed to have been undertaken primarily to amuse Shelby. The LA Auto Show brought the debut of Little Red, which had begun life as a notchback Mustang before being gussied up with GT500 bodywork, a Connally leather interior, and a 428 with twin Paxton superchargers. Before the *LA Times* Grand Prix in 1967, Shelby nonchalantly tossed the keys to the car to writer Charles Fox. A decade later, Fox immortalized his midnight run in what he called "Shelby's Folly" in a memorable column in *Car and Driver*.

"She was quick as the Vicar's daughter to a hundred, but the real magic came between a hundred and when the nose started to get airborne, which happened at 135–140 mph," Fox wrote.[34] "It was annoying to have to lift with fifteen hundred revs in hand. But we did a nice dance, Ol' Shel's Folly and I. With the road slick as slippery elm and she hanging onto the lip of the precipice by the tip of her pudgy paws, we went lunging into the damp night, a black panther, a phantom Helicon for my youthful imagination. I've had many good rides, and this was as good as any."

When Fox pulled into the parking lot of his Ramada Inn, he was greeted by a flotilla of police cruisers with lights flashing. The cops had been chasing him for the past hour. One of them rapped on his window with a long-barrel .357 Magnum. Fox was cuffed, ushered into a black-and-white, taken to the clink, and charged with reckless driving. It was only after he established his bona fides as a car reviewer that the threatened thirty-day sentence was knocked down to a $500 fine.

To satisfy another Shelby directive, Goodell built up a GT500 around a lightweight 427 Mark II engine with an aluminum head, solid lifters, bundle-of-snakes exhausts—the whole enchilada. This one was known as the Super Snake. It was trucked out to the high-speed Goodyear test track in San Angelo, Texas, where Shelby gave thrill rides to journalists at 150 mph. Then he handed his helmet to Goodell. "Freddie, I've got to go to Washington," he said.[35] "You'll have to finish this. Just wear my helmet, and nobody will know the difference." Goodell averaged 142 mph over 500 miles while maxing out at 170 mph. Don McCain, of GT350 Drag Unit fame, pitched Shelby with a proposal to build fifty Super Snakes. But the retail price of the car was so outrageously high that only one was sold before the project foundered.

Shelby also wanted Goodell to keep futzing around with the 427 Cobra even though no more chassis were being delivered by AC Cars. Shelby used to caravan up to Lake Tahoe with his renowned attorney, Stan Mullin, who owned a Ferrari 275 GTB. Mullin had been the first president of the California Sports Car Club, which was for several years a bitter rival of the SCCA, and he served as the corporate attorney for Lance Reventlow during the Scarab era. As the air got thinner on the drive to Nevada, the high-revving Italian V-12 had no trouble outrunning Shelby's 427 Cobra. Shelby wanted a more lethal weapon for these informal match races. Goodell retrofitted his car with a pair of Paxtons, a beefed-up Cruise-O-Matic three-speed automatic, and a hood scoop large enough to attract spelunkers. Paul Kunysz tested the car on local streets and freeways after helping to build it. "It was a very fast car, and it sounded bitchin'," he said.[36] "You'd get thumbs ups from the Highway Patrol while you were hauling ass."

Road & Track featured it in a story headlined "Cobra to End All Cobras."[37] At Orange County International Raceway, it boomed through the quarter mile in 11.86 seconds at 115.5 mph. With an estimated 800 horsepower, the car was too powerful to execute a brake stand, where the car is held in place with the brakes while the engine is revved. Mullin later reported, "The darn thing literally exploded past 140 mph, and actually accelerated faster at that speed than from a standstill. It ate my Ferrari alive."[38] Shelby claimed to have hit 190 mph and killed a buzzard with the windscreen. Not unexpectedly, the engine later sucked a valve. Kunysz bought the blown motor for $500, sleeved the cylinders and rebuilt it with primo Shelby and Mickey Thompson parts that he got for free. "I sold it for three grand," he said.[39] "That was the down payment on my first house."

As a public relations gesture, a virtual clone of Shelby's Cobra was given to Bill Cosby with a plate affixed to the dashboard: "This car is guaranteed to do 200 mph. Carroll Shelby." Cosby made it the centerpiece of a standup routine (and LP) titled, yes, "200 MPH." In it, he claimed that he'd lusted after the car because it had dual everything, including steering wheels, and was "faster than anything Steve McQueen owned."[40] But the moment he started it for the first time, he was terrified by the thunderous exhaust and violent vibration even at idle. "My scarf was limp.

My hair was standing straight up on my head. My Italian racing shoes had turned into sneakers. The fire extinguisher had emptied itself all over me," he said. "I had not put my foot on the gas pedal, and it was killing people," he said. After driving the car for a few seconds and barely missing a tree, he killed the ignition and told the guy who'd delivered the Cobra, "Take the keys and this car—its's all paid for—and you give it to George Wallace." Cosby wasn't joking. After taking delivery of the car and driving it for a grand total of a half mile, he gave it to his manager.

Although most of the 250 or so people working at Shelby American didn't know it, their days at LAX were numbered. The company's lease was due to expire in September, and after the boondoggle with the ill-fitting GT350 and GT500 hoods, there was no appetite for continuing to build Shelby Mustangs in Southern California. Goodell and Kerr looked into putting something together near the Ford assembly plant in San Jose. When this option didn't pan out, they negotiated a deal to build the 1968 model-year cars at the A. O. Smith plant in Michigan, and they established an engineering office in a vacant Buick building a block away.

It was time for a change of scenery. Since the move from Venice, the magic had been evaporating from Shelby American like air seeping out of a balloon. The LAX facility was so big and unwieldly and impersonal that what had once seemed like a family now felt more like a factory. "The whole atmosphere had changed," said Jim Marietta, who'd once jumped over fences to work for the race team for free.[41] "Everybody working so closely together promoted an electric sense of congeniality. Once we got to the airport, everything was so spread out. They hired a bunch of new people, of course, and it just didn't have the same rah-rah attitude. It seemed like we lost that esprit de corps."

Once upon a time, Butler had taught himself how to heliarc weld by surreptitiously watching Eaton, then practicing on his own after hours, just as Jere Kirkpatrick had honed his machining skills by studying, and then emulating, the mastery of Mahlon Lamoureux. Now, even Shelby American employees were barred from the race shop unless they had a special pass. Cliques were established—race versus production, GT40 versus Mustangers—and mixing between them was discouraged. As Boxx, a Trans-Am crewman, put it: "We were treated like outlaws,

MARCH 23, 1968

SEBRING

12 HOURS OF ENDURANCE FOR THE ALITALIA AIRLINES TROPHY   PRICE: $1.00

You gotta love the product placement. Not only is Alitalia Airlines part of the official race name, but the about-to-be-introduced Lincoln Continental Mark III is parked incongruously alongside the bright yellow Mark IV that Andretti and McLaren drove to victory in the car's first race, at Sebring in 1967. *John Gabrial Collection*

and all those guys would think of was those fuckin' Le Mans cars. We couldn't use any of the equipment in the shop, and everything was a big fuckin' deal. There was absolutely no cooperation between most of the guys on the two teams. We even had to buy all of our own power tools. We couldn't even get those cheap bastards to buy us team shirts."[42]

Most of the old-timers blamed Ford for the changes. Bureaucrats derisively referred to as "white shits" or "Fairlaners" were constantly dispatched from Dearborn to tour the facilities, asking questions and taking copious notes. Shelby himself wasn't around as often, and when he was, he seldom strolled around the shop the way he used to, slapping backs and bucking up the troops. In public, he inhabited the role of the glib corporate pitchman, and he insisted that each new Shelby-Ford product was better than the last one even as they strayed ever further from the crude but honest Cobras. But in private, he told his old friend John Christy, "It's gotten too big, and it isn't as much fun anymore.

There's too much money and too much work—and too many Ivy League suits runnin' around the damn place."[43]

As the spring of 1967 wound down, Shelby American was making one last push for road-racing glory on the international stage. Two brand-new Mark IVs were being prepared for Le Mans, along with a single Mark IIB, mirroring the work being done in Charlotte at Holman & Moody. When Gurney came in for his seat fitting in the car he'd be co-driving with Foyt, he couldn't even sit in the cockpit with his helmet on. Eaton fabricated a dome in the roof out of three pieces of aluminum. But even that didn't provide enough clearance, so the seat was lowered as well. "The floor panel was one-inch-thick aluminum honeycomb," Mike Donovan said.[44] "We cut the upper layer right where his butt cheeks would sit to get him down about another inch and removed part of the floorboard underneath him. There was only a thin sheet of aluminum between his butt and the ground."

Shelby American traveled with a crew chief and two mechanics per car plus several specialists (engine, fabrication, etc.) and the big Four—Shelby, Remington, Dowd, and Smith. Altogether, the Ford contingent consisted of more than 137 bodies occupying ten hotels, not counting Henry Ford II's retinue, and the expeditionary force included everything from interpreters and helicopter pilots to a coffee maker and American toilet paper. Housed in a leaky hangar with cobblestone floors, the operation seemed less like a race team than an army bivouacked in preparation for battle.

The Ford crew arrived at Le Mans feeling invincible. Forty-five minutes into the first practice session, it absorbed a punch in the gut when Andretti pitted with a cracked windshield. An hour later, Denny Hulme's windshield broke in a Holman & Moody Mark IV. Then Foyt's. Then McLaren's—while his car was parked in the pits! Turned out that the extra-hard temper applied to the glass to increase resistance to flying debris was too brittle. Frantic calls to Corning Glass in New York were rewarded with a commitment to knock out a rush order of new windshields in time for the race, but the cars would have to qualify as is and hope for the best.

Another issue popped up early on. The cars had to roll over a four-inch-tall block of wood to ensure that they weren't running lower than the minimum ride-height. But the Shelby American drivers found that their cars performed better when the ride-height was set at 3.5 inches. No problem. Remington told the guys to hammer wood shims between the coils of the springs to raise the ride height. Later, while ostensibly checking the brakes, they yanked the shims out to let the car settle.

The Fords were fast in qualifying, and McLaren was fastest of all. He'd given the Mark IV its maiden win at Sebring, so he knew what he wanted from the car. "Don't change a fuckin' thing," he told his crew after the first practice session.[45] "That son of a bitch is perfect." He pipped Hill to take the pole by three-tenths of a second. Other Fords were third, fourth, fifth, and sixth. Strangely, the slowest of the Shelby American and Holman & Moody cars was the big red No. 1 driven by Gurney and Foyt, whom everybody had assumed would be the fastest of the bunch. Exactly why they were off the pace is one of the great mysteries of Le Mans 1967.

Among armchair generals, the most popular theory is that Gurney didn't push as hard as usual because he didn't want to embarrass Foyt. The most prominent proponent of this proposition was Shelby himself. "Foyt never knew how fast Gurney could go," Shelby said.[46] "I didn't tell Gurney to do that. He figured it out himself." For the record, Gurney explicitly refuted this hypothesis. And history reflects that Foyt was a pretty fair road racer. In fact, while driving a Scarab for John Mecom Jr. in 1963, he trounced the Shelby American King Cobras driven by Dave MacDonald and Bob Holbert to win the big Nassau Trophy race in the Bahamas.

Gurney insisted that he was slow in practice because he wanted to be. "By 1967, I'd realized that Le Mans was more of an endurance contest than it was a race," he said.[47] "So I decided to emulate Briggs Cunningham, who used to beat me every year [by driving conservatively]. I knew that, if the car had an Achilles' heel, it was the brakes. At the end of the Mulsanne straight, I was doing two hundred ten, two-thirteen as I approached the hairpin, and I could have destroyed the brakes in about ten laps. So I made a solemn vow to emulate Briggs braking at the hairpin. I backed off maybe three hundred yards sooner than I needed to and let the drag and engine braking bleed off sixty miles per hour, or something like that, and then I hit the brakes."

Gurney also said that he spent practice working on car setup rather than pace to make sure that he—and Foyt, who barely got a chance to drive the car because of the windshield snafu—had a comfortable race car come race day. "I knew it was critical to be able to get through the Mulsanne kink without lifting," Gurney said.[48] "I spent a long time working on the car during practice until I could go through there one-handed, and we qualified way down in ninth. Of course, the Ford guys expected A. J. and me to be fighting each other to be fastest. So they kept saying 'What's wrong with the car?' I kept telling them, 'Hey, the car is great.'"

The third theory holds that Foyt and Gurney were what Shelby called "fiddle fuddlers"—drivers who couldn't stop messing around with the setup of their cars.[49] "Gurney tended to try to overengineer everything," said mechanic Kerry Agapiou, Charlie's older brother.[50] "When he drove the coupe with Jerry Grant in '65, he must have tried about ten sets of springs, but we ended up going back to the ones he started with originally."

Ford engineer Roy Lunn grew increasingly exasperated during practice. "Gurney and Foyt have to be, from my point of view, the worst development drivers when it comes to setting up a car," he said.[51] "And to have the two of them in one car, both with different ideas of how the cars should be set up . . . They got the car really screwed up." So screwed up, in fact, that at least one Ford engineer was convinced that they were planning to pull a clutch job—holding in the clutch and spinning the motor until it popped—in the race.

Friday night, after the team returned to its garage, Smith walked over to crew chief John Collins and Donovan and Phil Henny, the mechanics on the No. 1 car being driven by Gurney and Foyt. "He tore a page out of his little book and gave it to us,' said Henny, a Swiss master machinist who'd joined the team a few months earlier.[52] "And he said, 'You guys put all the adjustments from the McLaren car on the No. 1.' And we did. We took everything apart at two o'clock in the morning. And when Dan Gurney took the start the next day, it was a totally new race car."

The Fords also had new windshields. They were flown to France—though not, as legend has it, in first-class seats—and arrived Friday. That afternoon, product manager Bob Stahl and his technical assistant, Terry Johansen, were sent from the Dow Corning office in Brussels on a chartered Cessna 310 to install the windshields using a special silicone sealant. In the end, the windshields performed better than the cars they were in.

Come race day, Ronnie Bucknum, driving hard in a Shelby American Mark IIB, led the first hour until his engine overheated. Gurney inherited the lead, and he and Foyt never looked back. If they had, they would have seen a lot of chaos in their rear-view mirror. Only sixteen of the fifty-four starters finished the race, and most of the DNFs did not go gentle into that good night.

Hulme slid into the sand at the Mulsanne hairpin in the Mark IV he was sharing with Ruby. After Hulme manage to extricate the car, Ruby beached it for good. This left three Holman & Moody cars in the race—temporarily. At 3:34 in the morning, on his out lap after a pit stop for brake pads, Andretti stabbed the brake pedal of his Mark IV as he approached the Esses. His car veered sharp right and plowed into a sand embankment, ripping off the nose before lurching to a stop in the middle of the track. Andretti said the Holman & Moody mechanics had installed a brake pad backward. The crew claimed that Andretti had failed to warm up the brakes adequately before nailing them. He said, they said. Dazed and hurt, Andretti scampered to safety just before Roger McCluskey's Mark IIB barreled into the Esses—and clobbered the remains of Andretti's Mark IV. Fifteen seconds later, Jo Schlesser arrived on the scene in another Mark IIB and plowed right into the wreckage. Incredibly, the last three Holman & Moody entries had been eliminated in less than a minute.

Ferraris were running two-three-four, but Gurney was still loping along in the lead in a car he likened to big American highway cruiser. Ferrari team manager Franco Lini ordered driver Mike Parkes to get into Gurney's head. What happened next was one of the strangest incidents in racing history. "Parkes pulled in behind me and started flicking his lights, flashing his brights," Gurney recalled.[53] "He wanted me to gas it, hoping that I'd break the car. I was so tempted to blow him off, but I knew what his mission was. This went on for at least three laps. Finally, I pulled over onto the grass at Arnage, and damned if he didn't pull off right behind me!" There, they idled in the middle of the 24 Hours of Le Mans like two Uber drivers waiting for their customers to show up. "We sat there for maybe fifteen or twenty seconds—seemed like longer than that—until he pulled back out. Then I pulled out, and in about four laps later, I caught and passed him."

Shortly after dawn Sunday, McLaren was startled by an almighty *boom!* behind him. "Then I remembered I had a big engine, so I thought, 'Big engine, big noise.' It must have blown up," he said.[54] "But then I checked the oil gauge and found I still had pressure, so I thought it might be the transmission. But I checked that and found I still had a gearbox. So, I thought, 'Maybe it's an axle.' So I gave the throttle a few blips and satisfied myself that I still had axles. That got me puzzled, so then I looked in my rear-vision mirror, and there I saw a lot of daylight that hadn't been there before. The body had blown off. So I motored back to the pits and told them that I'd lost the back of my car, and they said, 'Yes, we can see that you have, and if you don't mind, we'd like you to go back and get it.' So off I went, and sure enough I found it halfway down the Mulsanne straight looking pretty sad and sorry."

Holding the bodywork with one hand and steering the car with the other, McLaren crawled back to the pits. There, the bodywork was secured with yards and yards of duct tape. "That race tape is good shit, you know," Charlie Agapiou said.[55] "But then the Frenchman in the pits started to blow his bloody whistle. 'No, No, No! You have to be able to open the car.' Then I had an idea, and I whipped off my belt, and Big Five whipped off his belt, and Homer Perry and one of the other Ford guys gave us their belts." Even Shelby pitched in, reluctantly donating his expensive alligator belt to the cause. (Only Remington refused to contribute to the cause, for some unknown reason.) After the belts were used as makeshift hinges and the tail was fortified with pop rivets, Donohue returned to the track. He and McLaren would finish fourth.

Foyt ran into only two glitches during an otherwise trouble-free race. During the night, he hit oil in the White House section of the track. "That thing got so damn slick, I like to run off there," he said.[56] "I over-revved the motor a little bit, but I was grabbing everything trying to stop." Then, when he pitted at the end of his shift, Gurney was nowhere to be found. This wouldn't have been a problem except that the seat wasn't adjustable, so Foyt—who was several inches shorter than Gurney—had been forced to adopt an uncomfortable straight-arm driving position. "I said, 'Man, my arms are killing me,'" he said.[57] "And they said, 'Oh, A. J., you gotta get back in. We're leading this race.' I said, 'Hot damn, I don't know if I can go another shift!'"

He did, of course. The Ferraris ran flat out the rest of the way, hoping to break the Ford, but the big, red Mark IV continued to circulate with almost monotonous reliably. Gurney and Foyt covered 3,251.57 miles at an average speed of 135.48 mph, 10 mph faster than the winning Mark IIA had gone the previous year. The 427 Ford also won the Index of Thermal Efficiency, an eccentric award that the ACO had created largely as a prize for itty-bitty French cars. "Shucks, that wasn't so tough. Indy was harder," Foyt declared afterward. "Le Mans ain't nothing but a little old country road."[58]

Nobody thought Gurney and A. J. Foyt were going to win Le Mans in 1967. The smart money said that if they didn't blow up their Mark IV trying to outrun the Ferraris, they'd blow it up trying to outrun each other. Instead, Foyt—driving the big, red No. 1—and Gurney rumbled to a thoroughly convincing win. "Le Mans ain't nothing but a little old country road," Foyt said afterward.
Revs Institute / Eric della Faille Photograph Collection

Unlike 1966, when the celebration had been muted because of the bungled finish, there was unrestrained joy on the faces of the winners. "I didn't plan to spray everybody with champagne after the race," Gurney said.[59] "But as I was standing on the victory rostrum, I looked down at the photographers and thought, 'Those guys look like they expect something.' Somebody handed me that big old magnum, and I said to myself, 'Well, let's let 'em have it.' Then I turned around and got just about everybody up on top. I had no idea that I would start a tradition. I was beyond caring and just got caught up in the moment. It was one of those once-in-a-lifetime occasions when things turned out perfectly."

Gurney's spontaneous gesture was a fitting climax to Ford's Le Mans program. "We have nothing left to prove," the Deuce declared after the

Everybody loves a winner! Gurney sits on the roof while Foyt steers their Mark IV toward the victory rostrum at Le Mans. That's Donovan on the right front fender, Phil Henny on the left rear fender, and John Collins hanging out the door. Nobody has any idea who the dude in the white vest or the three kids behind Gurney are. The dominant Mark IV was outlawed two days after winning Le Mans. *Dave Friedman*

race.[60] A week later, Frey announced that the company was pulling the plug on its endurance-racing operation. GT40s would continue to race at Le Mans—and win the next two years, as a matter of fact—but no longer under the Ford banner. It was time to put the shiny toys away and get back to the business of selling cars.

The victory at Le Mans in 1967 with a car designed, built, and engineered entirely in the United States was the greatest American achievement ever in international motorsports. It also represented the pinnacle of Shelby American's success. But now that Shelby had reached the top of the mountain, the only way forward was down. The fall would come fast, and the landing would be hard.

The Le Mans crew returned to Los Angeles and confronted a company that was in the process of imploding. Although GT350s and GT500s were still rolling down the assembly line, Shelby American employees and Ford bean counters were scurrying around the two hangars at LAX in a frenzied effort to inventory and dispose of tons—literally—of parts and equipment that had been accumulated over the past five years. It wasn't the fall of the Roman Empire, and there were no barbarian hordes beating on the doors, but it was ugly. "It was probably the worst sight I ever saw," Goodell said.[61] "And it was pretty confusing. There was stuff all over the place, and nobody was sure what was what. There were about fifty 427 engines that disappeared and were never seen again."

Ford didn't sever its relationship with Shelby, but the gravy train stopped running, and stricter financial controls were instituted. Shelby American was carved into three separate entities, each with its own financial ledger—Shelby Automotive to build Mustangs, Shelby Racing to run the motorsports programs, and Shelby Parts and Accessories to sell items ranging from tubular exhaust manifolds to Pit Stop, which was marketed as "a real man's deodorant" and was said to be "recommended for everyday use by non-race drivers too." Shelby Automotive was moving to Ionia, Michigan. Despite the name, Shelby would have virtually nothing to do with the new Mustangs. "But I'm not crying," he told *Road & Track*.[62] "Production was taking too much of my time anyway." The racing and parts divisions were relocated to an eighty-four-thousand-square-foot building at 4320 190th Street in Torrance, south of LA, leased from Standard Brands Paint. Shelby himself set up shop in a four-story office building in Playa del Rey.

The final GT500 left LAX in late July 1967, with all engineering cars and prototypes following three weeks later. Smith insisted on working up until the end, and he was still at it when Henny forklifted his desk away. By the beginning of September, the hangars at LAX were deserted. Other than senior managers and those with a need to know, most employees had been blindsided by the move, and the general sense was bewilderment rather than bitterness. As Henny recalled, "Carroll came in with all the envelopes and said, 'Guys, I'm sorry, but I have to let you go.'"[63]

The vast majority of Shelby American employees got pink slips. The production side fared the worst, obviously, and while some people were offered jobs in Michigan, there weren't many takers. "Four people went up there, and in a month and a half, they were back," said Lonnie Brannan, who helped run the production line.[64] "They asked me to go, and I told them I didn't lose nothing in Michigan, and I'm not going there looking for nothing."

The racing department took a much milder hit. Shelby Racing went into business with new letterhead stationery featuring the names of Shelby, Remington, and Dowd at the top and a motto—"World's Finest Competition Automobiles"—at the bottom. The Trans-Am season was still in full swing, and Shelby was about to unveil an all-new entry in the Can-Am series. He was also mulling over an Indy 500 program, and Smith was lobbying to get him interested in Formula A. There was plenty of work for the thirty-five or so people staffing the new company.

Shelby himself seemed conflicted about what to do next. Even as he was vacating the premises at LAX, he sent Lee Iacocca the results of a market research survey he'd commissioned. Titled "A Study of the Popularity and Influence of Carroll Shelby on Young Americans," the paper was based on interviews with one hundred male college students at four universities, one hundred and four young men attending an NHRA meet, and four magazine editors. It was a weird document combining encomiums from *Road & Track* editor Jim Crow with answers from respondents to questions about how willing they would be to buy Carroll Shelby equipment at a department store. It's not clear whether Shelby was trying to protect old turf or carve out new territory. But the mere existence of the survey suggests that Shelby was eager to maintain some sort of relationship with Ford even if he wasn't sure what it might be.

The post–Shelby American era began, fittingly enough, with the car that was supposed to update the Cobra with a cutting-edge mid-engine design. But instead of pointing the way to a promising and profitable future, the car ended its short, unhappy life as an orphan unwanted by either of its parents. Code-named the Cobra III back in 1965, it had been envisioned as a joint Shelby-Ford alternative to the Corvette and E-type Jaguar. Although Shelby kept a scale model of the car in his office, he wasn't gung-ho about the project. Early on, he signaled his reservations by having Jim McLean inform Ford that Shelby American didn't have the resources to take on the project. Instead, it was entrusted to Len Bailey, who'd been one of the four Ford engineers assigned to the original Ford GT40 program. Bailey drew up a mid-engined two-seater with a removable T-top and room to accommodate any one of a number of Ford's small-block engines. Square tubing and sheet metal were used to create a monocoque, which was assembled by the British company that built the tubs for the GT40s. The running gear was provided by John Wyer's J. W. Automotive Engineering, which was also responsible for the flamboyant white interior.

The car arrived in LA in June 1967. Because Shelby had sold the rights to the Cobra name to Ford, the car was renamed the Lone Star in honor of Shelby's heritage. This was an odd name for a car. Then again, it was an odd car, whatever the name. Seen from the right angle, it looked like a cross between a Lotus Europa and a Ferrari 330 P4. Viewed from a less flattering perspective, it looked more like the love child of a dachshund and a VW-based kit car. With 300 or so horsepower and a curb weight of 2,400 pounds, performance should have been impressive. (Wind-tunnel tests with a scale model suggested a top speed in excess of 200 mph.) But it was hard to get into and even harder to get out of, and with a price tag in the neighborhood of $15,000, it promised to be a tough sell. The prototype was sent to Dearborn for evaluation and returned to sender without comment.

It's easy to take pot shots at the Lone Star. But it's worth noting that the Lamborghini Miura, generally regarded as the first mid-engine supercar, had gone into production just a year earlier. And three years later, Lincoln-Mercury dealers would start selling another mid-engine coupe packing a small-block Ford V-8—the De Tomaso Pantera. So maybe it's best to think of the Lone Star as the victim of poor timing rather than an outright blunder. After returning to Torrance, it made the rounds of the show circuit and served as a prop on the cover of a Shelby Accessories catalog. Then it sat in a corner and collected dust. "I lost interest in it completely when I saw that it was just another car with gas tanks along the sides that you had to step over and that you could never be comfortable in." Shelby said.[65]

When it became clear that the 427 Cobra's days were numbered, Len Bailey, a British engineer who'd worked on the original GT40, was hired to design a successor, the Cobra III. Bailey created a sleek mid-engine coupe with somewhat ungainly proportions. By the time it reached the States in 1967, Shelby had lost the rights to the Cobra name, so the car was rechristened the Lone Star, and it sank without a trace. *Road & Track*

Dowd eventually advertised it in *Autoweek* with a come-hither headline: "FOR SALE—SEX ON WHEELS!!" This evidently was enough to get the Lone Star off of Shelby's hands. In 1969, the car was spotted by *Motor Trend* editor A. B. Shuman at a Fiat dealership off the beaten path, where it had been taken in on trade for a Ferrari. "The car is said to have been shipped to Ford for study early in its career to be considered for possible production but apparently it flunked its final exam," Shuman wrote.[66] "So now it languishes on a used car lot in Santa Barbara, looking for a very understanding person."

Whatever the Lone Star's flaws, it looked like a triumph compared to Shelby's next project, a scratch-built Can-Am car that completed a grand total of three laps in two races before being kicked unceremoniously to the curb. Those who worked on it used phrases like "one big disaster,"[67] "the worst car I ever worked on,"[68] and "a real piece of shit."[69] The King Cobra, as it came to be known, was a perfect illustration of why race car designers tend to be conservative by nature, building on prior success rather than trying to reinvent the wheel with each new creation. Innovation is a good thing, obviously, but too much of a good thing can be a recipe for an epic fail.

The Canadian-American Challenge Series had been inaugurated the previous year with great fanfare. With a no-holds-barred rules package and generous sponsorship from Johnson Wax, it had already staked its claim to being the biggest and best professional road-racing series in the country. Shelby wanted in, and Ford was happy to provide engines, but chassis options were limited. Chaparrals weren't for sale, McLarens were, but only last year's model. Lola T70s were available to anybody who wanted them, so, by definition, they were commonplace. To get an edge over the competition, Shelby decided to commission a brand-new chassis. But from whom?

In 1965, with financial backing from Goodyear, Shelby and Dan Gurney had formed All American Racers. "He had all the stock," Gurney joked, "and I had all the work!"[70] Gurney put together a small crew and opened a shop in Santa Ana, down in Orange County, and Shelby had little to do with the operation before being bought out in 1967.

British engineer Len Terry designed the first generation of AAR Eagles, which won races in both the Indy car and F1 series. Since then, Terry had teamed up with Frank Nichols, the founder of Elva Cars, to form Transatlantic Automotive Consultants. Shelby commissioned TAC to design a blue-sky Can-Am car.

Ultimately, the Can-Am series would be dominated by big, honking motors hogged out to seven, eight, nine liters and wedge-shaped bodies augmented with appendages designed to prevent cars from flying into outer space. Terry chose a different road. His T-10 was built around a potent but underpowered small-block V-8. The bodywork was smooth and flat, almost pancake-like, less concerned with producing downforce than minimizing drag. Under the aluminum skin was a conventional monocoque and a very unconventional suspension. Instead of having vertically mounted coil springs at each corner, Terry drew up a clever but unproven alternative featuring two transverse-mounted coil springs—one at the front and one at the rear—attached to lever arms or bell cranks. The idea was to isolate the roll rate from the spring rate. In theory, this would make it easier to tune the suspension. But theory and reality don't always align.

The car arrived at Shelby American shortly before the team moved from LAX but too late to compete in the first Can-Am races of the season. From the start, everything that could go wrong did go wrong, and the car was a constant work in progress. One of the changes, seemingly insignificant, symbolized some of the T-10's larger flaws. Although it was originally called the Cougar-Cobra, this sounded clunky and confused everybody. It was quickly renamed the King Cobra, in part because it resembled the Shelby-modified Cooper Monacos that Mac-Donald and Jones had driven famously in the West Coast Fall Series races that predated the Can-Am Series. Of course, that had been several years earlier, and the fundamental design of the Cooper Monaco itself dated back to the late 1950s. Speaking of the new version of the King Cobra, Collins said, "It was obsolete before we finished it."[71]

Testing spotlighted problems too varied to enumerate fully. "The car broke every time we went out," Collins said.[72] "We'd fix one thing, and something else would go wrong." The unusual cooling system didn't cool the car or the disgruntled driver, Jerry Titus, and the radiator had to be relocated and then re-relocated. The rear transverse spring popped out in Turn One at Riverside, and only a miraculous save by Titus prevented the car from being wrecked. "Additionally," mechanic Mark Popov-Dadiani said, "the rear suspension lower pickup points were in single shear, not supported on both sides of the heim joint. These points would bend and change the alignment, making things inconsistent. After modifying the front and rear suspension to coilover shocks, the tub up front began to bend around the pickup points."[73]

Another test at Riverside was aborted after Collins said, "Hey, Rem, somethings's wrong with that thing. See those lumps there?"[74] When they took a closer look, they saw the sway bar was hitting the body. "We pulled the driver in and intended to get a hammer and knock the body out," Collins said. "When we pulled the nose off, we saw the front end had collapsed."

The King Cobra finally made its debut at Riverside at the second-to-last Can-Am race of the season. Titus qualified thirteenth, 4.7 seconds off the time Gurney had set in a Lola T70 prepped by AAR. The long list of cars that outran the King Cobra included two Lolas owned by former Shelby American GM Peyton Cramer and the notoriously atrocious Honker entered by arch-rival John Holman for Andretti. Aside from unpredictable handling, Titus was also hamstrung by a lack of torque. The team was running a 351-cubic-inch Ford with Gurney-Weslake heads, and while it was a slick package, using a small-block engine was like bringing a pocketknife to a gunfight. Titus lasted three desultory laps before the fuel pump failed.

The car's next appearance, at Las Vegas two weeks later, was even more embarrassing After Titus posted the twelfth-fastest time during practice, the rear bottom link tore out of the chassis, sending the car spinning out of the Esses. The King Cobra was withdrawn, never to be seen again in competition. Even *Sports Car Graphic*, normally a diehard Shelby booster, couldn't dredge up anything nice to say. "The Ford effort as a whole, we feel, suffered through lack of preparedness and through the dispersal of available brainpower and resources into too many projects."[75] Remington, as usual, was blunter. "It was a fiasco," he said flatly.[76] "We tried to make it work, but it was awful. We finally gave up on it."

This image sums up the sad story of Shelby Racing's Can-Am entry in 1967—languishing in the pits while bewildered mechanics struggled to figure out what went wrong this time. Designed by Len Terry, the T-10 was a disaster from start to finish. During the car's debut here at Riverside, Titus managed only three desultory laps. Two weeks later, at Las Vegas, he didn't even take the start. Exit T-10. *Revs Institute / Albert R. Bochroch Photograph Collection*

But if the foray into Can-Am racing proved to be underwhelming, Shelby Mustangs remained the gold standard in Trans-Am. Titus finished second to Jones in the non-points July 4th night race at Daytona despite being eased off the track on the first lap and losing time making repairs. The series resumed for real at a glorified go-kart track in Bryar, New Hampshire. Joining the team on the road was a blue-and-white Ford Econoline van with 14-inch Shelby aluminum 10-spoke wheels and bold white "COBRA" lettering just below the windshield. This was the mobile office that John Timanus, former chief instructor at the Carroll Shelby School of High Performance Driving (and, later, SCCA's longtime technical director), used to run the Shelby Race Assistance Program, which sold parts at cost to race car owners.

As usual, Titus grabbed the pole. But in the race, making up time after stopping to change to rain tires, he was punted by a local hot shoe (driving a Shelby-built customer Mustang, ironically). His car bounded off an embankment, vaulted into the air, and spun so violently that nobody was sure how many times he went around. Four? Six? Eight? Titus smacked his head on the door frame and was knocked out. When he came to thirty seconds later, he rocked the car out of the mud and wobbled back to the pits. His crew didn't even bother with triage, much less emergency surgery. "The car was a throwaway," Schwarz said.[77] "It had hit the rear quarter panel so hard that it buckled the frame and turned the rear axles around to the point where the rear tire was rubbing against the back seat!"

The incident inspired Titus to write an earnest but ill-advised column in *Autoweek*. "I'd like to get on the soapbox about the quality of drivers they let run the Trans-Am," he wrote.[78] "Not the guys who run the whole circuit, but the local yuk who joins in for a lark when it comes to his area. Hopelessly uncompetitive but anxious to bore his friends during the winter months about how he diced with so-and-so. They've tried hard to kill me twice this year and we wouldn't want it any closer." Even in that pre-Twitter era, the blowback was fast and fierce, and it didn't take long for fans to start showing up at Trans-Am races mocking Titus by wearing "I'm a local yuk" buttons.

Titus won his third race of the season at Continental Divide. Afterward, Thompson surprised everybody by announcing his retirement from racing. A dentist by trade, he'd straddled the line between professional and amateur competition for twenty-five years, and few had done it better, but there was no longer much room for drivers like him in the upper echelons of the sport. He was replaced by Bucknum, who'd been a core member of Ford's Le Mans program. Titus made it back-to-back victories with what Cantwell called "just a perfect race" at Crow's Landing Naval Auxiliary Air Station near Modesto.[79] (Obviously, Trans-Am hadn't hit the big time yet.) But the next two races didn't go so well, and Shelby began to worry. Because the Mustangs and Cougars had performed so well over the course of the season, Ford already had the manufacturers' championship in the bag. But Shelby Racing and Bud Moore Engineering were still fighting over bragging rights, and the points title was going to come down to a one-race shoot-out at Kent.

Shelby made arrangements to borrow the Mustang of privateer John McComb just in case Titus needed it. He needed it. During practice,

Ford wasn't the only company to get mileage out of the successes of the GT40. Here, Marchal trumpets—in French!—the use of its headlights on the Foyt/Gurney Mark IV that won at Le Mans in 1967. *John Gabrial Collection*

42 ANNEES DE SUCCES !

1925
1967

un Palmarès unique !

31 VICTOIRES
aux 24 H. DU MANS

Les phares et projecteurs de complément S.E.V. MAR
CHAL sont les seuls à avoir triomphé 7 fois consécuti-
ves à la distance (de 1960 à 1967) avec FERRARI
el FORD.

MARCHAL a été le premier au monde, en 1962, à ex-
périmenter avec succès en compétition.

L'ÉCLAIRAGE A IODE

S.E.V. MARCHAL

9 FOIS CHAMPION DU MONDE

Titus had his third savage wreck of the season. Steaming around a blind corner, he found a Camaro on the racing line. He took evasive action, ran up an embankment that launched the car in the air as high as a telephone pole. Titus's Mustang crash-landed ass first, shortening the car by several feet, then rolled several times for good measure. Donohue gave Titus a lift back to the pits. "All this grass was stuffed under the front edge of his helmet, so you could tell he'd been through some-thing," Cantwell said, "but the car was the worst I've ever seen. I mean, it was just really mangled up. We stripped it and got rid of it. Some guy there wanted the car, so we said, 'Okay, it's yours.'"[80]

Shelby, looking incongruously resplendent in a blue blazer with white piping, gray slacks, alligator shoes, and a flawless black Stetson, persuaded McComb to let Titus drive his car. Donohue led majest-ically from start to finish in his Penske Camaro. Behind him, it was a street fight between Cougars and Mustangs. Titus's engine blew up. Then Jones broke, but not before he dropped a wheel and kicked up a rock that smashed Gurney's windshield. With Gurney driving one-handed while pushing back on the windshield to prevent it from caving in on him, Bucknum pulled clear. Then the water temperature gauge in Bucknum's Mustang started to climb. Bucknum was a calculating driver—he used to monitor his own lap times by checking his watch—so he backed off to keep the engine from overheating. But he paced himself well enough to finish second, forty seconds ahead of Gurney, and clinch the title for Shelby Racing. "In retrospect," Titus wrote in a post-season recap in *Autoweek*, "we started this season with a definite advantage of experience in chassis preparation but down on horsepower. This was corrected by Daytona. Chevy had the horsepower, but not the stopping or the handling. By Mid-Ohio they were stopping, by Bryar they were handling, and I can only assume that various foul-ups kept them from being real trouble until the last two races. The Cougars looked right from the start and got better. They had equal horsepower and brakes to the Mustangs immediately, but it took them a few races to get the chassis working well."[81]

Shelby later said that the 1967 Trans-Am season was the last time he cared seriously about racing. Which was a good thing because it was the last championship he would ever win.

CHAPTER SEVEN

HARD TIMES

1968

Carroll Shelby had unfinished business at the Indianapolis Motor Speedway. In 1958, he'd been contacted by Jack Ensley, a prominent local businessman and longtime SCCA road racer. Ensley had acquired an Offy-powered Kurtis roadster. He planned to take his rookie test in the car as a lark, but he wanted Shelby to drive it for real in the 500. Shelby was game. He showed up shortly after the track opened at the start of May and started going through the required phases of the rookie test, turning laps at 110 miles per hour, 115 mph, and 120 mph before being black-flagged. When he stopped in the pits, chief steward Harlan Fengler informed him that two drivers couldn't take their rookie tests in the same car. Since Ensley had already driven the car, Shelby was out. Shelby was convinced that Fengler, a not-so-benevolent dictator with no use for sports car drivers, had made up the rule on the spot. "The hell with it," Shelby snapped.[1] "I have plenty of jobs that I can drive in Europe." That night, he caught an airplane to New York, and he raced a factory Aston Martin DBR2 for John Wyer at Spa the following weekend.

Ford Motor Company had become interested in the Indy 500 about the same time that it began supplying engines to Shelby for the Cobra. Ford's Indy car program would eventually produce the four-cam Indy Ford, one of the most successful engines in American history. By the time Shelby had enough bandwidth to even consider taking another shot at Indy, Ford already had all the teams it needed. But in 1967, there were two developments that changed Shelby's thinking. First, the Ford Le Mans program ended, which left him with a cadre of mechanics and engineers who were all dressed up with no place to go. Second, an English aerospace engineer by the name of Ken Wallis designed an asymmetrical Indy car around a Pratt & Whitney jet turbine and four-wheel drive. Entered by Andy Granatelli, sponsored by STP and Paxton, and driven by Parnelli Jones, the so-called Whooshmobile came within three laps of winning the Indy 500.

The Indy establishment was horrified. New rules were immediately promulgated by the USAC to limit the inlet size of turbines to the point that they were no longer thought to be competitive. Wallis got crossways with Granatelli and quit. But Wallis remained convinced that, despite the new regulations, he could build a car capable of winning Indy. And in addition to being a clever engineer, he was an even better salesman. Wallis got the attention of Ted Halibrand. Best known for his magnesium wheels, Halibrand had been an engineer at Douglas Aircraft and was still an aviation aficionado. He'd already built an Indy car of his own, the Shrike, which Eddie Sachs had been driving when he and Dave MacDonald were killed at the Speedway in 1964. In the run-up to the 1968 Indy 500, Halibrand leased a shop with 12,800 square feet of space in Torrance, a couple of miles from Shelby Racing, to Wallis Engineering.

Although Wallis started building a new car on spec, he needed sponsors to pay for the program and a race team to run the car. Shelby ticked all the right boxes. "Ted Halibrand kind of got that thing going," Phil Remington said.[2] "I used to do a lot of work with him, wheels and stuff for the Cobras. He was an aircraft nut who had his own 310 Cessna. He said, 'How would you like to do a turbine car? You guys have got plenty of money, and Ford's got money. Why don't you talk to your boss?' So I approached Shelby, and he talked to Goodyear, and they said they'd go along with it. It was mostly Goodyear's money."

At the time, Goodyear was in the middle of a titanic tire war with Firestone. In 1967, Goodyear had won the Indy 500 for the first time since 1919. But it had been a freak victory made possible only because Parnelli's Firestone-shod turbine car broke with three laps to go. Now, to cover its bases, Goodyear wanted a Whooshmobile of its own. The public announcement of the program on January 12, 1968, generated plenty of media buzz, including a laudatory story in the *LA Times*. Two cars were being built, one for Bruce McLaren and the other for Denny Hulme, the reigning World Driving Champion. When Shelby signed on, the program was budgeted at close to $1.0 million. Later, Botany 500, which sold high-end menswear, came on board as the title sponsor, with plans for an ambitious advertising campaign that would blanket the country. Ultimately, more than $1.5 million was spent trying to get the cars into the show.

Wallis began by procuring three General Electric T58 turboshaft engines, the first turbines certified by the Federal Aviation Administration for civilian helicopters. In aviation form, the engine made close to 1400 horsepower. But to race at Indy, the annulus—the intake feeding air into the turbine compressor—of the T58 had to be squeezed down from the stock 41.6 square inches to 15.999 square inches. Wallis knew that getting power out of the choked-down turbine would be a challenge, but he had a workaround in mind, and he commissioned compressor fan blade modifications from GE that met the letter, if not the spirit, of USAC's annulus rules.

The transmission was often described as "hydrostatic drive," which was a fancy way of saying that it transmitted energy using hydraulic fluid. This particular transmission was built around an ingenious hydraulic system patented by Einar Jonsson for industrial applications. The turbine shaft ran through a reduction gear to shafts for the front and rear axles. Each wheel was equipped with a planetary gearset with a hydraulic pump. When one wheel started spinning, it would force hydraulic fluid to the other wheels to maintain drive. "The trickery was in the hydraulic control unit, which decided how to split torque between the other three wheels," said Dave Norton, a young engineer who worked with Jonsson on the turbine project.[3]

The rest of the car was equally complex. The body came from Dick Troutman and Tom Barnes, the team that had helped build the original

Scarabs, but the chassis was built in-house. A large frame, roughly eight feet by eight feet by sixteen feet, was formed out of angle iron and then used as a jig. The chassis consisted of sheets of 2024 T6 aluminum, an ultra-strong alloy common in the aerospace industry. Each panel had to be cleaned beforehand in a steaming vat of ethylene glycol, a powerful solvent. Since this grade of aluminum can't be welded, the sheets were held together with cleko fasteners, then glued and blind-riveted with so-called cherry rivets—another typical aerospace practice. The suspension pieces hooked onto flanges attached to steel brackets that were glued and pop-riveted to the ends of the chassis. The result was a car that was very stout but also very heavy—more than four hundred pounds overweight.

By conventional race car standards, the build was insanely labor-intensive. Wallis Engineering employed about fifty people. "The stuff was complicated, heavy, and just impossible to work on," Remington said.[4] "Wallis had done the turbine car for Granatelli. But then he got too big for his knickers and got all these dreams about hydraulic drive. He had a whole bunch of trick engineers and was spending money as fast as he could. You could see from the start that it was going to be a fiasco." [7-1]

Shelby wasn't so sure. But he wanted some of his own guys on-site both to help out and to protect his interests. He chose two of his top fabricators, Bill Eaton and Ron Butler. Eaton walked away mid-project because he felt it was "a bit of a charade."[5] He was replaced by Steve Shuttack, who'd joined the team the previous year to work on the Ronnie Bucknum/Paul Hawkins Mark IIB at Le Mans. "I liked it because it was an all-new type of fabrication to me with aircraft plumbing, aircraft wiring, et cetera," Shuttack said.[6] "Different tools and skills were needed. Later, when I was laid off, I probably could have worked at Boeing, if I'd thought about it."

Butler was less enthusiastic than Shuttack, not because of the type of work but because of the inhuman workload. "We were way behind on the job when I started," he said.[7] "I worked ninety hours a week for seven months with no days off. Can you imagine that? That's two weeks in one! We weren't even allowed to go to lunch. They paid me a per diem of twenty-five dollars a day, but they brought in lunch to eat at the shop, so I banked that twenty-five dollars, and on top of that, we

Dowd leans over to talk to aerospace engineer Ken Wallis, the designer of the turbine-powered single-seater that Shelby—and Goodyear—had commissioned to win the Indy 500 in 1968. Wallis built the car around a General Electric T58 turboshaft engine, more typically used to power helicopters. To circumvent restrictions implemented to slow down the turbine cars, he resorted to skullduggery inside the huge air intake in the nose. *Ron Butler Collection*

were getting time-and-a-half. I made about ten thousand bucks on that lot. That's how I paid for all the machinery I bought from Shelby later."

Shelby was having problems of his own at the beginning of 1968. On February 6, in a move that rocked the American automotive establishment, GM executive vice president Semon E. "Bunkie" Knudsen was named president of Ford Motor Company. At GM, Knudsen had been in charge of all high-performance activities, including racing. He and Shelby had sparred many times over the past five years, and theirs wasn't a friendly feud. Shelby was convinced that his days at Ford were numbered once Knudsen arrived. But even if Knudsen had wanted to, Ford couldn't cut Shelby loose right away because Shelby Automotive was providing design and engineering input for the 1968 GT350 and GT500 while Shelby himself, not to mention the broader Shelby brand, remained a core element of Ford's marketing campaign for the cars. Ford's demographic research had discovered that the typical buyer wasn't, as expected, a young would-be racer. Looking suave in a casual pullover, Shelby was pictured in print ads as the personification of the target customer—a prosperous and discerning middle-aged iconoclast seeking speed with style. "Carroll Shelby designed his COBRA GT to go like it looks," the ad copy read. Most observers agreed that the car delivered on the looks front. "Go" was another matter.

Cars built at A. O. Smith initially came off the Ford assembly line in Metuchen, New Jersey, before being shipped by rail to Ionia, Michigan. Mechanically, there was very little to distinguish them from stock Mustangs; better shock absorbers and modest engine upgrades were the biggest differences. Most of the components unique to the GT350 and GT500 were bolt-on pieces designed to fit seamlessly in place of items that were deleted on the assembly line. The rear end of the car looked largely unchanged from 1967 other than the addition of sequential taillights from the 1965 Thunderbird. But the front end featured an even longer hood with a nearly full-width scoop and a reprofiled grille. The interior got the deluxe treatment, and options such as air conditioning and a swing-away steering wheel were offered. The big news, though, was the addition of a convertible with a very slick rollbar covered in hard plastic so that it looked like a targa top. The convertible was a hit, accounting for nearly one third of the 4,450 Shelby Mustangs sold during the 1968 model year—the most ever in Shelby history.

With the Hi-Po 289 no longer being built by Ford, the GT350 graduated to a 302 with an aluminum Cobra intake rated at 250 horsepower and 333 lb-ft of torque. The GT500 retained the 428 Police Interceptor that had been used the previous year, with a single 715 CFM Holley four-barrel replacing the less effective—and more finicky—dual-carb arrangement. About halfway through the model year, Ford introduced the Cobra Jet, which was basically a 428 Police Interceptor block with the medium-rise heads and crank from a 427. Although Ford officially rated it at 335 horsepower, it was an open secret that the engine made an honest 400 horsepower. (Ford admitted to 440 lb-ft of torque at 3400 rpm.) When the Cobra Jet became available, Shelby used it as the power plant for a new model that he called the GT500 KR, for King of the Road. "Look for 0 to 60 times that will snap your eyeballs!" an overcaffeinated copywriter wrote.

Exactly how this name was chosen is a favorite piece of Shelby lore. For years, it was thought that the sobriquet was inspired by Roger Miller's country hit. But the song had been released way back in January 1965, and as the lyrics made clear, the king of the road in Miller's lyrics was actually a hobo. ("I'm a man of means by no means, king of the road.") Shelby himself popularized another version that sounds only slightly less fanciful. As the story goes, Shelby heard a rumor that Chevrolet was planning to use "King of the Road" as the name of a hot, new version of the Corvette. Or maybe it was the Camaro. Or even the Chevelle. Whatever. Shelby supposedly called up his attorney and asked him to find out whether GM had trademarked the name. The attorney said he'd get back to Shelby in a week. Shelby told him if he didn't provide the answer in an hour, he'd be fired. Shelby got the answer in an hour. He also got the trademark.

This origin myth obscures the contributions made by Bob Tasca, an influential Rhode Island Ford dealer who was a major force in the drag-racing world. (He also sold a couple of the first Cobras.) In 1967, Tasca was looking to weaponize the Mustang, and the 390—the biggest engine offered at the time—just didn't pack enough muscle to do the job. Working with Bill Gilbert, a local mechanic and drag racer, Tasca ordered a 428 Police Interceptor short block and more or less completed the engine with 427-spec pieces. He stuck the mongrel motor in a Mustang drag-race car he called the KR-8, for King of the Road, 1968. He later showed the engine to Ford engineers in Dearborn, who used it as the foundation of the Cobra Jet.

Notwithstanding its name or its derivation, the King of the Road wasn't. In many respects, the GT350 and GT500 were the antithesis of what Shelby had gone into business to create back in 1962. The Cobra was a rude, no-compromises sports car that exposed the contemporary Corvette as a pretender to the throne. Like the Corvettes of yore, the modern Shelby Mustangs of 1968 were boulevardiers rather than the real thing. "Maybe the racetrack characteristics of the old GT350 make

Shelby shows off a 1968 GT350 with sequential taillights from a '65 T-Bird and the first convertible to bear the Shelby imprimatur. By this time, the name was just about all the input Shelby provided for the cars. Production had moved from Southern California to Michigan. And even though a King of the Road model would be introduced later in the year, the Shelby Mustang was more touring car than sports car. *Ford Motor Company*

the 500 look like a bull in a china shop," *Sports Car Graphic* wrote in an article that bent over backward to praise the car, "but you can take this latest Shelby and your surfboard to the beach or let it idle outside your girl's house in the winter with the heater on and not wake up the neighborhood. Besides, it's always good for fast getaways when her father comes racing outside in his nightshirt, waving a shotgun."[8] Car reviews have come a long way in the past half century.

Even this faint praise was undercut by a photo of a GT500 in action, plowing through a corner like a Trabant with bald front tires and incurable alignment issues. While *Sports Car Graphic* tactfully referred to this as "an appreciable amount of understeer," *Road & Track* was less willing to let Shelby slide on the basis of past accomplishments.[9] "In the early days of Shelby Mustangs, the GT350 seemed a serious and partially successful attempt to make a sporting car out of the Mustang," it wrote, "but now if anything it accentuates most of the Mustang's inherent shortcomings. And, what's worse, the Camaro Z-28 is a better example of the same sort of car—for less money."[10] How hath the mighty fallen!

With Shelby's blessing, chief engineer Fred Goodell was able to sneak at least one cool special project past the corporate killjoys. Ford had used a '68 notchback as the prototype for the Mustang GT/CS, aka California Special, which was purely an appearance package designed to make a stock Mustang GT look like a GT500. This car was then given to Goodell, who hot-rodded it with an experimental Cobra Jet "X" engine with an unproven Conelec fuel injection system, a heavy-duty F-350-based automatic transmission, independent rear suspension, and rear disc brakes. Although the so-called EXP 500 never got anywhere remotely close to production, it posted a 0-to-60 time of 5.7 seconds and averaged 157 mph over twenty miles at Ford's test track in Romeo, Michigan. In honor of its performance, not to mention three coats of Gold Lustre Green Lacquer paint, it was nicknamed the Green Hornet.

Bunkie Knudsen wasn't interested in Shelby's new toy. He had his own ideas about how to pump up Ford's high-performance image. (They would eventually take shape as the Boss 302 and Boss 429 versions of the Mustang.) Shelby saw the writing on the wall, so he was open to the notion of teaming up with another carmaker. As it happens, Toyota Motor Sales had just built its American headquarters in Torrance, making it Shelby Racing's neighbor. Although Toyota sold only twenty-six thousand cars in the States in 1967, it was about to become a major player in the US market. (In 1971, Toyota rang up 404,000 sales.) Goodyear wanted to get in on the ground floor, and the company used its association with Shelby to sweeten its sales pitch.

During the course of conversations with executives in Japan, talk naturally turned to racing. Shelby was surprised to learn that Toyota planned to race its jewel-like 2000GT in the States the next year, and he was shocked to discover that the motorsports operation was going to be run by none other than Peter Brock. Since leaving Shelby American in 1965, Brock had put together a successful racing program for Hino, another Japanese manufacturer that recently had been acquired by Toyota. Brock Racing Enterprises seemed like the perfect team to lead Toyota's first motorsports foray on American soil. But Toyota execs were seduced by the possibility of hooking up with a genuine international celebrity. It's not clear exactly how the deal went down. But when the smoked cleared, Shelby got the contract and Brock didn't.

"I've got the shop set up," Brock said.[11] "I've got a new dyno. I've hired new guys. I've gone to the bank. I'm really hung out—and the cars aren't showing up. I get a phone call. It's one of the guys I knew at Shelby's. He said, 'Pete, nobody's supposed to know this, but the 2000GTs are here.' And I said, 'Hey, I've got a signed contract right here!' And he said, 'Well, we're preparing them to go racing.' I couldn't believe what I was hearing, but it was true."

The 2000GT was Toyota's stab at creating a modern sports car with global appeal. Two decades later, Mazda would build the MX-5 Miata, which combined the carefree appeal of a classic British roadster with bulletproof Japanese reliability and became the most popular two-seater ever built. The 2000GT, on the other hand, was designed to showcase Toyota's ability to match the quality and creativity of any carmaker in the world. Built around a Lotus Elan-style backbone chassis, it featured exquisite bodywork and an exotic twin-cam engine. Only 337 cars were sold over four years, but thanks in part to its rarity and build quality, the car is now considered a lodestar of Japanese manufacturing.

Three 2000GTs were shipped to Shelby in the summer of 1967. One was to be used as a development mule while the other two would be raced in SCCA's C Production class against Porsche 911s—the current champ—and Lotus Elans, Datsun 2000s, and Triumph 250s. Engineer Rich Erickson, a SoCal club racer, was hired to run the program, and Shuttack and Butler were named crew chiefs. John Dunn was in charge of engine development, of which there would be plenty. Several Japanese engineers traveled to the States at various times to work on the program, and at least one was attached to the team at all times.

The crew made the usual racing modifications, lightening the car where possible and strengthening it where necessary. The bumpers were deleted, Konis installed, heim-joined anti-roll bars added, the cooling system upgraded, and bushings swapped from rubber to nylon. Other improvements included a differential cooler and replacing the six-into-one exhaust with two tracts with individual megaphones. When early tests uncovered braking issues, the Dunlops were switched out in favor of race-spec Girlings. Remington got Halibrand to cast special 15-inch magnesium wheels to mount experimental low-profile Goodyear tires that the team hoped might be a magic bullet. "A nice little car," Remington said, which was, for him, high praise.[12]

The weak link was the engine. The 2.0-liter inline-6 featured the iron block found in the top-of-the-line Toyopet Crown. To this, Yamaha—the Japanese engineering firm better known for its motorcycles—grafted an aluminum head with dual overhead cams, an aluminum oil pan, and valve covers sporting a black crinkle finish, à la Ferrari. Fitted with triple Webers, the engine made an impressive 205 horsepower at 7200 rpm and 240 lb-ft of torque at 4400 rpm. Unfortunately, the SCCA nixed the Webers, and the team had to revert to a trio of side-draft dual-throat Mikuni carburetors. This cost about ten horses, and while Dunn tried mightily, he was never able to make up the deficit.

Bucknum did the initial testing and logged lap times roughly equal to the Porsches. But Toyota wanted to run a low-key program without any high-profile drivers. After several drivers were auditioned at Riverside, Scooter Patrick and Dave Jordan got the rides. Patrick was coming off back-to-back Under 2.0-Liter USRRC titles in a Porsche 906 while Jordan had won the Southern Pacific C Production title and finished second in the American Road Race of Champions in a 911, so they were familiar with the competition.

On the other hand, the guys at Shelby weren't familiar with Japanese customs, and this led to a serious culture clash. "We had a lot of assistance from the Toyota people," Al Dowd said.[13] "We even had a resident engineer assigned to us who couldn't speak any English. And they do things differently. You couldn't turn around without asking them for permission. We had a little guy named Mr. Miki from Japan whose English was terrible. You know, you ask those people. 'Is it okay if we do this?' and they say, 'Yes.' That means, yes, they understand what you want to do, but, no, was the answer. So he'd say, 'Yes,' and we'd go ahead and do it, and we were always in trouble with him."

Besides having a lot of "weird" meetings—Dowd's description—Japanese conventions led to some odd practices. "They were really into rituals," Butler said.[14] "When we got to the track, everybody had to stand in line, at attention, while we unloaded the cars." Remember, the country was only a generation removed from World War II, and

Remington had actually fought against the Japanese. Some of these demands didn't sit well with the Shelby American mechanics, and at least one of them quit rather than work on the Toyota program.

The season opened at Stardust Raceway at Las Vegas, where Patrick finished second and Jordan fourth. Neither of them had anything for defending national champion Alan Johnson, in a Richie Ginther Porsche 911S with all sorts of factory development bits. It was, unfortunately, a harbinger of things to come, and the next few races confirmed it. "The Toyota was a good race car with a nicely done, beautifully running engine with overhead cams and all that stuff," Jordan said, "but it just didn't have the bottom-end grunt that the Porsche had."[15] Eventually, it became clear that the team would have to start racing elsewhere in the country to gather enough points to qualify for the year-end national championship race at Riverside.

Shelby didn't attend any of these races. The Toyota program was a significant profit center for the company; Shelby Racing billed more

The Toyota 2000GT was a lovely two-seat coupe with a jewel-like twin-cam motor. But even though they were beautifully turned out and expertly driven by Scooter Patrick and Dave Jordan, the two Shelby Racing entries lacked the grunt to beat the Porsche 911s in C Production. Here, Jordan gets all he can out of his right-hand-drive race car, but the program was done after a single year.
Revs Institute / Robert Tronolone Photograph Collection

than $175,000 for preseason testing alone, and by the time the 1968 season was over, Toyota had spent more than $500,000. But after going to Le Mans in the vanguard of the Ford armada, Shelby had no interest in enduring weekends in desolate club tracks in places like Stuttgart, Arkansas, and Warbonnet, Oklahoma. So he left the program in the hands of Erickson, Dowd, and Remington.

Trans-Am was higher up on Shelby's to-do list, though, to be honest, he wasn't chomping at the bit to attend these races either. But while Shelby seemed increasingly ambivalent about the whole racing enterprise, Ford was determined to claim a third straight title. Since the engineers at Kar-Kraft were no longer responsible for the Le Mans program, Ford put them to work on designing a new Trans-Am car. One of Shelby's 1967 Trans-Am cars was shipped to Michigan. There, Ed Hull—the man who'd designed the J-Car—cataloged its faults and came up with a host of improvements that would be incorporated into a pair of new Mustangs.

Hull focused first on the rear suspension. In 1967, the rear tires rubbed up against the leaf springs under load—not a good thing. He went to a narrower leaf spring to provide more clearance, and to make up for the loss of lateral control he added a Watts linkage. Another issue at the rear was brake-pad knockback, which occurred when the live axle deflected. Hull's solution was to install a NASCAR-style full-floating rear axle with moveable axle shafts. He also upgraded the brakes, cleaned up the roll cage, and used lightweight body panels. Meanwhile, senior project engineer Lee Dykstra improved the suspension geometry (and longevity) by hiding a larger spherical bearing inside the rubber boot around the front tie strut bushing. "Essentially," Dykstra said, "we made it into a proper race car."[16]

Shelby Racing started the season with a pair of brand-new Mustangs built on surface plates at Kar-Kraft. At first, the crew wasn't thrilled about using a turn-key chassis rather than one they'd developed them-selves, but in all fairness, Hull's platform was so good that they didn't complain about it for very long. The engine, on the other hand, was something they complained about from the instant it arrived, leaking oil by the quart, until the moment the last one mercifully exploded.

For 1968, to take advantage of new regulations, the venerable 289 was stroked to 302 cubic inches. Even so, it had become painfully clear during the last half of the previous Trans-Am season that the engine couldn't match the breathing qualities of the small-block Chevy. Ford engineers knew that if more air could be flowed through the ports, the engine could spin faster and develop more horsepower. They designed a new series of motors featuring round intake ports that were absolutely huge. "The ports are so bloody big," Keith Duckworth, co-creator of the Cosworth DFV Formula 1 engine, told Ford's Don Coleman, "you could send a [little person] down them."[17]

Not a small person, as it turned out, but a tunnel. To maximize airflow, the ports ran directly from the manifold to the cylinder instead of being routed around the pushrods. The pushrods were then encased in brazed tubes that tunneled right through the heart of the gargantuan intake ports, hence the name tunnel port. It seemed to be a brilliant solution, but events proved otherwise. "Ford decided to build a better mousetrap for 1968. But the mousetrap snapped on the wrong head, because the engines Ford came up with were absolute pieces of shit," mechanic Bobby Boxx said.[18] "Those engines leaked oil everywhere, and they exploded faster than you could put them into the cars. The engine situation got so bad that we used to start a pool to see which lap they'd decide to saw themselves in half."

Boxx insisted that Shelby Racing blew up fifty-seven tunnel-port 302s during the 1968 season. More conservative sources put the number at "only" thirty-two. (Chuck Cantwell said thirty-seven.) Lew Spencer, who again managed the team, started describing race weekends in terms of how many engines had grenaded, so a two-engine weekend meant that two engines had popped. Thus, Continental Divide was a *six*-engine weekend—two blown in practice, two blown in qualifying, and two blown in the race. "We changed oil pans by the hundreds," Jerry Schwarz said.[19]

The beauty of the tunnel port was that it allowed drivers to rev the engines to 8500 rpm and above—an extraordinary feat for a pushrod motor, even by modern standards. But drivability was abysmal. Tunnel-port technology was well-suited to NASCAR, where a narrow power band wasn't an issue because drivers turned high engine speeds for long periods of time. But that was the wrong paradigm for road racing, with its mix of fast straights and slow corners. "Those engines ran good at about 8000 or 8500 rpm," Cantwell said.[20] "But they didn't have any power or throttle response down low." So even when the tunnel ports weren't blowing up, the drivers hate-hate-hated them.

The mechanics hated them even more. The oil pickup in the stock oil sump was so far forward that the engine suffered from catastrophic starvation under acceleration, when the oil shifted to the rear of the pan. Mitch Marchi at Kar-Kraft developed a slick sheet-metal alternative with a second pickup at the rear of the oil pan and a second oil pump piggybacked to the main one. One pump supplied oil to the engine, the other to the sump. In other words, there was an illegal dry sump hidden inside the legal wet sump. Pure genius.

Like all great horror movies, Shelby's 1968 Trans-Am season began on a sunny, almost cheerful note. The first race was at Daytona, which was held as part of the twenty-four-hour enduro for the first and last time. By this point, the Terlingua Racing Team fiction had been dropped, and Shelby Racing entered two cars, with Jerry Titus paired with Bucknum in one and a pair of Australians, Horst Kwech and Alan Moffatt, in the other. Kwech's engine leaked oil like a sieve during practice while Titus's was dry as sand. In the race, it was the reverse. The crew added two or three quarts of oil to the Titus/Bucknum car every pit stop. The situation was so dire that mechanics kept crawling into the cockpit to wipe down the oil-soaked pedals! But the engine miraculously stayed together for twenty-four hours, and Titus and Bucknum finished first in class and an amazing fourth overall. The other car DNFed with a broken front spring structure. Mechanic Mark Popov-Dadiani complained to the Ford Engine & Foundry people about poor build quality. For speaking truth to power, he was fired.

The following month found the Trans-Am series at Sebring, where the cars would be running a race-within-a-race in the 12 Hour. By this time, Ford had identified the valve covers as the source of the worst of the oil leaks, and a new breather system had been implemented. Nevertheless, engines blew up left and right during practice, and Kwech lost another one in the race. Once again, the motor in the Titus/Bucknum car defied expectations and kept on going to the finish, third in class

Titus, co-driving with Bucknum, gives Shelby Racing a win at Daytona in the first Trans-Am race of 1968. (They were also fourth overall in the twenty-four-hour enduro.) With a slick chassis from Kar-Kraft and a promising tunnel-port V-8 from Ford, the team had high hopes for the season. Alas, engines blew up so often that the crew used to bet on when they would saw themselves in half. *Revs Institute / Eric della Faille Photograph Collection*

behind a pair of Roger Penske Camaros. Not great, but not terrible. All things considered, the season had started reasonably well. Like the clueless patsies who walk blithely into the woods in slasher flicks, the Shelby team didn't foresee the bloodbath to come.

Schwarz, the Mustanger with more time on the program than anybody other than Cantwell, stopped traveling with the team shortly after that. While a lot of the original Shelby guys thought the move to LAX was the beginning of the end, Schwarz thought *leaving* LAX was where it all went wrong. "When we moved to Torrance, it seemed to go downhill from there," he said.[21] "There was a lot going on with budgets and everything, and things just changed. Racing became less and less fun and more and more . . . it's hard to explain."

But there were still lighter moments. Schwarz remembers working alongside Remington on the Trans-Am cars. He'd brought an expensive radio to the shop and cranked up the volume to listen to acid rock.

Remington kept turning it down, and Schwarz kept turning it back up. This loop continued until the radio suddenly exploded into a thousand pieces. "Phil never said a word, just kept on working. I got the message loud and clear," Schwarz said.[22] "Phil evidently did not like acid rock music and turned it off with an M-80."

At the time, Shelby Racing employed twenty-four hourly and eleven salaried employees. All of them were busy as the summer of '68 approached. The Trans-Am and Toyota programs were about to get going hot and heavy, and a full crew would be needed at Indy to support the Wallis turbine car. But first, Shelby wanted to collect what looked like some low-hanging fruit in the USRRC series, which was more or less Can-Am Lite—Group 7 cars but without the mighty McLaren and Chaparral teams gobbling up all the prize money.

Shelby American's former general manager, Peyton Cramer, had rejoined Shelby as a "racing consultant." The previous year, Cramer had run Peter Revson in Can-Am, without much success. Shelby acquired the remains of the program, which consisted of several Lola T70s in various states of disarray and a collection of spares of dubious utility. John Collins cobbled together a raceable car, and Jim O'Leary built up a 378-cubic-inch Ford V-8 with a Gurney-Weslake head. Revson came with the program, much to the chagrin of Carroll Smith. Handsome and worldly, Revson was the son of a founder of the Revlon cosmetics empire. Although he'd been around for several years, he was regarded as a playboy rather than a serious driver, and he was more famous for his beauty queen girlfriends than his racing exploits. Smith wasn't expecting much when he headed down to Mexico City for the first race of the season.

Just getting to the track turned out to be a protracted ordeal. Smith spent four days marooned with the car in El Paso before finally bribing officials to get across the border. There hadn't been time for Revson to test the car, so Smith had scared himself silly shaking it down. Afterward, racing in a car he'd never sat in on a track he'd never seen before, Revson dialed up a banzai lap as qualifying was ending to claim the pole. He was running away from the field when he had to pit with a loose battery cable. He then came from nineteenth to finish third. "He did the most magnificent, professional job of driving a race car that I'd seen in years," Smith said.[23] Shelby was so pleased by the outing that he decided to invest in a more competitive McLaren M6B to make a serious run at the Can-Am championship in the fall.

Alas, Mexico City was the highlight of the Shelby Racing USRRC effort. At Riverside, in the next race, Revson qualified third before losing an engine early. The team missed three consecutive races before showing up at Pacific Raceways in Kent with a fancy-schmancy aluminum 427 that Ford had provided. Revson stuck it on the pole. But the engine was leaking so much oil that the crew attached a one-gallon catch can to the back and jury-rigged a pump to send oil back to the engine. Ford's Homer Perry told Revson, "We don't care if you finish the race or not—just lead it."[24] Revson duly led the first lap before retiring with what was officially listed as—nudge, nudge, wink, wink—a gearbox failure. And with this DNF, Shelby's USSRC dreams went up in smoke.

The month of May was approaching, which meant the Indy car became the top priority. Turbines were trending in 1968. Even though USAC had restricted the size of the annulus from 23.999 square inches to 15.999 square inches, three car owners were convinced that they could still build a competitive turbine-powered car. After splitting with Wallis, Granatelli had commissioned a clean-sheet design from Colin Chapman, the mastermind behind Lotus Cars. Chapman came up with one of his most innovative creations, the arresting wedge-shaped Lotus 56. To drive it, he lined up his current F1 superstars, former World Champions Jim Clark and Graham Hill. Also, Jack Adams, a prominent aircraft dealer who'd been trying to get a turbine car into the race for several years, was touting a new chassis. Altogether, nine turbine-powered chassis were entered. "We appear to be on the threshold of the jet age of auto racing," Forrest Bond wrote in *Sports Car Graphic.*[25]

The Shelby/Wallis car got plenty of local attention, including several stories in the *LA Times.* The newspaper's racing columnist, Bob Thomas, attended the press preview at Riverside in mid-March and reported, somewhat credulously, that the car had hit 208 mph on the backstraight and smoked all four tires with Wallis at the wheel. At the time, the engine was still being operated with an unrestricted annulus of 41.6 square inches rather than the restricted inlet that would be required at Indy, so the self-reported top speed was plausible, though most observers dismissed it as wildly optimistic. A few days later, during a Goodyear tire test at the Indianapolis Motor Speedway, McLaren topped out at 158 mph—a good 3 mph less than the minimum speed to qualify for the 500 and at least 10 mph off the expected pole. When Wallis asked him what he thought of the car, McLaren hemmed and hawed before finally admitting, "All right. If you *really* want to know, it's a cross between a Sherman tank and a Formula Ford."[26]

Adding injury to insult, Jonsson, the car's transmission designer, made the tactical error of getting into an argument with A. J. Foyt in the Holiday Inn Northwest bar over the merits of turbine cars. Although Jonsson may have won the debate, he lost the ensuing war, and he returned to Torrance after a trip to the hospital to get thirty-two stitches in his face. He later filed a $200,000 lawsuit alleging that Foyt struck him "with a sharp and deadly weapon"—to wit, a broken beer bottle—while fellow Indy car driver Roger McCluskey inflicted "numerous bruises and contusions."[27] Chief mechanic Jack Beckley, who would later become technical director of the Indy 500, was also named as a defendant.

The plot thickened when Wallis gave Butler a blueprint for work to be done to the starter motor. The car featured a chisel nose into which a V-shaped air intake had been cut. Within the intake sat a stainless-steel nosepiece housing the starter motor. Attached to the bullet-shaped nosepiece was a ring resembling a doughnut cut in half the long way. This ring was sized to reduce the annulus from the stock opening of 41.6 square inches to the 15.999 square inches permitted by USAC. The blueprint called for Butler to attach four springs to the front of the starter motor and cut an O-ring groove in the side of the body. This would allow the nosepiece to slide smoothly up and down over the starter motor. The motor itself was secured with a pair of quarter-inch-diameter bolts that extended through the housing. Butler rifled-drilled one of them—an exacting job—and added a -2 AN fitting to the end. AN fittings are usually attached to hoses or tubes, which got Butler to thinking, "What the hell is going on here?" After asking around and learning more about how gas turbines worked, he cottoned on to

Wallis's scheme. When the engine started up, air would be blown from the second-stage compressor through the tiny hole he'd rifled-drilled through the bolt. The nosepiece and the doughnut ring attached to it would slide forward over the starter motor. This would allow air to flow in behind the doughnut, thereby circumventing the annulus restriction. The engine would appear to be legal at tech inspection, but it would operate illegally on the track.

Butler confronted Wallis. "You sons of a bitches are cheating!"[28]

Wallis didn't bother denying it. "We've got a million dollars from Botany 500 and all the money from Shelby and Goodyear," he said. "What would you do?"

"That's not my problem. You shouldn't have done this to start with."

"Well, we can't stop now. I tell you what I'm going to do. You're going to quit working for Shelby, and you're going to work for Wallis Engineering, and you're going to sign a nondisclosure thing that says you're not allowed to say anything about the stuff that went into the motor. And on top of that, I'm going to give you a twenty-five-cent [-an-hour] raise."

Butler naively accepted the offer. But as is so often the case with so many sub-rosa enterprises, secrets tend to frustrate even the most vigorous efforts to suppress them, and truth won out. In this particular case, Wallis ran afoul of another turbine expert with car-racing experience— Craig Breedlove. In 1965, two weeks after his record-setting runs at Bonneville in a Cobra Daytona Coupe, Breedlove drove his General Electric J79 jet turbine-powered *Spirit of American Sonic I* to a land-speed record of 600.601 mph. Like Wallis, he wanted to use a GE T58 as the basis of an Indy car, and like Wallis, he figured out a foolproof method of bypassing USAC's annulus restriction. Breedlove pitched the project to Granatelli. When Granatelli questioned the ability of the T58 to be competitive at Indy, Breedlove explained the cheat and told him that Wallis was using the same workaround. Granatelli turned him down because he was already committed to Chapman and the Lotus 56. But the elephantine Granatelli never forgot.

There was even more drama before the team left for Indy. Back then, the entire month of May was devoted to the 500. The Speedway was set to open for practice on Wednesday, May 1. "We saw the cars loaded up on Friday, and we came in on Monday and found the doors locked with a legal note on the door," said Norton, the junior Jonsson engineer.[29] "They had cleaned out the shop—lathes, mills, rollaway toolboxes, everything." Turned out that Jonsson had filed a writ of attachment against Wallis Engineering over what he claimed were $30,000 in unpaid bills. Shelby settled the debt, and the attachment was "lifted in a matter of hours," according to the Los Angeles County Sheriff's Office, but the fun was just beginning.

Shelby Racing showed up at the Speedway with two nicely turned-out cars—McLaren's No. 66, painted gold with a royal blue center stripe, and Hulme's No. 69, with the paint scheme reversed. McLaren was out in his car on the first day, and he completed his rookie test on day two. Hulme did several runs in his teammate's car and started shaking down his own machine the following Monday. "The New Zealand 'Can-Am twins' McLaren and Hulme are in and out of the No. 69 Shelby turbine, but can't reach one hundred sixty," Donald Davidson wrote in his day-by-day report for *Floyd Clymer's 1968 Indianapolis 500 Yearbook*.[30] "Designer Ken Wallis said earlier that he was aiming for the pole, but the cars haven't shown speed. Apparently, the drivers are complaining of severe handling problems. All is not well in the Shelby camp and rumors are that both McLaren and Hulme are looking around for another ride."

McLaren had signed onto the project primarily because Goodyear was paying him $50,000 to help develop the car and an additional $20,000 for testing. But he wasn't a happy camper. Slowing down was one issue. Because the turbine didn't provide any engine braking, the overworked disc brakes got so hot that Remington kept cutting holes in the bodywork to provide additional cooling. More problematic was the suspension geometry. The lower heim joints attached to the rear uprights were only three inches apart, which is to say much too close together. When McLaren accelerated, the rear tires developed unwanted toe-in. When he braked, he got instant toe-out. In effect, the handling toggled between frightening and terrifying.

"The thing was doing two hundred twelve miles per hour on the straightaways, but it was four hundred pounds too heavy and couldn't get around the corners and the brakes were on fire," Butler recalled.[31]

"On the left side was the motor, and in the middle was this big bloody tank filled with the kerosene, and he's sitting on the right side between the two right-side tires in a little cradle made out of one-inch square tubing. Can you imagine doing two hundred twelve miles per hour with that little thing between you and the wall? He was scared shitless."

Meanwhile, back in California, Breedlove was puzzled by why Granatelli hadn't outed Wallis yet. After thinking it over, Breedlove became convinced that Granatelli was waiting for Shelby's cars to qualify. *Then*, Breedlove believed, Granatelli would go public with details about the cheat, thereby achieving the maximum embarrassment for Wallis (who'd quit him to form a rival company), Goodyear (he was a Firestone guy) and the Indianapolis Motor Speedway (which had won a lawsuit he'd filed against it). Breedlove was himself a Goodyear driver, and he was loyal to the brand. On Monday night, he called Larry Truesdale, the general manager of the Goodyear Racing Division. "You've got a big problem brewing out there," Breedlove told him.[32] "Are you aware that the engines in your turbine cars are illegal?" After Breedlove brought the mortified Truesdale up to speed, Remington said, "The garage is locked up right now, but we have a key. I'll go over there and tear down the front of the engine and see what's inside."[33]

Neither of the Shelby/Wallis turbines practiced on Tuesday as McLaren and Hulme had flown to Europe to compete in the Spanish Grand Prix the following weekend. But nobody really noticed because most eyes were on Mike Spence, an up-and-coming British F1 driver who was in the Granatelli Lotus 56 that Clark had been scheduled to drive before being killed at Hockenheim. Only four days after passing his rookie test, Spence clocked the fastest lap of the month, at 169.555 mph. But later in the afternoon, while making a run during Happy Hour, he crashed hard in Turn One and was pronounced dead of massive head injuries at 9:45 p.m.

Spence's wreck was a ghoulish godsend for the troubled Wallis turbine effort. An emergency meeting was convened in Shelby's hotel room. "Goodyear told Shelby, 'You better shut this off right away,'" Remington said.[34] "So he withdrew the cars before there could be any big stink about it. It would have been a real mess if anybody had gotten wind of what was going on." The crash of the Lotus served as a convenient alibi for the real reason the team abruptly ended the program. Two hours after Spence hit the wall, Shelby issued a statement through a PR functionary: "After complete and intensive testing, I feel at the present time it is impossible to make a turbine-powered car competitive with a reasonable degree of safety and reliability."[35]

Granatelli was understandably furious. Not only did the announcement imply that the Lotus had been responsible for Spence's crash, but it also buried the lede—that the Shelby/Wallis turbine was a cheater car that had been on the verge of getting busted. The Botany 500 garage in Gasoline Alley was padlocked, and Shelby and the crew hightailed it out of Indy on his DC-3 before any embarrassing follow-up questions could be asked. The unseemly and mystifying exit sparked plenty of scorn. "The gap between the few good cars in the Indy field and multitudes of poor ones was symbolized by two machines that weren't even there," Brock Yates wrote in a scorched-earth column in *Car and Driver.*[36] "They were the Ken Wallis/Carroll Shelby turbines that have to be included with the

Shelby Racing showed up at the Indianapolis Motor Speedway with a pair of Wallis turbines that were overweight, underbraked, and plagued by diabolical handling issues that unnerved McLaren and Hulme. The cars never showed enough speed to make the show, and they were abruptly withdrawn after a week when the team learned that Wallis was using a technical cheat in the turbine's intake system to game the system. *Revs Institute / Karl Ludvigsen Photograph Collection*

Titanic and the Gallipoli campaign as one of the great debacles of the Twentieth Century."

Of course, Yates didn't realize that, in addition to being uncompetitive, the car was a fraud. Although rumors immediately started making the rounds, several years passed before they were enshrined in print in a stunning piece of investigative reporting by Yates and co-author Karl Ludvigsen (writing under a pseudonym, Eric Nielssen) in a *Car and Driver* story titled "The Evil Phantom of Gasoline Alley."[37] No doubt this was one reason Wallis was able to promote his next project—a steam-powered Indy car funded by Bill Lear, which turned out to be another boondoggle. McLaren was thrilled to be relieved from having to drive a car that was trying to kill him. Hulme snagged a ride in a Dan Gurney Eagle and finished fourth.

Butler was fired for not informing the team about Wallis's cheat, and he couldn't have cared less. "I was so bloody exhausted, I went home, and I lay by the pool for three weeks," he said.[38] "After three weeks, the phone rings. It's Al Dowd. He said, 'Get your ass back down here. We want you to run the Toyota program.' I said, 'Well, what about all those other problems?' And he said, 'Oh, we've got that all taken care of.' It was swept under the rug like nothing had ever happened."

The Toyota program wasn't where Shelby had hoped it would be. The cars were good, the drivers were good, and the crew was good. They just weren't good enough to beat the Porsches driven by Johnson and Milt Minter. Under the circumstances, there didn't appear to be any chance that either Patrick or Jordan would be able to win the Southern Pacific divisional title. But in SCCA club racing, the national championship was decided on the basis of the winner-take-all American Road Race of Champions. The catch was that the ARRC was open only to drivers who finished in the top three in their division.

In June, Robert F. Kennedy was assassinated at the Ambassador Hotel near downtown Los Angeles, where Shelby had held numerous press conferences over the years. Even as the nation seemed to be self-destructing during a summer of discontent, Shelby Racing started criss-crossing the country in search of weaker regions where the team could beat up on the locals and score much-needed points in C Production. Patrick led one-two finishes in Stuttgart, Warbonnet, and Mid-Ohio while Jordan turned the tables in Odessa, Texas. It might have had something to do with the wedding-night celebration Dowd prepared for the newly married Patrick.

"I had all of this ammunition, and when we got to the hotel we booby-trapped Scooter's room," Dowd said.[39] "The legs fell off the bed when he got on it. And when you opened a drawer, we had it rigged so that the whole top blew off of the night table. We had cherry bombs underneath the toilet seat—all kinds of stuff. It cost $800 to repair all of the damage that we'd done to the room. We had a big battle, throwing cherry bombs. We had a regular war going on at three o'clock in the morning, after all the bars closed. I was barricaded in my room, and they were trying to get at me. Then things calmed down a little as people started to pass out, and eventually everyone got to sleep. The next morning, I called room service and asked them to bring me some coffee. The guy knocked on the door, and I had forgotten about the night before. They had bobby-trapped my door, and the screen door was blown right off the hinges when I opened it. And this poor guy, with a tray and everything, threw it up in the air and took off across the lawn, and I never saw him again. They asked us never to come back there, and I can't blame them."

Patrick finished third in the Southern Pacific divisional standings, which meant he qualified for the ARRC, but despite the win at Odessa, Jordan ended up fourth. This year, the ARRC was being held at Riverside, Patrick's home track. But any advantage he had in terms of familiarity was counterbalanced by the nature of the circuit, which favored the Porsches. Johnson and Minter ran in tandem all race, finishing first and second, with East Coast stalwart Bob Tullius a tick behind in his Group 44 Triumph TR250. Patrick finished a discouraging fourth, 33.5 seconds behind the leader and barely holding off another 911S.

This wasn't what Toyota had had in mind when it traded Brock for Shelby. The company ended the partnership and decided to focus on motorsports in Japan. Along the way, Shelby was offered a chance to become a Toyota distributor, but he turned it down based on advice proffered by Lee Iacocca. "Oh, forget it, Shel," he told him. "We're going to push the [Japanese] back in the ocean."[40] Shelby passed along the opportunity to his friend Tom Friedkin, who became a billionaire distributing Toyotas.

One other footnote: After losing the 2000GT program to Shelby, Brock immediately approached Datsun and persuaded the company to put him in charge of its puny American motorsports efforts. Racing in memorable red-white-and-blue livery, Brock Racing Enterprises won a pair of C Production national championships with Datsun 240Zs and back-to-back 2.5-Liter Trans-Am titles with Datsun 510s. And who was the driver? None other than fellow Shelby American refugee John Morton. So Datsun rather than Toyota became the first Japanese company to establish a high-performance image in the States, and it remained a major player in both professional and grassroots racing for many years to come.

Shelby's prospects weren't much brighter on the Trans-Am front. During the course of the season, the cars changed colors repeatedly—red, light blue, orange, Gawd-Awful Yellow and, finally, corporate dark blue. But no matter what the paint scheme, their fortunes were almost uniformly bleak. At War Bonnet Park Raceway, Jerry Titus blew an engine. Jones was filling in for Kwech. After a dispute over red-flag rules, he grabbed a steward by the neck and shook him like a tambourine before Cantwell and Spencer ran over to defuse the situation. "I don't think I made any friends, especially with SCCA officials," Jones allowed.[41] He finished third after an unscheduled pit stop to repair the throttle linkage.

Ford used the mechanical issue as an excuse to insist on building all engines in its production department instead of entrusting assembly to Shelby Racing. The company also embedded two engineers with the team, ostensibly to help out but, in reality, to make sure that the engines weren't touched. This was a supremely idiotic idea. Production car engines spend most of their time lazing along at less than 4000 rpm while race engines regularly scream to redline—8500 rpm, in this case—and beyond. The tolerances in race motors have to be finer, the attention to detail an order of magnitude greater. The build quality of an engine coming off a production-car assembly line can't stand up to the rigors of racing.

The oiling system remained a constant source of anxiety. Although the secret dry sump unit solved the oil-starvation problem, it prevented the crew from checking how much oil was actually in the engine—a major concern since oil tended to collect in the valve covers and blow out during hard cornering. Cantwell unenthusiastically agreed to serve as a brake marker during pit stops. "Our pit stops started with me standing in the pit lane with a pressurized oil bottle in my hands and Titus stopping at my knees, me pulling the hood pins, raising the hood, and plugging the oil bottle into an engine quick-fill and closing the hood and inserting the pins. That could be a little scary."

Dykstra, who attended all the races as Kar-Kraft's representative, blamed most of the engine failures on shoddy assembly by Ford workers accustomed to working on six-cylinder Mustangs. But even when the motors stayed together, the Mustangs couldn't keep up with the Penske Camaros. "What happened was that Chevrolet homologated spoilers in the front and the rear, and there was not a Ford homologation to match that," he said.[42] "So, in addition to the engine problems, there was an aero problem as well."

At Lime Rock, Titus was a distant second to Donohue despite receiving an official reprimand for rough driving. David Pearson was the guest driver. Although his engine didn't explode, it oiled down the track so thoroughly that he was black-flagged. At Mid-Ohio, Titus was second again, but one-and-a-half laps behind Mark Donohue. Kwech was back in the second car. Born in Vienna, he was raised in Australia, and he raced with a decal of a kangaroo on his helmet. He'd already won a Trans-Am championship, in an Alfa in the Under 2.0-liter class. Fast and tough, "Kwechie" was a favorite of the crew. Unfortunately, his return to the team coincided with another blown tunnel port—on the pace lap!

Bridgehampton was a disaster even before the crew got to the track. Hauling the cars to New York, the truck driver mistakenly got on a picturesque parkway instead of a more modern highway, and the top of the transporter clipped a lower-than-usual overpass. The roofs of the Mustangs were crunched, so the guys stayed up most of the night pounding out sheet metal. The team arrived at the track in a rented beer delivery truck. Both cars lost engines, one in the race, the other before it started. At Meadowdale, each motor amazingly remained in

NASCAR legend David Pearson makes a guest appearance at Lime Rock. But his engine lasts for less than thirty minutes before oiling down the track thoroughly enough to earn him a black flag. Titus finished second in the team's other car, but he was lapped twice by the winner. In a year, the Shelby Mustangs had gone from all-conquering to also-rans. *Revs Institute / Duke Q. Manor Photograph Collection*

one piece—something that happened only once all year—but the cars were way off the pace. Kwech blew engines at St. Jovite and Bryar, and Titus wasn't competitive at either circuit.

The underlying problem wasn't money, that's for sure. Ford originally agreed to stake Shelby with $300,000 for the program. The company ended up spending close to $800,000—and that didn't include free cars, parts, and engineering support. Then again, in a mid-season memo to Shelby, Spencer complained bitterly about Ford's "contributions" to the Mustang effort. He said that the powers that be insisted that the team run a host of illegal parts yet seemed more concerned about paint jobs than on-track performance. "A complete smokescreen has been thrown up since Sebring to obscure the fact that the engines are far below par," he wrote.[43] "Needless to say, team morale is very low. The crew is used to winning and no matter how hard they work or how many late nights they put in changing engines, it seems to be of no avail."

Watkins Glen was a rare highlight for the Mustangs. By this point, Cantwell and Spencer were so desperate to find the pace they needed to compete with the Donohue/Penske juggernaut that they were running Firestones despite Shelby's long association with Goodyear. But during practice, Titus blistered his tires, so a set of Goodyears had to be mounted at the last minute. These new tires were slightly smaller than the Firestones, which meant that the gear ratios should have been adjusted to prevent the engine from turning too many revs, but there wasn't enough time to make the change. In the race, Titus was forced to spin the motor to nine grand just to keep up. But Donohue ran into problems, and Titus was able to sneak past Sam Posey late in the race—Posey called it "the most beautiful pass I ever saw"—to score a surprising win.[44] "It's just a miracle that the engine lasted," Cantwell said. Especially since the engine in the second car had exploded again.

The season reached rock bottom at Continental Divide. Destroying six engines—six engines!—over the course of a single weekend was bad enough. But the cherry on top of the team's sundae of woe was the surprise crew chief Jack Aylesbury found when he opened a crate holding a factory-fresh tunnel port from Dearborn. Attached to it was the usual dyno sheet showing the usual numbers. But when he checked inside the valve covers, he realized that the engine was missing two pushrods and three rocker arms. "Am I supposed to run this piece of shit?" Boxx snarled at one of the Ford engineers who'd been assigned to the program.[45] "There ain't any pushrods in it." This was the last straw for Titus. After the next race at Riverside, he said, he was quitting the team.

In his last race in a Mustang, Titus battled valiantly with Donohue for the lead at Riverside before—fittingly—the motor exploded. Thoroughly disgusted, Shelby split before the race was over. But after Donohue broke, Kwech was the best of the rest. Spencer hung out a pit sign: "WATCH REVS THINK." Later, near the end of the race, he changed it to "WE LOVE YOU." Kwech rumbled to an immensely satisfying win. "John Dunn of Shelby Racing built the engine, and it never missed a beat," Kwech said.[46] "For this one race, we got the green light to build our own engines, and I won. That should have told Ford something, but it didn't."

The internal politics at Ford grew increasingly toxic. Corporate racing supremo John Cowley—who'd never been a Shelby fan—wrote cattily to Trans-Am chief Fran Hernandez, "If you would spend as much time fixing the failures as figuring out statistical failure rate, we might have an invincible machine. But, as they say in most competitive sports, the losers are always checking the statistics."[47] Hernandez wasn't letting this go without a riposte. "I believe you have the issues confused, because most of my time is spent in fixing failures and improving the vehicle and not in figuring statistics," he fired back.[48] "If the E&F Division comes up with any kind of an engine for 1969 you will have an invincible machine as we have had no chassis failures since the Daytona twenty-four-hour race."

The season ended on a down note at Kent, where Shelby had won the Trans-Am championship for Ford the previous year. Titus qualified on the pole—in a Pontiac Firebird, which was a bitter pill for the Shelby guys to swallow after all of his successes in their cars. Revson, who replaced him in the Mustang, blew yet another engine. Kwech saved himself the agony of losing a motor by wrecking early. Shortly after the race was over, Cantwell quit to manage the race shop and road-racing program for archrival Roger Penske. By the end of the year, Spencer was the last remaining member of the original band. "The 1968 season was frustrating for all of us," he said.[49] "We were used to winning, and when we started losing, it just tore the team apart. I came away from 1968 thinking, 'Well, I'm glad I did that. And I'm glad I don't have to do it again.'"

Shelby Racing had one last bullet in the chamber for 1968—the Can-Am Series, which featured six races, one every two weeks, starting in the fall. Ford was eager to raise its profile in the series, which had been dominated by Chevrolet. The company had been fooling around with an open-top Can-Am-eligible variation of the old J-Car, now designated the G7A. But extensive testing had shown that neither the car nor the highly experimental (read: impossible to keep together) three-valve Calliope engine were ready for prime time. All American Racers was planning to run Ford-powered cars for Gurney and his young protégé, Swede Savage, and the Agapiou brothers, Charlie and Kerry, were sticking a Ford in an old Lola T70 for Bucknum. But Shelby Racing would be operating as the quasi-factory team.

Shelby had bought two McLaren M6Bs for Revson to drive. Back when Shelby sold GT350s and Trans-Am Mustangs for customers, they had been identical (more or less) to the team cars raced by Titus. Bruce McLaren had adopted a different approach. His customer models featured last year's technology, while he saved the good stuff for the machines he and Hulme would be racing. Shelby and Carroll Smith understood that they were starting at a disadvantage. But they were hoping that some engine magic provided by Ford—and in-house engine builder Jim O'Leary—could give the team a shot at disrupting the Bruce and Denny Show. It didn't work out that way. "We had endless engine trouble—all or most of it due to some unwanted interference from Dearborn," Smith said.[50]

Shelby Racing unloaded at Elkhart Lake for the season opener with a pair of M6Bs that Eaton had modified to accommodate big-block Fords. The team also had two all-aluminum 427s with an exotic cross-ram intake and Hilborn injection similar to the system used on the four-cam Indy Fords. The car wasn't very impressive, largely because the alloy big-block suffered from chronic oiling issues. After practice, one 427 was swapped for another, apparently identical. Asked why the change was made, Remington said cryptically, "Because it's five o'clock Friday." Writing in *Autosport*, Pete Lyons reported, "This had every sign of [being] a political rather than a mechanical decision."[51] Revson started seventh and finished fourth, nearly two minutes behind the leader. This was the season writ small: McLaren and Hulme waltzed to victory while Revson scrapped with Jim Hall's Chaparral 2G and Mark Donohue's M6B for honors in the second-class division.

At Bridgehampton, Revson qualified an excellent third but was sidelined by a broken suspension. At Edmonton, he spun a bearing. Torrential rain fell at Laguna Seca, creating the conditions necessary for John Cannon—who was nearly six seconds off the pole in qualifying—to score a magnificent victory in his antiquated McLaren Elva Mk II. Revson had a dismal race, finishing laps down. At Riverside, the team lost two engines during practice. Before the start of the race, Shelby put his arm around Revson and apologized. He should have waited a few more minutes. On the first lap, Revson's oil pressure plummeted to zero, and he retired. "We never had the budget to really do it right," O'Leary explained.[52] "I was the only engine man on that car, and it was a lot of work because we never had enough money to buy the spare parts we needed. I ended up flying back and forth rebuilding engines, and that wasn't fun."

Las Vegas was another dud. Although Revson ran second early, he suffered a flat tire, which may have contributed to the suspension failing later in the race. That marked Revson's fifth consecutive DNF. But rather than slinking home to lick their wounds, the crew headed to Japan for the invitation-only World Challenge Cup Fuji 200. Heavily promoted by the Japan Auto Club, the one-off race brought together North American Can-Am cars and homegrown Group 7 machines. After all the crashes at Las Vegas two weeks earlier, McLaren, Hulme, Hall, and Gurney were no-shows. Revson qualified a close second to Donohue and diced with him for most of the race. When Donohue pitted with a fuel issue, Revson breezed to victory. And so it happened that the last Can-Am race ever contested by Shelby was also the only one he ever won.

With a customer McLaren M6B and an aluminum Ford 427 with an exotic cross-ram intake and Hilborn injection, Revson was as fast as anybody, other than McLaren and Hulme, during the 1968 Can-Am season. Here, he leads Donohue at Bridgehampton. But engine woes sabotaged his year—until the team flew to Japan for a one-off race at Fuji. There, Revson outlasted Donohue to score Shelby Racing's first—and last—Can-Am victory. *Revs Institute / Karl Ludvigsen Photograph Collection*

CHAPTER EIGHT

END OF THE LINE

1969

Historians generally fall into one of two camps. There are the Great Man types who believe that singular larger-than-life figures—Alexander the Great, Napoleon, Darth Vader—control the levers of history. On the other side of the divide are structuralists who argue that systemic forces such as economics or climate determine the course of events. Without Carroll Shelby, there was no Cobra, and without the Cobra, Ford's assault on Le Mans might have played out very differently. But Shelby American was also in the right place at the right time, as the emergence of the baby boomer generation created a cohort of consumers who were willing to pay a premium for high-performance vehicles.

By both measures—Great Man and structuralist—the Shelby empire was in decline as 1969 dawned. Shelby, the man, was diminished and disengaged. He'd distanced himself from day-to-day operations years earlier, and now there was no big picture to command his time and energy. Other than brand image, Shelby no longer supplied anything that Ford needed because Ford had adapted to the demographic shifts of the 1960s, and the roles once played by the GT350 and GT500 were now filled by the Boss 302 and Boss 429. As for the Cobra, it had long since been consigned to the dustbin of history.

From Ford's perspective, Shelby's most important function was showing the flag at races and media events and dressing up and posing for advertising shoots promoting his mildly modified Mustangs. The deal with Toyota had been a dead end. The effort to create a Can-Am car from scratch had been a humiliating bust. Ditto for plans to put a successor to the Cobra into production. Shelby Racing had a contract to race a pair of Mustangs in Trans-Am, but the commitment expired out at the end of the season, and neither party had shown any interest in negotiating an extension. Meanwhile, it was generally understood that, during 1969, Bud Moore Engineering was the stud in the Ford stable; Shelby was the pack mule bringing up the rear.

While Shelby piddled around with outside interests ranging from the Shelby Sky Terrace Motel in Lake Tahoe to the World Championship Chili Cook-off in Terlingua, Carroll Smith was desperate to get something going on the racing front. Working with Homer Perry at Ford, he put together a budget for a full-on Can-Am program with a customer McLaren M12 for Peter Revson. Ford agreed to supply a new 8.0-liter engine, and, at one point, there were fanciful discussions about developing a new gearbox and four-wheel drive to handle all the power. By the end of February, two new McLarens had been delivered to Torrance. But before they could be readied for racing, Smith clomped down the stairs from his office and announced, "You might as well put your tools away. There's no more Can-Am."[1]

Like everybody else at Shelby Racing, Smith had been blindsided by the abrupt cancellation of the program. As recently as February 27, he'd spoken to Perry and confirmed that everything was copacetic. A week later, Perry called to tell him to pay off Revson and stop working on the Can-Am cars. "I found out that you could take about a year and a half to make a program and about two hours to shut it down," Smith said.[2] "To this day, I have no idea of what happened."

The Trans-Am program was still solid, but the season wasn't scheduled to begin until May. "We were kind of in limbo," Ron Butler said.[3] "I know we weren't very busy because I was running a go-kart at the time, and I had time to piss around with that go-kart engine when no one was looking. We were just sort of filling in time."

But Smith wasn't ready to throw in the towel. Next, he put together a proposal to compete in the SCCA Continental Championship for Formula A cars. Known more popularly as Formula 5000, these were open-wheel cars with stock-block American V-8s. Smith wanted to run a Ford 302, and he placed an order with Trojan Ltd., which built customer cars for McLaren, for a Mk 10B for Revson to drive. For various reasons, the project was stillborn. But just when Smith figured he'd been hung out to dry, Shelby came through with a new job opportunity.

"He ran into this guy in a bar—typical Shelby—and the guy said, 'I own a Formula 5000 car (which Shelby had never heard of), and it's quick, but it can't finish races,'" Smith recalled.[4] "And Shelby said, 'Have I got a fix for you!'" Shelby essentially shipped Smith to the Milestone Racing team four races into the Continental Championship season. "It was a hell of a deal for me," Smith said. "I forget what I was making at the time, but Shelby rented me out for about six hundred bucks a month more." The car was an Eagle with a small-block Chevy, and the driver was Tony Adamowicz. "We won the championship," Smith said. "That's how my consulting company began."

While the race operation in Torrance spun its wheels, Shelby Automotive in Michigan was creating what appeared, at least from the outside, to be the wildest GT350 and GT500 ever. But looks can be deceiving, rarely more so than in this case. Now in their fifth year of production, the Shelby Mustangs had undergone a remarkable about-face. When the GT350 debuted in 1965, it had resembled a stock Mustang but performed like a race car. Now, though the Shelbys looked unique, they were little more than stock Mustangs with boy-racer touches.

By 1969, the last vestiges of Southern California input had disappeared. Convertibles and SportsRoofs—the new name for the fastback Mustang—were shipped from an assembly line in Dearborn to the A. O. Smith plant just 130 miles away. During the planning stages, there had been talk about several upgrades to enhance the street credibility of the Shelbys—Koni shocks, fuel injection, rear-wheel disc brakes, even a sliding roof and hideaway headlights—but all of them were dropped before the car went into production. As usual, the cars received a handful of "premium" touches, from extra gauges to functional rear brake ducts to a wood-grain automatic shift T-lever (whoopee!). To compensate for the lack of any legitimate performance credentials, the cars were festooned with what seemed to be an endless array of Cobra logos—on the wheels, on the steering wheel, on the grille, on the C pillar (or rear fender of the convertible), even on the shift lever. "Look at us," the badges shouted unpersuasively, "we're the real deal! Seriously!"

One great benefit of building the cars at A. O. Smith was that the far better build quality in Ionia allowed the stylists to be more ambitious. In 1968, the existing fenders had been lengthened with the addition of fiberglass extensions. Now, the cars got entirely new fenders, even longer and more dramatic than before. John Chun designed a new grille around Shelby-only bumpers, lower valances, and Lucas running lights. Chun soon moved to Chrysler, where he was assigned to (among other projects) the new-for-1970 Dodge Challenger. Put the Mopar pony car next to a 1969 GT350 or a GT500, and it's hard to miss the similarity of the wide-mouth front-end treatments. Strictly a coincidence? You make the call.

The most arresting feature of the new Shelbys was the fiberglass hood, which featured not one, not two, not three, not even four, but *five* functional scoops. The two rearmost ones, facing the windshield, exhausted hot air out of the engine bay. The three on the front of the hood were NACA ducts designed to channel cool air *into* the engine compartment. Developed in 1945 by the National Advisory Committee for Aeronautics, the predecessor of NASA, NACA ducts are air inlets that generate minimal drag, which make them very popular in the racing world. This was the first time they'd been used in a mass-market production car.

Fred Goodell opted for NACA ducts because he'd been unhappy with wind noise generated by the broad hood scoop on the 1968 models. The most effective of the three inlets was the one in the center, which was plumbed directly to the ram-air air cleaner and sealed with a rubber gasket on the underside of the hood. The Swiss cheese-style hood was very much a nothing-succeeds-like-excess design element. But that was just what the car needed. "In my opinion," Goodell said, "it's still the best-looking Shelby of them all."[5] (*Car Life* called it as "beautiful as

Raquel Welch."[6]) And if imitation is the sincerest form of flattery, then it's worth noting that Ford used the Shelby Mustang as the inspiration for the restyled Mach 1 that debuted a few years later.

On the other hand, the verdict on the performance front was a thumbs-down. "A garter snake in Cobra skin," *Car and Driver* declared.[7] There was nothing wrong with the engines, but there was nothing special about them either. The GT350 got a new 351-cubic-inch Windsor V-8 (290 hp at 4800 rpm and 385 lb-ft at 3400 rpm) while the GT500 was equipped with the 428 Cobra Jet (335 hp at 5200 and 440 lb-ft at 3400) that had been found in the previous year's King of the Road. Respectable numbers, to be sure, especially since the CJ really was making more than 400 ponies. But unless a buyer couldn't live without the elongated nose and or large collection of Cobra insignias, the same performance was available for far less in a properly optioned Mach 1.

The 1969 GT350 and GT500 were the most stylish—and arguably the best-looking—Shelby Mustangs ever built. But they were also the farthest from the original concept of transforming a mechanically humdrum sedan into a legitimate sports car. "They really weren't the cars we had started with," Shelby said. In June 1969, he asked Lee Iacocca to kill the program. After the 1970 model year, the Shelby Mustangs were history. *Ford Motor Company*

POWER BY *Ford*

Sitting still . . . it looks invincible

Turn it on and let it out and you'll see how that long, low, racy styling dares anything else to come close. When racing expert Carroll Shelby designs a car this way you don't expect him to build very many. He doesn't.

The Shelby GT isn't a car you buy simply because it's handsome and rare. You buy it, of course, to drive it.

Let out the famous ram air 428 Cobra Jet engine in the GT 500, and suddenly you'll know the meaning of the word "power". Wind up the 351 ram air V-8 in the GT 350, and you'll capture the true

feeling and excitement of Shelby motion. Take a corner at speed . . . stab the brakes, and feel how the car is slowed with the force of 11.3" power assisted front disc brakes. Ride through a curve . . . Heavy duty adjustable shock absorbers with competition type springs will keep the fat Polyglass belted tires in firm contact with the road thru all its bumps and dips. A heavy duty front stabilizer bar keeps the body tight and level against the force of cornering. That's race car handling . . . it's something built into every Shelby GT.

And it's available now at your local Shelby Ford Performance Center.

Shelby GT 350/500

Even Ford seemed to be unsure about what the car stood for or how it ought to be marketed. One print ad read "Uncommon . . . you might even call it rare!" Okay. A second ad featured another head-scratcher: "Sitting still . . . it looks invincible." Invincible? Even within the Mustang family, the GT350 was trumped by the Boss 302, and the GT500 was a slug compared with the Boss 429. Ford used every opportunity to play up the connection to Shelby, the racer, but the Shelby Mustang had devolved into a car without a constituency.

And then suddenly, shockingly, it was all over. In June 1969, Shelby flew to Dearborn and euthanized the Mustang program. "I went to Mr. Iacocca and asked him to cancel the program," Shelby said.[8] "I thought there were a lot of cars built by other companies that are similar, and the competition was much keener, including inside Ford Motors Company." At least, that was what he said at the time. Later, when he was less inclined to toe the party line, he elaborated on his reasoning: "We built the '65s and sold a few of them. Then we built the R-Models and only sold a handful of them. When we came to the '66s, we softened them up a little and added a few options and sold almost five times the number we had in 1965. In '67, the Mustangs got bigger, in '68 they got bigger, and in '69 they got bigger, and they really weren't the cars we had started with. I finally said the hell with it."

When Shelby said *no más*, there were still a few just-completed and not-yet-converted Mustangs languishing at A. O. Smith. Dealers didn't want new 1969 cars so late in the model year. Ford altered the VIN numbers (with the approval of the FBI) and sold the Shelbys as 1970 models. The only upgrades were the addition of two black stripes on the hood and a chin spoiler. This brought final-year production to 3,150. Over a five-year period, nearly fourteen thousand GT350s, GT500s, and GT500 KRs were built. By contrast, Cobra production petered out after a grand total of only 998 cars. The Shelby Mustangs don't boast the cachet of the Cobras. But for many years, they were the cars that paid most of the bills.

Still, it seems fitting that, even after quitting the new-car business, Shelby continued to race. The 1969 Trans-Am season promised to be the busiest and most competitive ever, with a dozen races being contested from coast to coast over a hectic five-month stretch. Despite the traumas of the previous year, the guys at Shelby Racing were upbeat going into the new season. Perry, a longtime Shelby ally, had been given control of the program. Better still, the wretched tunnel-port 302 wasn't returning for a sequel.

Toward the end of the 1968 season, a series of elaborate tests had been run at Riverside to evaluate engine options for 1969. The three basic configurations under consideration were an unloved tunnel-port, an old-school 289 topped with a new-wave Gurney-Weslake head, and a 302 with a poly-angle head that would later be used in the 351 Cleveland. The Gurney-Weslake motor produced the best lap times, and with Weber carburetors, it also boasted the best drivability. But this combination was too exotic and expensive to put into production, so there was no way it was going to be homologated. Next best was the canted-valve 302. Although mid-range torque was marginal, the stout four-bolt main-cap block, forged steel crank, and meaty connecting rods suggested good durability—a major selling point after the travails of the previous year. Officially designated the Boss 302, this was the engine that powered Trans-Am Mustangs in 1969.

Ford also addressed the other big gripe of 1968 and agreed to let the teams assemble their own engines. At Shelby Racing, John Dunn conducted a series of "very promising" flow bench tests. "The basic design of the 1969 Ford Gr. II engine would appear to be exceptionally good," he wrote in an internal memo.[9] But he saw some storm clouds on the horizon. "Preliminary dynamometer tests and subsequent vehicle track testing have definitely indicated a very inadequate power potential below 4000 rpm," he wrote. Drivability would prove to be a problem that vexed the drivers all season. As Dykstra explained, "There was still development there because they put two 1100 Holleys on the thing to start out with, so it was way over-carbureted. It wasn't until 1970 that we got a proper throttle-response engine."[10]

Mustangs built at the Rouge were shipped to Torrance along with kits filled with pieces Kar-Kraft had developed for the car—roll cages, chassis-strengthening mods, fuel tanks, fenders, hoods, and so on. After being assembled, the cars were painted an attractive shade of blue set off by white C-shaped stripes and bold meatballs for the race numbers on the flanks. Sitting low to the ground, with a ducktail rear spoiler and a front splitter, the finished product looked handsome and purposeful. Horst Kwech was back in one car while Jerry Titus had been replaced in the other by Revson, who'd demonstrated that he was more than a pretty face.

The season began with a tragedy that set the tone for what was to come. The race—"doomed from the start," according to *Sports Car Graphic*—was one of the first ever held at Michigan International Speedway.[11] A road course had been cobbled together by linking a portion of the banking with a section of twisties through the infield. It had rained for several days beforehand, and sleet fell during qualifying. Parnelli Jones grabbed the pole in a Bud Moore Mustang while sixth was the best Revson could do. Although it was dry when the field was flagged off, rain immediately started falling. On lap eight, while trying to execute a pass, Kwech slid onto the slick grass. "In retrospect, it seems incredible that no one could foresee the possible consequences of a car going off where Horst Kwech's Mustang did—with such particularly grisly effects," *Sports Car Graphic* reported.[12] Kwech understeered into a pair of parked Javelins, killing AMC employee Derwood Fletcher. Twelve other spectators were injured, several critically. Adios, one Trans-Am Mustang. Revson was nowhere before blowing a tire and retiring.

Revson missed the next race, at Lime Rock Park, because he was competing in the Indy 500. (He'd bumped his way into the field after a hang-on-for-dear-life, last-gasp qualifying run and then was named co-Rookie of the Year, with Mark Donohue, after finishing fifth.) On Revson's recommendation, Shelby hired Sam Posey to sub for him. What's interesting about this choice—and it says a lot about how far Shelby's attention had strayed from racing—is that Shelby had never heard of him even though Posey had raced against Revson in Can-Am the previous year and had run occasionally in Trans-Am as well. Posey's reputation at the time was modest, but Lime Rock was his home track, and it was the kind of circuit where local knowledge could pay big dividends.

With Revson, Donohue, Jones, George Follmer (Number Two to Jones), and Ronnie Bucknum (Number Two to Donohue), all at Indy, Kwech was fastest in qualifying—until Posey did a last-lap flyer and kept his foot in it despite dropping a wheel in the scary-fast downhill sweeper just before the finish. But in the race, Kwech was the class of the field, and he drove away from Posey—until his brake master cylinder failed. Posey seemed to be home free. But there was a complication. His seat had broken during the warmup, and the only replacement the team could fine on short notice was an old, bolt-upright stock-car number found in the upper reaches of Moore's transporter. "Within half an hour, I was in desperate back pain. Terrible pain," Posey remembered.[13] "I remained that way, almost in and out of consciousness." He was virtually delirious after two hours in the car. Thanks partly to quicker pit stops, he was maintaining a narrow but steady lead over Swede Savage in a Moore Mustang. Then, Posey's engine dropped a cylinder, and Savage started to run him down. Just about the time Savage was ready to sweep past, he cut a tire, and Posey hung on to score an unlikely victory. "I couldn't get out of the car," he said.[14] "Lew Spencer and a couple of the guys pulled me out through the window, and when I went to Winner's Circle, I was resting all of my weight on Lew. I just couldn't walk."

This was the last professional race Shelby would ever win.

After Lime Rock, the team slouched toward mediocrity. Mid-Ohio and Bridgehampton were both forgettable. Kwech was on form at Donnybrooke, where he outqualified Revson and pushed Donohue and Parnelli hard for the lead for most of the race until crashing heavily into a tree and totaling his Mustang. Revson was third to Donohue at Bryar two weeks later, but a lap down.

Even with the benefit of hindsight, it's hard to pinpoint the reason Shelby Racing fared so poorly while Moore was so much more competitive with essentially the same equipment. Spencer was still managing the team, and Jack Aylesbury was still the crew chief, supported by five mechanics, an engine man and a truck driver. "We had a very closely knit team," Spencer said.[15] "You know how some teams go to the races and no hotel owner wants them there? In the three years that I managed that team, we never had a team member get in trouble and we never stayed in a hotel that we weren't invited back to the next year. Of course, you couldn't say that about the Cobra team—those guys were hell-raisers from the beginning of that program to the end. Our program was entirely different, and our people were gentlemen in every sense of the word."

Sam Posey slices through the bucolic landscape at Lime Rock in 1969 in the Trans-Am Mustang usually driven by Revson, who was off racing in the Indy 500. Posey's teammate, Horst Kwech, led from the start. But when his car broke, Posey dominated the rest of the race despite suffering agonizing pain from a brutally uncomfortable seat. Posey's victory at Lime Rock was the last one ever recorded by Shelby. *Revs Institute / Duke Q. Manor Photograph Collection*

The biggest difference between 1968 and 1969 was probably the absence of Chuck Cantwell. Besides his technical acumen, Cantwell enjoyed the respect of everybody from Shelby Racing mechanics to top Ford management. After he defected to Penske, Chevrolet won seven races in a row en route to claiming the manufacturers' championship. The other big loss was Titus. Revson's pace wasn't the issue, but he never bonded with the team the way Titus had. The crew was always happy to go the extra mile for Titus, who'd been a mechanic himself and who was very much one of the guys. The jet-setting Revson got so crossways with the crew at one point near the end of the season that he literally parked his car in the middle of the race. *Sports Car Graphic* had a theory of its own. As Ted West wrote, "Moore was able to divert most of the corporate advisers, engineers, technicians, and resident wizards over to 'helping' poor ol' Carroll Shelby, who therefore had an appropriately rotten season."[16]

All of the team's negative karma came together with a terrible, horrible, no good, very bad day at St. Jovite. Follmer, the pole-sitter, blew a Boss 302 engine and spun in his own oil. Mayhem ensued on an industrial scale. No fewer than eight cars wrecked in that single corner. Kwech flipped, soared over the guardrail. and landed on all four wheels. Revson was the last to arrive. When he saw the frantically waving yellow flags, he got his car whoa-ed down to a canter, but the track was so slick that he slid into the pack anyway and ended up on top of the hood of a Firebird. When he got out of his car, he didn't realize he was so high above the ground, and he suffered minor ankle and shoulder injuries when he touched down. "I've never seen anything like that before," driver Johnny Rutherford said after he got back to the pits.[17] "That bunch of cars looked like they'd been dropped from an airplane."

Even after the team bottomed out at St. Jovite, the pendulum never really swung in the other direction. "We were pretty much history after that," Kwech said.[18] "The team never recovered after that, and the cars never ran or handled the same." Between the carnage at St. Jovite and Kwech's previous accidents at Michigan and Donnybrooke, Shelby Racing now had four totaled chassis. They were shipped back to Kar-Kraft, which performed heroic cut-and-paste surgery to create two reconstituted cars. The patients survived, but with limitations.

"We had trouble with the suspensions," Spencer said.[19] "It didn't seem to make any difference what we did—when we thought we had the setting just right, we'd go out and the car wouldn't handle. By that time, Chuck had left the team and went with Penske. I still believe that if Chuck had been there, it would have gotten sorted out, and we would have done all right. Some way or another—I don't know what magic he would have put on it—but somehow, we would have done okay. But to cut the cars up and then weld parts back together to build new cars just made them too flexible."

Still, at least some of the team's problems could be found by looking in the mirror. Shelby Racing fell behind Moore in terms of development during the season. Also, Revson and Kwech couldn't match the pace of Jones and Follmer, much less Donohue in the Penske Camaro, and Titus was often quicker in a Pontiac Firebird campaigned with far less factory support. The final chords were playing for the team, and everybody could hear them loud and clear.

Kwech didn't take the start at Watkins Glen, held a week before the Woodstock music festival would be staged on the other side of upstate New York. Revson did, but he crashed before reaching the finish. At Laguna Seca, Spencer sat Kwech down in favor of Dan Gurney, in the hopes of recapturing some of the old Shelby magic. It didn't work. Gurney finished third, a lap down, while Revson was fourth, two laps down. At Kent, the entire team contracted food poisoning. "Roger's revenge," the wags called it.[20] Revson was fourth, with Gurney tenth after two unscheduled stops to change the differential and replace a shattered windshield. Shelby, who by this time attended races only when Ford formally requested his presence, sat in the pits with his arms folded, wearing sunglasses and the expression of a man with a nasty case of indigestion. Even the news four days later that his old nemesis Bunkie Knudsen had been fired did nothing to lift his spirits.

In 1968, the Shelby Racing Trans-Am team had been victimized by the notoriously fragile and peaky tunnel-port engine. In 1969, the issue was a lack of pace. Here at Laguna Seca, the team drafted Gurney—a proven stud—to see if the drivers were the problem. Despite trying hard, the best he could manage was third place, a lap down to the leader. Shelby Racing closed its doors at the end of the year. *Dave Friedman*

In a last-ditch effort to salvage something of the season, Ford rented Sears Point Raceway for a day-long test before the Trans-Am race there. Gurney was a no-show. Rumors that he was signing with Mopar for 1970 started making the rounds. (They turned out to be true.) When Gurney showed up for the race, Ford scratched his entry. "Nobody, not even Dan Gurney, can come in and save a program in the last three minutes," said Jacque Passino, radiating disapproval while Shelby washed his hands of the spat.[21] "It was Ford's decision," he said.[22] Kwech, who'd languished on the bench for the last three races, was put back in a car, and he qualified an excellent third. Revson, mired in seventh, sat dejectedly on the wall after practice was over. In the race, he pitted after two laps, got in a fight with his crew, drove straight to the paddock, and abandoned the car. Kwech DNFed when his suspension failed.

Riverside was the end of the line for both the Trans-Am season and Shelby Racing. Revson and Kwech started fourth and ninth, and by odd coincidence, that's exactly where they finished—a quiet conclusion to eight noisy years on center stage. Shortly after the race, Shelby convened a meeting in the shop. "Well, we just sold out to Ford," he told the gathered employees. "We're done. We're closing down."[23] Asked why, he said, "Ford's takeover of the racing team took the fun out of it."[24] In December, the other shoe dropped when Henry Ford II announced that he was slashing the company's motorsports budget by 75 percent. When a reporter requested an explanation for this extraordinary shift of resources, the Deuce snapped, "Because we think we spend too much."[25] Next question. The Total Performance era was over, and with it, so was Shelby's tenure as one of the highest-profile and most influential people in the American automotive universe.

Years later, Shelby would reflect upon his stormy alliance with the suits in Dearborn with a mixture of pride and regret. In retrospect, he said, he should have "handled the goofy politics at Ford a lot differently than I did and not let the pitiful people like John Cowley and some of the little twerpheads who were very jealous stick their noses in. I wouldn't have put up with them and some of the crazy ideas that they had as long as I did, and I should have used Ford for what they were good for. I had such a beautiful relationship with Engine & Foundry.

They built the things that I needed. Ray Geddes did an excellent job of handling the company politics, but the political situation at Ford always took much more of my time than it should have. I guess that's just part of playing the game. You have to have a relationship with a big company to really get anything done, but you pay a tremendous price for it."[26]

But in 1969, Shelby just wanted out—not just out of his deal with Ford but out of the car business altogether. During the summer, he heard from a young Cobra enthusiast named Mike Shoen. A few years earlier, Shoen had bought a poster that reproduced a George Bartell painting of a Cobra Daytona Coupe at Sebring in 1965, and the artwork inspired him to embark on a quest to buy the car. Shoen eventually got in touch with Shelby and was invited to visit the shop in Torrance. When he got there, Shoen found two Daytona Coupes sitting side by side. One had been sold for $4,000 the previous week to a schoolteacher in Florida. The other car was in as-raced condition from its last competitive appearance, at Enna in 1965. Shelby referred to it as the team's Number One Car; Shoen later confirmed that it was CSX2299, which had five wins to its credit, the most famous being Le Mans in 1964 in the hands of Gurney and Bondurant. (Coincidentally, this was the car pictured in the poster that had kicked off Shoen's search.) Because of this history, Shelby was asking $7,500.

The negotiations took several months, not because they were so tortured but because this was pre-internet, and Shoen didn't want to spend money on long-distance phone calls, so all the back-and-forth was conducted via letters. Shelby and Shoen finally agreed on a purchase price of $5,100. By the time the deal was consummated, it was late December, and Shelby Racing had vacated the premises in Torrance. Shoen was told to pick up the car at 1042 Princeton Drive, the site of the original shop in Venice. The place was empty except for a clothes locker, two cardboard boxes on the mezzanine, and the man who greeted him.

"My name is Warren Davenport. I am the last employee of Shelby American. Here's your car," he said. Then, almost as an afterthought, he added. "Do you want to buy this double supercharged 427 over here for $12,000?"[27]

Shoen passed on the Paxton-powered Cobra, but he ended up with what just might be the most valuable race car in American history. Also, the people he met through Shelby provided the material for his wonderful history of the 1963, '64, and '65 racing seasons, *The Cobra-Ferrari Wars, 1963-1965*. Shelby couldn't find anybody willing to pay $12,000 for the Super Snake in 1969, so he grudgingly hung onto it. In 2007, it sold at auction for $5.5 million. As they say, timing is everything.

AFTERWORD

S helby was burned out by 1969. But he was too accustomed to life in the limelight to be content padding around the house in slippers. Although he spent much of the next decade on safaris in Africa and promoting his own brand of chili, it wasn't long before he returned to the car world. In 1971, he and Al Dowd ran a truncated and unsatisfying season of Indy Car races under the banner of Shelby-Dowd Racing. When Lee Iacocca moved to Chrysler, Shelby joined him and introduced a series of high-performance products. Later, after filing lawsuits against several companies building knockoffs of the Cobra, he started building copies of his own—except that he didn't call them copies. Instead, he sold them as "continuation Cobras," which adroitly evaded the thorny authenticity issue with his usual panache. Later still, he negotiated a deal with Oldsmobile to provide engines for his Series 1 two-seat sports car. Along the way, he had a heart transplant, acquired a new kidney, and went through several more marriages and lord knows how many more romantic entanglements. In 2005, amazingly, his career came full circle as he again collaborated with Ford on what would be new versions of the GT350 and GT500. Hertz even commissioned a modern take on its old Rent-a-Racer. By the time he died in 2012, at eighty-nine years old, he'd outlasted not only most of his contemporaries but also his own expectations.

Shelby mellowed as he aged. He became a fixture at car shows, signing tens of thousands of autographs. Wealthy at last and with nothing left to prove, he founded the nonprofit Carroll Shelby Foundation to do good works helping kids overcome medical issues. He was never an avuncular figure exactly, and he could still be cantankerous, but time softened his rougher edges. He was transformed into a character—the country boy who outsmarted the city slickers—and he thrilled audiences by trotting out the old stories on demand. He was beloved, for God's sake. Carroll Shelby beloved! How this would have shocked the people who knew him back in the day, when he was scheming to fashion something out of nothing, and he was willing do to just about anything to make his improbable dream of building the Cobra come true.

He didn't do it alone, of course. Hundreds of men and women worked with him at Ford and Shelby American over the years. For some, it was just a job. For others, it was a stepping-stone. Several grew into celebrities in their own right. Others, well known by the cognoscenti, became engineers, crew chiefs, team managers, race mechanics, engine builders, and restoration mavens whose influence stretched across the entire automotive landscape. For the better part of a decade, Shelby American was the biggest game in town, and it was a beacon of excellence that's been unrivaled in scale or scope ever since. As Ryan Falconer puts it, "My feeling always has been that, at one point, Shelby had the greatest mechanics in American working there."

Shelby was the sun around which everybody else revolved, and without him, the solar system he created would have spun out of control. The automobile and racing industries have produced many titans, from Henry Ford and Harry Miller at the turn of the twentieth century to Roger Penske and Elon Musk here in the twenty-first. But none of them could have accomplished what Shelby managed to pull off in the 1960s. It took a man wearing not just a black Stetson but also a unique combination of hats—salesman, wheeler-dealer, politician, gambler, proselytizer, boon companion. He was a larger-than-life entrepreneur with a grand vision and a wily rogue with a fluid relationship with the truth. His friends freely acknowledged that he wasn't a saint, and even critics who claimed he'd stabbed them in the back admitted that they craved his company.

Like all racing drivers, especially ones who survived the murderous 1950s, Shelby was adept at calculating risk versus reward. With unerring precision, he navigated a path between bottom-line bureaucrats, jealous rivals, impatient creditors, and skeptics dubious of his ability to deliver on his lofty promises. Shelby was dynamic, charismatic, mercurial,

Shelby was only forty-six when he "retired" in 1969 and set his sights on Africa. In fact, his dramatic life story would feature several additional acts, including a few more stints as an automobile manufacturer with Chrysler, General Motors, and, later, Ford. But it was during the 1960s, while he was running Shelby American, that he reached the zenith of his influence as both a racer and as a carmaker. *Ford Motor Company*

mercenary, and a little bit dangerous. He had to be. He was a man who succeeded on his wits alone. Against all odds, and without any money, he created a car company that built some of the most iconic automobiles in American history. It was Shelby American, more than any other entity, that demonstrated the possibilities of professional road racing, and the team's multi-million-dollar partnership with Ford established the paradigm for modern motorsports, where racers operate as collaborators with manufacturers rather than serving merely as hired hands.

And so, for a few glorious years in the mid-1960s, thanks to Shelby's singular talents, the center of the racing universe was a brick building nestled in an otherwise quiet neighborhood in Venice, California. Peer inside the window at 1042 Princeton Drive and you'll see the ghosts of Phil Remington poring over a blueprint, Ole Olsen throttling up a

289 on the dyno, Jerry Schwarz flaring a GT350 wheel well with an air hammer, and Charlie Agapiou preparing a cherry bomb attack. Overseeing it all is a lanky Texan who doesn't do a lick of manual labor but whose vision shapes everything coming out of the shop. He's standing in front of a red Cobra with whitewall tires and wire wheels. "There's a lot of designing, testing, and trial runs behind every new innovation and performance record," he says, speaking directly into a camera for a promotional movie produced by Ford. "How do I know? My name's Carroll Shelby, and performance is my business."

ENDNOTES

Introduction
1. Ted Sutton, interview by author.
2. Dave Friedman, *Remembering the Shelby Years—1962–1969* (Los Angeles, CA: Carroll Shelby Children's Foundation, 1998), 305.

Chapter One
1. *Road & Track*, December 1969.
2. Dave Friedman, *Remembering the Shelby Years—1962–1969* (Los Angeles, CA: Carroll Shelby Children's Foundation, 1998), 82.
3. Rinsey Mills, *Carroll Shelby: The Authorized Biography* (Minneapolis, MN: Motorbooks, 2012), 62.
4. Carroll Shelby, interview by author.
5. Carroll Shelby, interview by author.
6. Carroll Shelby, interview by author.
7. John Wyer, *The Certain Sound: Thirty Years of Motor Racing* (Lausanne, Switzerland: Automobile Year: Edita, 1981), 63.
8. Carroll Shelby, interview by author.
9. Mills, *Carroll Shelby*, 209.
10. Carroll Shelby, interview by author.
11. Carroll Shelby, interview by author.
12. John Lamm, "Scaglietti Corvettes: Italian Twist on America's Sports Car," *Collier Automedia*. https://www.collierautomedia.com/scaglietti-corvettes-italian-twist-on-americas-sports-car.
13. Peter Brock, interview by author.
14. Peter Brock, interview by author.
15. Peter Brock, interview by author.
16. Carroll Shelby, *The Cobra Story* (New York, NY: Trident Press, 1965), 191.
17. Mills, *Carroll Shelby*, 221.
18. Carroll Shelby, interview by author.
19. Carroll Shelby, interview by author.
20. *MotoRacing*, February 16–26, 1962.
21. Movieclips, "Print the Legend - The Man Who Shot Liberty Valance (6/7) Movie CLIP (1962) HD," *YouTube*, October 7, 2011. https://www.youtube.com/watch?v=363ZAmQEA84.

22. Doyle Gammell, interview by author.

23. Doyle Gammell, interview by author.

24. John Christy and Dave Friedman and John Christy, *Carroll Shelby's Racing Cobras* (Oxford, UK: Osprey Publishing, 1982), 8.

25. Friedman and Christy, *Racing Cobras*, 8.

26. Friedman and Christy, *Racing Cobras*, 9.

27. *Sports Car Graphic*, May 1962.

28. Bruce Junor, interview by author.

29. Doyle Gammell, interview by author.

30. Advertisement, *Playboy*, October 1962.

31. Fred Gamble, interview by author.

32. Fred Gamble, interview by author.

33. Robert D. Walker, *Cobra Pilote: The Ed Hugus Story* (Deerfield, IL: Dalton Watson Fine Books, 2017), 56.

34. Friedman, *Remembering*, 283.

35. Dan Gurney, interview by author.

36. Peter Brock, interview by author.

37. Peter Brock, interview by author.

38. Bill Eaton, interview by author.

39. Carroll Smith, interview by author.

40. Phil Remington, interview by author.

41. Friedman, *Remembering*, 268.

42. Carroll Shelby, interview by author.

43. Dan Gurney, interview by author.

44. *Competition Press*, September 8, 1962.

45. John Morton, interview by author.

46. *Los Angeles Times*, October 13, 1962.

47. Carroll Shelby, interview by author.

48. John Morton, *Inside Shelby American: Wrenching and Racing with Carroll Shelby in the 1960s* (Minneapolis, MN: Motorbooks, 2017), 49.

49. Friedman, *Remembering*, 234.

Chapter Two

1. Dave Friedman, *Remembering the Shelby Years—1962–1969* (Los Angeles, CA: Carroll Shelby Children's Foundation, 1998), 291.

2. Carroll Shelby, interview by author.

3. Susan Schafran, interview by author.

4. Joe Freitas, interview by author.

5. Lew Spencer, interview by author.

6. Carroll Smith, interview by author.

7. Red Pierce, interview by author.

8. *Competition Press*, February 9, 1963.

9. *The Shelby American #59*, 15.

10. *Road & Track*, June 1963.

11. *Road & Track*, May 1963.

12. Peter Brock, interview by author.

13. Friedman, *Remembering*, 285.

14. *The Shelby American #46*, 19.

15. Carroll Shelby, interview by author.

16. Phil Remington, interview by author.
17. *Car and Driver*, October 1963.
18. *Motor Trend*, September 1963
19. *Sports Car Graphic*, November 1963.
20. Jere Kirkpatrick, interview by author.
21. Tony Stoer, interview by author.
22. Tony Stoer, interview by author.
23. Charlie Agapiou, interview by author.
24. Friedman, *Remembering*, 156.
25. Allen Grant, interview by author.
26. Allen Grant, interview by author.
27. Allen Grant, interview by author.
28. Wally Peat, interview by author.
29. *Seattle Times*, September 30, 1963.
30. Friedman, *Remembering*, 246.
31. Allen Grant, interview by author.
32. Allen Grant, interview by author.
33. Allen Grant, interview by author.
34. Wally Peat, interview by author.
35. *The Shelby American #42*, 19.

Chapter Three

1. Peter Brock, interview by author.
2. Peter Brock, interview by author.
3. Dan Gurney, interview by author.
4. Carroll Shelby, interview by author.
5. Carroll Shelby, interview by author.
6. Peter Brock, interview by author.
7. Peter Brock, interview by author.
8. Peter Brock, interview by author.
9. Peter Brock, interview by author.
10. Peter Brock, interview by author.
11. Peter Brock, Dave Friedman, and George Stauffer, *Daytona Cobra Coupes* (Blue Mounds, WI: Stauffer Publishing, 1995), 128.
12. Ted Sutton, interview by author.
13. Brock, Friedman, and Stauffer, *Daytona Coupes*, 130.
14. Peter Brock, interview by author.
15. Dave Friedman, interview by author.
16. Dave Friedman, "Dave Friedman Interview," by Hugh Milstein, *Dave Friedman Archive*, https://davefriedmanarchive.com/about-dave-friedman/interview/.
17. John Morton, interview by author.
18. *The Shelby American #56*, 19.
19. Dave MacDonald, "February 16th, 1964 - Dave MacDonald at the Daytona Continental 2000km at Daytona International Raceway," davemacdonald.net. https://www.davemacdonald.net/gallery/closeups/daytonacobracontinental2000.htm
20. *The Shelby American #33*, 31.
21. Charlie Agapiou, interview by author.
22. Charlie Agapiou, interview by author.

23. John Morton, interview by author.

24. Michael Shoen, *The Cobra-Ferrari Wars 1963-1965* (Vancouver, BC: CFW, 1988), 103.

25. John Morton, *Inside Shelby American: Wrenching and Racing with Carroll Shelby in the 1960s* (Minneapolis, MN: Motorbooks, 2017), 126.

26. Ted Sutton, interview by author.

27. John Morton, interview by author.

28. *The Shelby American*, 14.

29. John Morton, interview by author.

30. Jim Marietta, interview by author.

31. Jim Marietta, interview by author.

32. Red Pierce, interview by author.

33. Peter Brock, interview by author.

34. *Sports Car Graphic*, November 1964.

35. *The Shelby American #46*, 19.

36. Friedman, *Remembering*, 295.

37. *The Shelby American #46*, 46.

38. Jere Kirkpatrick, interview by author.

39. Tony Stoer, interview by author.

40. Tony Stoer, interview by author.

41. Tony Stoer, interview by author.

42. Jere Kirkpatrick, interview by author.

43. Jere Kirkpatrick, interview by author.

44. Ralph Falconer, interview by author.

45. Wally Peat, interview by author.

46. *Competition Press*, March 21, 1964.

47. Dan Gurney, interview by author.

48. Friedman, *Remembering*, 59.

49. Bob Bondurant, interview by author.

50. Carroll Shelby, interview by author.

51. Bob Bondurant, interview by author.

52. Peter Brock, Dave Friedman, and George Stauffer, *Daytona Cobra Coupes* (Blue Mounds, WI: Stauffer Publishing, 1995), 293.

53. Shoen, *Cobra-Ferrari Wars 1963-1965*, 197.

54. Brock, Friedman, and Stauffer, *Daytona Coupes*, 306.

55. Shoen, *Cobra-Ferrari Wars*, 211.

56. Carroll Shelby, interview by author.

57. Parnelli Jones, interview by author.

58. Parnelli Jones, interview by author.

59. Parnelli Jones, interview by author.

60. *Sports Car Graphic*, January 1965.

Chapter Four

1. *The Shelby American #61*, 19.

2. Randy Leffingwell, *Shelby Mustang: Racer for the Street* (Minneapolis, MN: Motorbooks, 2011), 52.

3. Chuck Cantwell, interview by author.

4. Chuck Cantwell, interview by author.

5. Peter Brock, interview by author.

6. *The Shelby American #51*, 14.

7. *Sports Car Graphic*, March 1965.

8. Chuck Cantwell and Greg Kolasa, *Shelby Mustang GT350* (Phoenix, AZ: David Bull Publishing, 2017), 58.

9. Michael L. Shoen, *The Cobra-Ferrari Wars 1963–1965* (Paradise Valley, AZ: CFW, 1990) 248.

10. Peter Brock, interview by author.

11. Brock Yates, *Enzo Ferrari, The Man, the Cars, the Races, the Machine* (New York, NY: Doubleday, 1991), 303.

12. Leo Levine, *Ford: The Dust and the Glory: A Racing History* (New York, NY: Macmillan, 1968), 485.

13. Don Frey, interview by David Crippen, *Benson Ford Research Center*, January 1986.

14. Levine, *Dust and the Glory*, Page 501.

15. Bruce Junor, interview by author.

16. Ron Butler, interview by author.

17. *Car and Driver*, May 1965.

18. Ralph Falconer, interview by author.

19. Ralph Falconer, interview by author.

20. Phil Henny, *Phil Remington: REM, Remembered by His Friends* (Portland, OR: Editions Cotty, 2015), 37.

21. Dave Friedman, *Remembering the Shelby Years—1962–1969* (Los Angeles, CA: Carroll Shelby Children's Foundation, 1998), 290.

22. Ron Butler, interview by author.

23. Bob Bondurant, interview by author.

24. *The Shelby American #46*, 20.

25. *The Shelby American #46*, 20.

26. Bruce Junor, interview by author.

27. Dick Lins, interview by author.

28. Andre (Gessner) Capella, interview by author.

29. Peter Crane, interview by author.

30. *Car and Driver*, February 1967.

31. *Sports Car Graphic*, July 1968.

32. Friedman, *Remembering*, 296.

33. Chuck Cantwell, interview by author.

34. Bernie Kretzschmar, interview by author.

35. Chuck Cantwell, interview by author.

36. Bernie Kretzschmar, interview by author.

37. Levine, *Dust and the Glory*, 510.

38. Rinsey Mills, *Carroll Shelby: The Authorized Biography* (Minneapolis, MN: Motorbooks, 2012), 377.

39. Frank Lance, interview by author.

40. Chris Amon, interview by author.

41. Chris Amon, interview by author.

42. Ryan Falconer, interview by author.

43. Karl Ludvigsen, *The Inside Story of the Fastest Fords: The Design and Development of the Ford GT Racing Cars* (Turin, IT: Style Auto Editrice, 1971), 34.

44. Walter Hayes, *Henry: A Life of Henry Ford II* (New York, NY: Grove Weidenfeld, 1990), 94.

45. *The Shelby American #43*, 12.
46. "Ford Division Program of Racing and Related Activities for the Model Year 1966" memo, July 13, 1965.
47. Friedman, *Remembering*, 291.
48. Fred Gamble, interview by author.
49. Bob Bondurant, interview by author.
50. Allen Grant, interview by author.
51. Bob Bondurant, interview by author.
52. Allen Grant, interview by author.
53. Charlie Agapiou, interview by author.
54. Alan Mann and Tony Dron, *Alan Mann: A Life of Chance* (Croydon, UK: Motor Racing Publications, 2012), 144.
55. Shoen, *Cobra-Ferrari Wars*, 350.
56. Carroll Shelby, interview by author.
57. Mann and Dron, *Life of Chance*, 145.
58. Charlie Agapiou, interview by author.
59. Peter Brock, interview by author.
60. Peter Brock, interview by author.
61. Brock, Friedman, and Stauffer, *Daytona Coupes*.
62. Brock, Friedman, and Stauffer, *Daytona Coupes*.
63. Ron Butler, interview by author.

Chapter Five

1. *The Shelby American #58*, 18.
2. Dennis Eshelman, interview by author.
3. Leo Beebe to Don Frey, "Racing Reminders for Donald N. Frey" memo, January 5, 1966.
4. Don Coleman, interview by author.
5. Tim Foraker, interview by author.
6. Tim Foraker, interview by author.
7. Allen Grant, interview by author.
8. Jere Kirkpatrick, interview by author.
9. Dave Friedman, *Remembering the Shelby Years—1962–1969* (Los Angeles, CA: Carroll Shelby Children's Foundation, 1998), 168.
10. Diana (Trampe) Geddes Day, interview by author.
11. Diana (Trampe) Geddes Day, interview by author.
12. Diana (Trampe) Geddes Day, interview by author.
13. Mark Waco, interview by author.
14. *The Crew Tells How They Won the 1966 Le Mans Endurance Race with the Ford GT40*, Jim Marietta (2016; private production; copy 22 of 50) DVD.
15. Bernie Kretzschmar, interview by author.
16. Bernie Kretzschmar, interview by author.
17. Don Frey, interview by David Crippen, *Benson Ford Research Center*, January 1986.
18. Leo Beebe to Don Frey, "Racing Reminders for Donald N. Frey" memo, January 5, 1966.
19. *The Shelby American #43*, 14.
20. Friedman, *Remembering*, 59.
21. *The Shelby American #57*, 14.
22. Leo Beebe to Don Frey, memo, January 5, 1966.

23. Mark Donohue and Paul Van Valkenburgh, *The Unfair Advantage* (New York, NY: Dodd, Mead, and Company, 1975), 53.

24. Bill Eaton, interview by author.

25. Charlie Agapiou, interview by author.

26. Dave Friedman, interview by author.

27. Chuck Cantwell, interview by author.

28. *Sports Car Graphic*, May 1966

29. *Sports Car Graphic*, May 1966.

30. *Sports Car Graphic*, May 1966.

31. *The Shelby American #51*, 15.

32. *Car and Driver*, May 1966.

33. Chuck Cantwell, interview by author.

34. Bernie Kretzschmar, interview by author.

35. *Motor Trend*, September 1966.

36. Robert Krauss, interview by author.

37. Andre (Gessner) Capella, interview by author.

38. Bob Carlson, interview by author.

39. Andre (Gessner) Capella, interview by author.

40. Andre (Gessner) Capella, interview by author.

41. Ron Butler, interview by author.

42. Ron Butler, interview by author.

43. Bernie Kretzschmar, interview by author.

44. Chris Amon, interview by author.

45. Leo Beebe, interview by David L. Lewis, *Benson Ford Research Center*, October 12, 1988.

46. *Road & Track*, September 1966.

47. Dave Friedman, interview with Dick Hutcherson.

48. Leo Beebe to John Mayhew, Ford Motor Company memo, April 21, 1966.

49. Walter Hayes to John Mayhew, Ford Motor Company memo, April 4, 1966.

50. John Wyer, *The Certain Sound: Thirty Years of Motor Racing* (Lausanne: Automobile Year: Edita, 1981), 152.

51. Dick Attwood, interview by author.

52. *The Shelby American #57*, 19.

53. Chris Amon, interview by author.

54. *The Shelby American #43*, 15.

55. Chris Amon, interview by author.

56. *The Shelby American #43*, 15.

57. Eoin Young, *McLaren Memories: A Biography of Bruce McLaren* (Auckland, Australia: HarperCollins Publishers, 2005).

58. Young, *McLaren Memories*.

59. Friedman, *Remembering*, 240.

60. Dave Friedman, interview with John Collins.

61. Dave Friedman, interview with Carroll Smith.

62. Dave Friedman, interview with Charlie Agapiou.

63. Charlie Agapiou, interview by author.

64. *The Shelby American #43*, 15.

65. *The Shelby American #42*, 19.

66. Mills, *Authorized Biography*, 428.

67. *Car and Driver*, September 1966.

68. *The Shelby American #42*, 19.

69. Dave Friedman, interview with Jacque Passino.
70. Paul M. Preuss, interview by David L. Lewis, *Benson Ford Research Center*, May 30, 1989.
71. *United Press International*, June 20, 1966.
72. Peter Miles, interview by author.
73. Carroll Shelby, *The Cobra Story* (New York, NY: Trident Press, 1965).
74. Friedman, *Remembering*, 296.
75. *The Shelby American #53*, 16.
76. *The Shelby American #53*, 16.
77. *The Shelby American #53*, 16.

Chapter Six

1. Bernie Kretzschmar, interview by author.
2. *Car and Driver*, May 1965
3. *The Shelby American*, Winter 2015, 64.
4. Dave Friedman, *Remembering the Shelby Years—1962–1969* (Los Angeles, CA: Carroll Shelby Children's Foundation, 1998), 111.
5. Chuck Cantwell, interview by author.
6. Charles McHose to Don DeLaRossa, Ford status report, August 1, 1966.
7. Chuck Cantwell, interview by author.
8. Chuck Cantwell, interview by author.
9. *The Shelby American*, Winter 2010, 51.
10. Chuck Cantwell, interview by author.
11. *Sports Car Graphic*, March 1967
12. *Road & Track*, February 1967.
13. *Car and Driver*, February 1967.
14. *Car and Driver*, February 1967.
15. Friedman, *Remembering*, 296.
16. *The Shelby American #65*, 21.
17. Friedman, *Remembering*, 312.
18. Dave Friedman, interview with Bill Eaton.
19. *Car and Driver*, May 1967.
20. Phil Remington, interview by author.
21. Phil Remington, interview by author.
22. Bill Eaton, interview by author.
23. Mario Andretti, interview by author.
24. Phil Remington, interview by author.
25. Ron Butler, interview by author.
26. Chuck Cantwell, interview by author.
27. Bernie Kretzschmar, interview by author.
28. *Sports Car Graphic*, July 1967.
29. *The Shelby American #51*, 18.
30. Friedman, *Remembering*, 312.
31. Friedman, *Remembering*, 23.
32. Don Coleman, interview by author.
33. *Car and Driver*, May 1967.
34. *Car and Driver*, April 1978.
35. *The Shelby American #53*, 15.
36. Paul Kunysz, interview by author.

37. *Road & Track*, February 1968.
38. Richard Kopec, *World Registry of Cobras & GT40s* (Sharon, CT: Kopec/Eber Publishing, 2008), 497.
39. Paul Kunysz, interview by author.
40. dwcobb43, "Bill Cosby 200MPH," *YouTube*, May 23, 2011. https://www.youtube.com/watch?v=3-JQksYxgM0.
41. Jim Marietta, interview by author.
42. Friedman, *Remembering*, 22.
43. Dave Friedman and John Christy, *Carroll Shelby's Racing Cobras* (Oxford, UK: Osprey Publishing, 1982), 196.
44. Mike Donovan, interview by author.
45. Friedman, *Remembering*, 40.
46. Carroll Shelby, interview by author.
47. Dan Gurney, interview by author.
48. Dan Gurney, interview by author.
49. Dave Friedman, interview with Carroll Shelby.
50. Kerry Agapiou, interview by author.
51. Eoin Young, *McLaren! The Man, the Cars & the Team* (Newport Beach, CA: Bond/Parkhurst Publications, 1971), 95.
52. Phil Henny, interview by author.
53. Dan Gurney, interview by author.
54. *Sports Car Graphic*, September 1967.
55. Charlie Agapiou, interview by author.
56. A. J. Foyt, interview by author.
57. A. J. Foyt, interview by author.
58. Bill Libby, *A. J. Foyt* (New York, NY: Hawthorn Books, 1974), 193.
59. Dan Gurney, interview by author.
60. *Motor Trend*, September 1967.
61. *The Shelby American #53*, 18.
62. *Road & Track*, January 1968.
63. Phil Henny, interview by author.
64. Lonnie Brannan, interview by author.
65. *The Shelby American #40*, 22.
66. *Motor Trend*, December 1969.
67. Friedman, *Remembering*, 265.
68. Kopec, *World Registry*, 1542.
69. Dave Friedman, interview with John Collins.
70. Friedman, *Remembering*, 126.
71. *The Shelby American #56*, 22.
72. *The Shelby American #56*, 22.
73. Mark Popov-Dadiani, interview by author.
74. *The Shelby American #56*, 22.
75. *Sports Car Graphic*, January 1968.
76. Phil Remington, interview by author.
77. *The Shelby American #51*, 19.
78. *Autoweek*, November 4, 1967.
79. Chuck Cantwell, interview by author.
80. Chuck Cantwell, interview by author.
81. *Autoweek*, October 28, 1967.

Chapter Seven

1. Carroll Shelby, *The Cobra Story* (New York, NY: Trident Press, 1965), 115.
2. Phil Remington, interview by author.
3. Dave Norton, interview by author.
4. Phil Remington, interview by author.
5. Dave Friedman, *Remembering the Shelby Years—1962–1969* (Los Angeles, CA: Carroll Shelby Children's Foundation, 1998), 72.
6. Steve Shuttack, interview by author.
7. Ron Butler, interview by author.
8. *Sports Car Graphic*, February 1969.
9. *Sports Car Graphic*, February 1969
10. *Road & Track,* June 1968.
11. Peter Brock, interview by author.
12. Rinsey Milles, *Carroll Shelby: The Authorized Biography* (Minneapolis, MN: Motorbooks, 2012), 473.
13. *The Shelby American,* Winter 2011, 36.
14. Ron Butler, interview by author.
15. Dave Jordan, interview by author.
16. Lee Dykstra, interview by author.
17. Don Coleman, interview by author.
18. Friedman, *Remembering*, 23.
19. *The Shelby American #51*, 19.
20. Chuck Cantwell, interview by author.
21. *The Shelby American #51*, 19.
22. Phil Henny, *Phil Remington: REM, Remembered by His Friends* (Portland, OR: Editions Cotty, 2015), 45.
23. *The Shelby American #57*, 17.
24. *The Shelby American #56*, 22.
25. *Sports Car Graphic*, May 1968.
26. *Car and Driver*, June 1974.
27. Associated Press, May 25, 1968.
28. Ron Butler, interview by author.
29. Dave Norton, interview by author.
30. *Floyd Clymer's 1968 Indianapolis 500 Yearbook* (Indianapolis, IN: Floyd Clymer, 1968).
31. Ron Butler, interview by author.
32. Samuel Hawley and Craig Breedlove, *Ultimate Speed: The Fast Life and Extreme Cars of Racing Legend Craig Breedlove* (Chicago, IL: Chicago Review Press, 2018), 168.
33. Hawley and Breedlove, *Ultimate Speed*, 168.
34. Phil Remington, interview by author.
35. *Sports Car Graphic*, August 1968.
36. *Car and Driver*, August 1968.
37. *Car and Driver*, June 1974.
38. Ron Butler, interview by author.
39. *The Shelby American*, Winter 2011, 37.
40. Rinsey Mills, *Carroll Shelby: The Authorized Biography* (Minneapolis, MN: Motorbooks, 2012), 473.
41. Tom Madigan, *Follmer: American Wheel Man* (Duarte, CA: ejje Publishing Group, 2013), 172.

42. Lee Dykstra, interview by author.
43. Lew Spencer to Carroll Shelby, "Group II Program Problems and Comments" memo, July 10, 1968.
44. Daniel Lipetz, *The Trans-Am Era: 1966-1972 in Photographs* (Phoenix, AZ: David Bull Publishing, 2016), 79.
45. Friedman, *Remembering*, 23.
46. Friedman, *Remembering*, 179.
47. David Tom, John Cowley to Fran Hernandez, Ford Motor Company memo, October 4, 1968 in *The Cars of Trans-Am Racing: 1966–1972* (Forest Lake, MN: CarTech, 2020).
48. Charlie Henry, Fran Hernandez to John Cowley, Ford Motor Company memo, October 15, 1968 in *Kar-Kraft: Race Cars, Prototypes and Muscle Cars of Ford's Special Vehicle Activity Program* (Forest Lake, MN: CarTech, 2017).
49. *Vintage Motorsports*, November/December 1995.
50. *The Shelby American #57*, 17.
51. *Autosport*, September 6, 1968.
52. Dave Friedman interview, with Jim O'Leary.

Chapter Eight

1. *The Shelby American #56*, 22.
2. *The Shelby American #57*, 18.
3. Ron Butler, interview by author.
4. *The Shelby American #57*, 18.
5. Dave Friedman, *Remembering the Shelby Years—1962–1969* (Los Angeles, CA: Carroll Shelby Children's Foundation, 1998), 59.
6. *Car Life*, October 1968.
7. *Car and Driver*, February 1969.
8. *The Shelby American #61*, 20.
9. John Dunn, "1969 Gr. II 302 Engine Intake Development Arrangement" memo.
10. Lee Dykstra, interview by author.
11. *Sports Car Graphic*, July 1969.
12. *Sports Car Graphic*, July 1969.
13. *The Shelby American #60*, 16.
14. *The Shelby American #60*, 16.
15. Friedman, *Remembering*, 296.
16. *Sports Car Graphic*, March 1970.
17. Daniel Lipetz, *The Trans-Am Era: 1966-1972 in Photographs* (Phoenix, AZ: David Bull Publishing, 2016), 120.
18. Friedman, *Remembering*, 179.
19. *The Shelby American #46*, 24.
20. *Vintage Motorsports*, January/February 1996.
21. *Autoweek*, October 11, 1969.
22. *Autoweek*, October 22, 1969.
23. Lonnie Brannan, interview by author.
24. *Vintage Motorsports*, January/February 1996.
25. *Los Angeles Times*, December 28, 1969.
26. *The Shelby American, #61*, 18.
27. Mike Shoen, interview by author.

SHELBY AMERICAN TIMELINE

December 1960: Carroll Shelby retires from racing after driving a Birdcage Maserati to a second-place finish at Laguna Seca and clinching the USAC Road Racing Championship.

January 1962: Shelby tests an AC Ace fitted with a 221-cubic-inch Ford V-8 at Silverstone.

February 1962: The first chassis is flown from AC Cars in England to Los Angeles International Airport and assembled at Dean Moon's shop in Santa Fe Springs with a 260-cubic-inch Ford V-8. This becomes the Cobra prototype.

April 1962: Painted yellow by car customizer Dean Jeffries, the lone Cobra is featured at the New York International Auto Show.

June 1962: Shelby American moves into the shop at 1042 Princeton Drive in Venice where Lance Reventlow's celebrated Scarab race cars had been built.

August 1962: Shelby American is incorporated.

October 1962: First race for the Cobra. Billy Krause is leading the Chevrolet Corvette Z06s at Riverside when the left rear hub breaks.

November 1962: The first Shelby American production Cobra leaves the Venice shop. Several other Cobras have already been completed by Ed Hugus at European Cars in Pittsburgh.

February 1963: Dave MacDonald scores the Cobra's first victory, at Riverside, with Ken Miles second. The car's first FIA race, at Daytona later that month, doesn't go as well.

March 1963: Although Cobras are now fitted with rack-and-pinion steering and 289-cubic-inch Hi-Po engines, they fail early and often at Sebring.

April 1963: MacDonald finishes second behind Bill Sherwood's Corvette at Del Mar. This is virtually the last time a Sting Ray will beat a Cobra all year.

July 1963: After Cobras place one-two-three in the A Production race at Lake Garnett, Kansas, Miles cheekily enters the modified race and wins it as well.

September 1963: Driving a Cobra at Bridgehampton, Dan Gurney becomes the first American to win an FIA race in an American car since John Fitch and Phil Walters drove a Cunningham C-4R to victory at Sebring in 1953. One week later, Bob Holbert wins from the pole at Mid-Ohio to earn the US Road Racing Championship over Miles. Shelby American also claims the manufacturers' title.

October 1963: Driving a King Cobra, MacDonald waxes a sterling international field to win the *Los Angeles Times* Grand Prix at Riverside. A week later, he triumphs again at Laguna Seca.

February 1964: After leading handily during its debut at Daytona, the Cobra Daytona Coupe driven by Holbert and MacDonald catches fire during a pit stop and retires.

March 1964: Holbert and MacDonald give the Daytona Coupe its maiden win in the 12 Hours of Sebring. On the other hand, the debut of the 427 roadster, driven by Miles and John Morton, is a disaster.

April 1964: The prototype Sunbeam Tiger races unhappily for the first time at Tucson. Car and driver Lew Spencer don't see eye to eye.

May 1964: Holbert retires from racing after a bad wreck at Kent. Three weeks later, MacDonald dies in a ghastly accident in the Indy 500 that also claims the life of Eddie Sachs.

June 1964: A Daytona Coupe driven by Gurney and Bob Bondurant wins the GT class and finishes fourth overall at Le Mans. Back at Riverside, Jere Kirkpatrick sets a class record in the Dragonsnake's first official drag strip outing.

August 1964: Gurney eviscerates the Ferrari 250 GTOs at Goodwood, prompting Enzo Ferrari to start noodling over a devious political solution to beat the Daytona Coupes.

September 1964: Cobra roadsters reign supreme in the States as they dominate back-to-back five hundred-kilometer events at Road America and Bridgehampton. Nevertheless, Ferrari still secures the GT World Championship.

October 1964: At Riverside, Parnelli Jones scores the last win ever for the King Cobra. The car crashes and burns the next week at Laguna Seca.

December 1964: Shelby American takes delivery of two GT40 Le Mans prototypes and 101 Mustangs to be transformed into GT350s.

January 1965: Shelby American signs a lease for two hangars at LAX previously occupied by North American Aviation.

February 1965: The GT350, with Miles behind the wheel, wins at Green Valley, near Dallas, in its first SCCA outing. Two weeks later, Miles earns a much bigger trophy as he and co-driver Lloyd Ruby take the checkered flag at Daytona in a GT40.

March 1965: The move from Venice to LAX is completed.

April 1965: While the GT40s struggle, the Daytona Coupes cruise from win to win in FIA competition, starting with Bondurant and Allen Grant galloping home first at Monza. But the FIA refuses to homologate the 427 Cobra, rendering it a white elephant.

June 1965: Debacle at Le Mans. After being fastest and leading by miles, all of the Ford GTs break. Ditto for the Shelby American Daytona Coupes. Ten of the eleven factory-backed entries fail to finish.

July 1965: Bondurant and Jo Schlesser clinch the GT title for Shelby American by winning at Reims in their Daytona Coupe. This is the first championship ever won by an American manufacturer in international competition.

August 1965: Jerry Titus continues to clean up in B Production by driving his R-Model GT350 to wins at Candlestick Park and Oregon International Raceway.

November 1965: Craig Breedlove and Bobby Tatroe set twenty-three speed records in a Daytona Coupe at the Bonneville Salt Flats. Two weeks later, Titus wins the SCCA's American Road Race of Champions at Daytona to claim national B Production honors for the GT350.

December 1965: Shelby American delivers the first GT350Hs to Hertz.

January 1966: The first of twenty-nine 427 S/C Cobras is sold. It takes nearly a year to move the rest of them.

February 1966: Shelby American Mark IIAs finish one-two-five at Daytona, with Miles and Ruby reprising their victory of the previous year.

March 1966: Miles and Ruby make it two in a row by winning Sebring in the open-top X-1 after Gurney, leading by a lap, suffers an engine failure one corner before the finish.

June 1966: Ford Mark IIs finish one-two-three at Le Mans, but everybody is confused and nobody is happy after Bruce McLaren and Chris Amon are declared the winners of a controversial dead-heat finish and Miles and Denny Hulme are demoted to second place.

August 1966: Miles is killed at Riverside while testing the J-Car. This month also marks the first test of the big-block GT500.

September 1966: Racing a hastily prepared Shelby Mustang, Titus wins at Riverside to secure the inaugural Trans-Am championship for Ford.

October 1966: The first fiberglass pieces for the 1967 GT350s arrive at LAX—and don't fit properly. This turns out to be a sign of hellish production woes to come.

December 1966: The last 427 Cobras are delivered to Shelby American.

February 1967: All but one of the Mark IIBs break at Daytona as Ferrari scores a humbling one-two-three victory with its new 330 P4. The Shelby American Trans-Am program, operating as the Terlingua Racing Team, also lays an egg in the opening race of the season.

March 1967: Titus wins at Sebring in a Trans-Am Mustang painted Gawd-Awful Yellow.

April 1967: The next day, still at Sebring, the freshly christened Mark IV—essentially a J-Car with more aerodynamic bodywork fashioned by Phil Remington—wins straight out of the box, with McLaren and Mario Andretti sharing the honors.

June 1967: Gurney and A. J. Foyt win Le Mans in the all-American Mark IV. Two days later, the car is banned by the FIA, and the Mark IV retires with a perfect record—two races, two victories. Meanwhile, the Lone Star prototype, envisioned as a mid-engined replacement for the Cobra, arrives in LA from the UK.

July 1967: The last Shelby Mustangs are built in Southern California. Production subsequently moves to the A. O. Smith plant in Ionia, Michigan.

August 1967: Shelby American starts vacating the hangars at LAX. Shelby Racing moves to a new shop in Torrance.

September 1967: Titus scores his fourth and final Trans-Am win of the season, at Crow's Landing Naval Auxiliary Air Station near Modesto. Meanwhile, Shelby Racing's Toyota 2000GT is tested for the first time at Riverside in preparation for the 1968 SCCA season.

October 1967: By finishing second at Kent in the last race of the season, Ronnie Bucknum clinches a second consecutive Trans-Am manufacturers' championship for Ford.

November 1967: At Las Vegas, the star-crossed Can-Am car that Shelby had commissioned from British designer Len Terry makes its second and last desultory appearance. A mechanical failure prevents Titus from even taking the start.

January 1968: At a press conference in Riverside, Shelby announces his plans to enter the Indy 500 with a turbine-powered car designed by Ken Wallis, whose previous Whooshmobile had nearly won the race in 1967.

February 1968: A tunnel-port engine defies the odds at Daytona and lasts for twenty-four hours, allowing Bucknum and Titus to win the Trans-Am race and finish an impressive fourth overall in the enduro.

March 1968: Peter Revson finishes third in the USRRC Race at Mexico City in a Ford-powered Lola T70. Alas, it's all downhill from there.

April 1968: The Toyota 2000GT scores its first win in SCCA C Production competition, at Stuttgart, Arkansas, with Scooter Patrick leading Dave Jordan to a one-two finish.

May 1968: Fiasco at Indy. The turbine cars driven by McLaren and Hulme are dead slow. Then the team discovers that Wallis had designed a cheat into the intake system, and the cars are hastily withdrawn after a week of practice to prevent the fraud from coming to light.

August 1968: Two weeks after Titus scored a miraculous win at Watkins Glen, the Trans-Am team reaches rock bottom while blowing up six tunnel-port engines during practice, qualifying and the race at Continental Divide Raceway, near Denver.

September 1968: Titus's tunnel-port motor breaks as usual, but Horst Kwech's survives, improbably, and he scores an enormously popular win in the Trans-Am race at Riverside.

November 1968: Patrick finishes fourth in the American Road Race of Champions at Riverside, closing the books on the disappointing Toyota 2000GT program. After unsatisfying Can-Am performances in the States, Revson ends the year by winning in Japan, at Fuji, in his McLaren M6B.

March 1969: Ambitious plans to run the Can-Am season are abruptly canceled when Ford unexpectedly pulls the plug on the program. This leaves Shelby Racing with nothing on its plate other than Trans-Am.

May 1969: Sam Posey, subbing for Revson, scores an unlikely victory after Kwech breaks in the Trans-Am race at Lime Rock. It's the last win Shelby will ever record.

June 1969: Shelby asks Lee Iacocca to kill the Shelby Mustang program at the end of the 1970 model year. The deed is done.

August 1969: Revson and Kwech total their Mustangs when they both hit oil in the same turn at St. Jovite. The team never recovers from this calamity.

September 1969: The 1970 GT350 and GT500 are introduced. They are the last of the Shelby Mustangs—until a new series of Shelby-ized Ford Mustangs debuts in 2007.

October 1969: Revson finishes fourth and Kwech ninth in the Trans-Am race at Riverside, marking the end of the line for Shelby Racing.

December 1969: Shelby is officially out of the car business, though he retains several Cobras, his profitable Goodyear distributorship and the shop at 1042 Princeton Drive in Venice.

THE CARS OF SHELBY AMERICAN

Leaf-spring Cobra (1962–1964): Originally designed around a 260-cubic-inch Ford V-8, the leaf-spring Cobra reached its classic form with a Hi-Po 289. Built for both street and track. Production: 655.

Cobra Daytona Coupe (1964–1965): Designed by Peter Brock, the Daytona Coupe was a race car created by enveloping an upgraded leaf-spring Cobra chassis with enclosed aerodynamic bodywork. Production: 6 (included in the 655 above).

Dragonsnake (1964): The first Shelby American drag-racing car was a tired street Cobra modified for quarter-mile duty in 1963. The next year, four Dragonsnakes were built on leaf-spring frames—one raced by the team and three sold to customers. Production: 4 (also included in the leaf-spring total above).

King Cobra (1963–1964): A Cooper Monaco T61 sports racer modified to accept a 289-cubic-inch Ford V-8. Five were raced by Shelby American, one entered as the Lang Cooper, and two sold directly to Comstock Racing in Canada. Production: 8.

Sunbeam Tiger (1964): Prototype race car consisting of a Sunbeam Alpine chassis retrofitted with a 260-cubic-inch Ford V-8 (and, later, a 289). Production: 1.

Coil-spring Cobra (1964–1966): Built on a wider, stouter version of the leaf-spring Cobra frame, coil-spring Cobras were fitted with big-block V-8s split roughly between race-derived 427s and street-oriented 428s. Built for both street and track. Roughly twenty-nine cars were sold as 427 S/Cs. Production: 343.

Type 65 (1965): Essentially the next iteration of the Daytona Coupe, the Type 65 was a race car designed by Brock around a coil-spring Cobra frame and a big-block 427. Production: 1 (incomplete).

1965 GT350: Heavily modified Ford Mustangs with Hi-Po 289s, built in the Shelby American shops in Venice and at Los Angeles International Airport. Production: 526.

1965 GT350 Competition: Designated as the R-Model, this was a GT350 modified for SCCA B Production racing. Two were raced by Shelby American, the rest sold to customers. Production: 36.

Ford GT40 (1965): A Le Mans prototype built by Ford Advanced Vehicles in the UK around a steel monocoque and a small-block V-8.

Ford GT40 Mark II (1965): A GT40 modified to accept a big-block 427-cubic-inch Ford.

427 Dragonsnake (1966): A factory-built 427 Cobra optimized for drag racing and offered to customers. Production: 1 (included in the coil-spring total above).

1966 GT350: A more refined version of the 1965 model. Production: 2,378.

1966 GT350H: A mildly customized iteration of the 1966 GT350 sold to Hertz to be part of the company's rental-car fleet. Production: 1,001.

1966 Trans-Am Ford Mustang: A Mustang hot-rodded with GT350 R-Model components. After building one prototype, Shelby American produced four so-called Group I cars for international rallying and sixteen Group II cars for SCCA sedan racing, either amateur (A Sedan) or professional (Trans-Am). Production: 21.

GT40 Mark IIA (1966): An upgraded version of the Mark II.

Twin-Paxton Cobra (1967): A big-block Cobra modified with dual Paxton superchargers. One built for Shelby, the other for comedian Bill Cosby. Production: 2 (included in the coil-spring total above).

1967 GT350: A fresh take on the GT350 based on the new-for-1967 Ford Mustang. Production: 1,175.

1967 GT500: Essentially the same car as the 1967 GT350, with a 428-cubic-inch Ford V-8 replacing the small block engine found in its little brother. Production: 2,050.

1967 Super Snake: A GT500 fitted with a full-tilt 427 race motor. It turned out to be too expensive to get beyond the prototype stage. Production: 1 (included in the GT500 total).

Ford GT40 Mark IIB (1967): An upgraded version of the Mark IIA.

1967 Trans-Am Ford Mustang: Shelby American built four team cars, and twenty-one cars for customers eager to race in Trans-Am and/or A Sedan. Production: 25.

Ford Mark IV (1967): A rebodied version of the J-Car—a Le Mans prototype built by Kar-Kraft with an aluminum-honeycomb monocoque and the ubiquitous big-block 427.

Lone Star (1967): A mid-engined two-seat sports car commissioned by Shelby American as a successor to the 427 Cobra. Designed by Len Bailey and built in England. Production: 1.

T-10 King Cobra (1967): A Can-Am race car commissioned by Shelby American. Designed by Len Terry and built in England. Production: 1.

1968 GT350: An upgraded version of the 1967 model, now equipped with a 302-cubic-inch V-8. Built at the A. O. Smith factory in Ionia, Michigan. Production: 1,457.

1968 GT500: An upgraded version of the 1967 model, also built at the A. O. Smith plant in Ionia, Michigan. Production: 1,422.

1968 GT500KR: About halfway through the 1968 model-year production cycle, the more powerful Cobra Jet version of the 428 became available. The Cobra Jet engine was stuffed into a GT500, which was then renamed GT500KR, for King of the Road. Production: 1,571.

1968 Trans-Am Ford Mustang: Built by Kar-Kraft in Brighton, Michigan, around Ford's troublesome tunnel-port 302.

Toyota 2000GT (1968): Race cars built by Toyota in Japan and campaigned by Shelby Racing in SCCA C Production competition in 1968.

Lola T70 (1968): A customer Can-Am race car campaigned by Shelby Racing in the US Road Racing Championship in 1968.

McLaren M6B (1968): A customer Can-Am race car campaigned by Shelby Racing in the Can-Am series in 1968.

Shelby/Wallis Turbine (1968): A turbine-powered single-seater commissioned by Shelby Racing to race in the Indy 500 in 1968. Designed and built by Ken Wallis in Southern California. Production: 2.

1969/1970 GT350: The final iteration of the Shelby Mustang. For 1970, a chin spoiler and hood stripes were added. Production 1,281.

1969/1970 GT500: The big brother of the 1969/1970 GT350. Production 1,869.

1969 Trans-Am Ford Mustang: Built by Kar-Kraft, with a Boss 302 replacing the reviled tunnel-port engine. Largely identical cars were raced by Bud Moore Engineering.

ACKNOWLEDGMENTS

I t's a cliché to say that I stand on the shoulders of giants, but that doesn't make it any less true. The Shelby American story has been told—magnificently—on many occasions, by many writers. Some of them were in the trenches back in the day, while others have made chronicling the company's saga their life's work. Shelby American was covered comprehensively in its heyday. Since then, it's been the subject of thousands of magazine articles, dozens of books, and Google only knows how many blogs, podcasts, and YouTube videos. The ground has been thoroughly plowed by many who came before me, and I'm grateful for all the material they've uncovered.

Sixty years have passed since the Cobra roared to life. Sadly, most of the people who worked at Shelby American are gone. I've done my best to talk to the ones who are still around, and to those I missed, I apologize for not getting in touch. Although I had no idea that I would someday be writing a book about this subject, I had the good fortune to interview several of the major players in years past—Phil Remington, Al Dowd, Carroll Smith, Lew Spencer, Bill Eaton, Bob Bondurant, Dan Gurney, Phil Hill, Chris Amon, and, of course, Carroll Shelby. But there were many questions I never asked them, so this is a project I couldn't have undertaken without a lot of help from a lot of people.

The first is my collaborator on two previous books, Dave Friedman. As Shelby American's longtime staff photographer, Dave was there in Dean Moon's shop when the first Cobra was being assembled in early 1962, and he was still shooting when the company ceased to exist in the summer of 1967. Anybody who's familiar with Cobras on even a cursory basis has seen his work, and anyone with a deep appreciation for the marque probably owns some of his photos. But Dave has also done yeoman's work interviewing drivers, mechanics, administrators, and other Shelby American stalwarts. Material gleaned from those interviews provides most of the text in the dozen or so books he's written about this era. The transcripts also are the foundation of his magnum opus, *Remembering the Shelby Years, 1962-1969*. Dave has graciously allowed me to quote liberally from this book, and I've taken full advantage of his generosity. (Citations for all quotes used in the text are listed in the endnotes.)

Second are Rick Kopec and the über-knowledgeable enthusiasts at the Shelby American Automobile Club. Founded in 1975, SAAC is the go-to resource for anybody interested in the cars and legacy of Carroll Shelby. Besides hosting an annual national convention and producing a quarterly magazine, *The Shelby American*, SAAC publishes the *World Registry of Cobras & GT40s*, the *SAAC Shelby Registry, 1965-1966-1967*, and the *SAAC Shelby Registry, 1968-1969-1970*. These are extraordinary works of academic history and automotive archaeology filled with in-depth (and entertaining) entries covering every imaginable aspect of Shelby American arcana as well as chassis histories of each Cobra, GT40, GT350, and GT500 ever built. It's hard to imagine any serious fans of these cars, much less any owners, who don't own at least one edition of the registries. Thanks especially to three of SAAC's so-called registrars—Howard Pardee, Vincent Liska, and Dave Mathews—for reviewing portions of my manuscript, as well as a fourth registrar, Greg Kolasa, for providing photographs. Equally invaluable to my research were the "Cobrasations" in *The Shelby American*—Q&As with more than fifty people who were crucial to the Shelby American story, from the best-known characters to those whose names are familiar only to the most devoted students of the marque. These Q&As were a trove of information, and I want to acknowledge Rick's generosity for granting me access to this material.

I also want to give a shout-out to a quartet of incomparably charitable former Shelby American employees who've written memoirs covering the time they spent in the race shops in Venice, El Segundo, and Torrance. John Morton's *Inside Shelby American* provides the best sense of what everyday operations looked and felt like during the Cobra's glory years. Peter Brock covers some of the same events in *Daytona Cobra Coupes* while also offering the definitive history of the development of the car initially known as "Brock's Folly." *Shelby Mustang GT350* by Chuck Cantwell with Greg Kolasa is a remarkably clear-eyed and revelatory history of Shelby's Mustang-related legacy, on both road and track. Phil Henny, meanwhile, has established a cottage industry writing about this era in the books *Just Call Me Carroll*, *Phil Remington*, *Dan Gurney Nostalgie*, *Dave MacDonald*, *Bob Bondurant*, and, most recently, *The Mighty Ford MkIV*.

And then there are all the people who patiently and cheerfully answered questions that, over the years, they've heard hundreds if not thousands of times before. Thank you, Charlie Agapiou, Kerry Agapiou, Mario Andretti, Sonny Balcaen, Lonnie Brannan, Ron Butler, Andre (Gessner) Capella, Bob Carlson, Don Coleman, Peter Crane, Diana (Trampe) Geddes Day, Mike Donovan, Lee Dykstra, Dennis Eshelman, Ralph Falconer, Ryan Falconer, Tim Foraker, A. J. Foyt, Joe Freitas, Doyle Gammell, Allen Grant, J. L. Henderson, Parnelli Jones, Dave Jordan, Bruce Junor, Jere Kirkpatrick, Robert Krauss, Bernie Kretzschmar, Paul Kunysz, Frank Lance, Dick Lins, Jim Marietta, Ralph Mora, Dave Norton, Wally Peat, Red Pierce, Mark Popov-Dadiani, Steve Shuttack, Tony Stoer, Ted Sutton, Mark Waco, and Susan Schafran Warne. Whatever I got right in the book is in large part because of you. Whatever I got wrong is completely my fault.

I also owe a big tip of the hat to Mike Shelby, Carroll's son; Aaron Shelby, Carroll's grandson; Peter Miles, Ken's son; Rick Titus, Jerry's son; Lynn Park, aka Mr. Cobra; Mike Shoen, author of *The Cobra-Ferrari Wars*; Bruce Meyer, the nicest guy in the collector car world, and his curator, Tom Kenney; Drew Serb and Emily Lambert, founder and managing director of The Cobra Experience; John Gabrial, for providing the memorabilia; and chief archivist Laura Fisher at the Petersen Automotive Museum. Special appreciation to Ted Ryan, Jamie Myler, and John Clinard for opening up Ford Motor Company's remarkable archive of documents and photos. Also, Scott George, Paul Kierstein, and Bryan Gable of the Revs Institute went far above and beyond the call of duty in providing photos and research material. Much appreciated.

Of course, this book wouldn't exist were it not for Lee Klancher, the publisher of Octane Press, who greenlighted and helped shape the project. Ambitious books about racing are a tough sell, yet Octane manages to make them pencil out. Thanks also to endlessly patient production editor Faith Garcia, marketing specialist Catherine Zinser, and publicist Jo Snyder.

At this point, you'd think there couldn't be anybody left for me to mention. But, in fact, I've saved the best for last. Thanks most of all to my longtime companion, Emily Young. Hardly a day goes by that I don't reflect on how implausibly lucky I am that the love of my life should also be the world's most sympathetic and thorough editor. Emily deserves credit for inspiring me to embark on this project, and without her help I never would have finished it. I owe her a debt of gratitude I can never repay.

BIBLIOGRAPHY

Brock, Peter, Dave Friedman, and George Stauffer. *Daytona Cobra Coupes*. Blue Mounds, WI: Stauffer Publishing, 1995.

Bruce, Gordon. *The First Three Shelby Cobras: The Sports Cars that Changed the Game*. Tenbury Wells, UK: Porter Press International, 2018.

Cantwell, Chuck, and Greg Kolasa. *Shelby Mustang GT350*. Phoenix: David Bull Publishing, 2017.

Comer, Colin. *The Complete Book of Shelby Automobiles: Cobras, Mustangs, and Super Snakes*. Minneapolis: Motorbooks, 2009.

———. *Shelby Cobra Fifty Years*. Minneapolis: Motorbooks, 2011.

———. *Shelby Mustang Fifty Years*. Minneapolis: Motorbooks, 2014.

Cotter, Tom, and Al Pearce. *Holman-Moody: The Legendary Race Team*. St. Paul: Motorbooks International, 2002.

Craft, John. *Bud Moore: Man and Machine*. Daytona Beach: Carbon Press, 2009.

Donohue, Mark, and Paul Van Valkenburgh. *The Unfair Advantage*. New York: Dodd, Mead, and Company, 1975.

Evans, Art. *Carroll Shelby: A Collection of My Favorite Racing Photos*. Forest Lake, MN: CarTech Books, 2016.

———. *Ken Miles*. Redondo Beach, CA: Photo Data Research, 2004.

Evans, Art, and Dave Friedman. *The Shelby American Story*. Yellow Springs, OH: Ertel Publishing, 2019.

Farr, Donald. *Ford Mustang: America's Original Pony Car*. Minneapolis: Quarto Publishing Group, 2017.

Ferrari, Enzo. *Le Briglie del Successo*. San Lazzaro di Savena: Poligrafici il Borgo, IT, 1970.

Friedman, Dave. *Remembering the Shelby Years, 1962-1969.*
Los Angeles: Carroll Shelby Children's Foundation, 1998.
———. *Shelby American Racing History.* Osceola, WI. Motorbooks
International, 1997.
———. *Shelby American: Up Close and Behind the Scenes.* Minneapolis:
Motorbooks, 2017.
———. *Shelby GT40.* Osceola, WI: Motorbooks International, 1995.
———. *Trans-Am: The Pony Car Wars 1966-1971.* Minneapolis:
Motorbooks, 2001.
Friedman, Dave, and John Christy. *Carroll Shelby's Racing Cobras.*
Oxford: Osprey Publishing, 1982.
Gabbard, Alex. *Fast Mustangs.* Lenoir City, TN: Gabbard, 1990.
Gozzi, Franco. *Memoirs of Enzo Ferrari's Lieutenant.* Milan:
Giorgi Nada Editore, 2002.
Hammill, Des. *Ford Small Block V8 Racing Engines 1962 to 1970:
The Essential Source Book.* Poundbury, UK: Veloce Publishing, 2014.
Hawley, Samuel, and Craig Breedlove. *Ultimate Speed: The Fast
Life and Extreme Cars of Racing Legend Craig Breedlove.* Chicago:
Chicago Review Press, 2018.
Hayes, Walter. *Henry: A Life of Henry Ford II.* New York:
Grove Weidenfeld, 1990.
Henry, Charlie. *Kar-Kraft: Race Cars, Prototypes and Muscle Cars of
Ford's Special Vehicle Activity Program.* Forest Lake, MN: CarTech
Books, 2017.
Henny, Phil. *Dan Gurney Nostalgie.* Portland: Editions Cotty, 2018.
———. *Dave MacDonald: Cobra Man, The Will to Win.* Portland:
Editions Cotty, 2017.
———. *Just Call Me Carroll.* Portland: Editions Cotty, 2004.
———. *Phil Remington: REM, Remembered by His Friends.* Portland:
Editions Cotty, 2015.
Henny, Phil, Bill Riley, and Mike Teske. *The Mighty Ford MKIV.*
Portland: Editions Cotty, 2021.
Kolasa, Greg. *The Definitive Shelby Mustang Guide 1965-1970.*
Forest Lake, MN: CarTech Books, 2012.
Kopec, Richard. *SAAC Shelby Registry: 1965-1966-1967.* Sharon, CT:
Shelby American Automobile Club, 2011.

————. *SAAC Shelby Registry: 1968-1969-1970*. Sharon, CT: Shelby American Automobile Club, 2014.

————. *World Registry of Cobras & GT40s*. Sharon, CT: Kopec/Eber Publishing, 2008.

Leffingwell, Randy, and David Newhardt. *Shelby Mustang: Racer for the Street*. Minneapolis: Motorbooks, 2005.

Legate, Trevor. *Cobra: The First 40 Years*. Minneapolis: Motorbooks, 2006.

————. *Ford GT40: Production & Racing History, Individual Chassis Record*. Dorchester: Veloce Publishing, 2001.

Lerner, Preston, and Dave Friedman. *Ford GT: How Ford Silenced the Critics, Humbled Ferrari and Conquered Le Mans*. Minneapolis: Quarto Publishing Group, 2015.

————. *Scarab: Race Log of the All-American Specials, 1957-1965*. Osceola, WI: Motorbooks International, 1991.

Levine, Leo. *Ford: The Dust and the Glory: A Racing History*. New York: Macmillan, 1968.

Levy, George, and Pete Biro. *Can-Am 50th Anniversary: Flat Out with North America's Greatest Race Series 1966-74*. Minneapolis: Motorbooks, 2016.

Libby, Bill. *A. J. Foyt*. New York: Hawthorn Books, 1974.

Lipetz, Daniel. *The Trans-Am Era: 1966-1972 in Photographs*. Phoenix: David Bull Publishing, 2016.

Ludvigsen, Karl E. *Can-Am Racing Cars: Secrets of the Sensational Sixties Sports-Racers*. Hudson, WI: Iconografix, 2005.

————. *The Inside Story of the Fastest Fords: The Design and Development of the Ford GT Racing Cars*. Turin, IT: Style Auto Editrice, 1971.

Lyons, Pete. *Can-Am*. Osceola, WI: Motorbooks International, 1995.

Madigan, Tom. *Follmer: American Wheel Man*. Duarte, CA: ejje Publishing Group, 2013.

Mann, Alan, and Tony Dron. *Alan Mann: A Life of Chance*. Croydon, UK: Motor Racing Publications, 2012.

Mills, Rinsey. *Carroll Shelby: The Authorized Biography*. Minneapolis: Motorbooks, 2012.

Morton, John. *Inside Shelby American: Wrenching and Racing with Carroll Shelby in the 1960s*. Minneapolis: Motorbooks, 2017.

Schorr, Martyn L. *Ford Total Performance: Ford's Legendary High-Performance Street and Race Cars*. Minneapolis: Motorbooks, 2015.

Shelby, Carroll. *The Cobra Story*. New York: Trident Press, 1965.

Shoen, Michael L. *The Cobra-Ferrari Wars 1963-1965*. Vancouver: CFW, 1988.

Spain, Ronnie. *GT40: An Individual History and Race Record*. London: Osprey Automotive, 1986.

Tom, David. *The Cars of Trans-Am Racing: 1966–1972*. Forest Lake, MN: CarTech Books, 2013.

Walker, Robert D. *Cobra Pilote: The Ed Hugus Story*. Deerfield, IL: Dalton Watson Fine Books, 2017.

Wyer, John. *The Certain Sound: Thirty Years of Motor Racing*. Lausanne, CH: Automobile Year: Edita, 1981.

Wyss, Wallace A. *Shelby's Wildlife: The Cobras, Mustangs and Dodges*. Osceola, WI: Motorbooks International, 1987.

———. *Shelby: The Man, The Cars, The Legend*. Yellow Springs, OH: Ertel Publishing, 2007.

Yates, Brock. *Enzo Ferrari, The Man, the Cars, the Races, the Machine*. New York: Doubleday, 1991.

Young, Eoin S. *Forza Amon! A Biography of Chris Amon*. Auckland: HarperSports 2003.

———. *McLaren Memories: A Biography of Bruce McLaren*. Auckland: HarperCollins Publishers, 2005.

———. *McLaren! The Man, the Cars & the Team*. Newport Beach: Bond/Parkhurst Publications, 1971.

Yoshikawa, Shin. *Toyota 2000GT: The Complete History of Japan's First Supercar*. Tokyo: Tachibana, 2002.

INDEX

CPSIA information can be obtained
at www.ICGtesting.com
Printed in the USA
LVHW112115190822
726431LV00003B/18/J